Thomas Jefferson on Taste and the Fine Arts

M. Andrew Holowchak

Series in American History

www.vernonpress.com

In the Americas:
Vernon Press
1000 N West Street, Suite 1200
Wilmington, Delaware, 19801
United States

In the rest of the world:
Vernon Press
C/Sancti Espiritu 17,
Malaga, 29006
Spain

Series in American History

Library of Congress Control Number: 2022939769

ISBN: 978-1-64889-478-7

Table of contents

List of Figures

To a very cherished and dear friend, Vivienne Kelly,
who is a sculptor of no small talent!

Preface

"*De gustibus non est disputandum;* that is, there is no disputing against Hobby-Horses; and, for my part, I seldom do; nor could I with any sort of grace, had I been an enemy to them at the bottom; for happening, at certain intervals and changes of the Moon, to be both fiddler and painter, according as the fly stings." ~Laurence Sterne, *The Life and Opinions of Tristram Shandy, Gentleman*[1]

While touring the pleasure gardens of England with John Adams, Jefferson was at times awed by the resplendent beauty, but at other times, taken aback by cumbrous superfluity. While at the garden at Cheswick, he writes, "The garden shows still too much of art." At Blenheim, he says the same, "Art appears too much."[2]

That sentiment was no *obiter dictum.* It was written with due circumspection. Art could be overdone. That he learned from reading and assimilating Lord Kames', William Hogarth's, Edmund Burke's, and Hugh Blair's views on beauty, sublimity, the art of criticism, and taste, as well as Thomas Whately's critical comments in his very popular *Observations on Modern Gardening*—a sort of critical guide to the aesthetics of pleasure gardening. In the words of Whately, when gardening is overdone, there is "a jealousy of art" and "art then intrudes."[3] A new science, to be dubbed by Alexander Baumgarten "aesthetics" in 1735, was birthed.[4]

Kames and Blair noted that taste required the right amount of the right sort of aesthetic stimulation: too little, and it would be underdeveloped and unappreciative of beauty and sublimity; too much (e.g., French rococo), and it would be overindulged to such an extent that its judgments would be forced and without an appreciation of the practical aspects of beauty and sublimity.

---

[1] Laurence Sterne, *The Life and Opinions of Tristram Shandy, Gentleman,* ed. Melvyn and Joan New (New York: Penguin Books, 2003), 14.

[2] Thomas Jefferson, "A Tour of the Gardens of England," in *Thomas Jefferson: Writings,* ed. Merrill D. Peterson (New York: Library of America, 1984), 623 and 627.

[3] Thomas Whately, *Observations of Modern Gardening,* ed. Michael Symes (Woodbridge, UK: Boydell Press, 2016), 119–20.

[4] Peter Lamarque, "History of Aesthetics," *Oxford Bibliographies,* https://www.oxfordbibliographies.com/view/document/obo-9780195396577/obo-9780195396577-0002.xml, accessed 2 Apr. 2022.

Like Kames and Blair, Jefferson sought an aesthetic mean, yet his was an American sense of that aesthetic mean. That mean was to be serviceable for what he envisaged would be a predominantly agrarian nation—one without the degradation that occurred in overcrowded cities, like London, in which manufacture predominated and the overburdened laborers often "rejuvenated" themselves through gambling, drinking, and prostitution. Jeffersonian republicanism was to be a corrective to the centuries-old abuses of heavy-handed, intrusive government.

That corrective was a movement toward greater liberty and equality and that movement demanded not only political, moral, and educational reforms, but also—and this has been eschewed in major works of Jefferson's political thinking—aesthetical reforms. No nation could be great without its citizens having some appreciation for beauty.

What amount of art was needed for Jefferson's American aesthetic mean?

Art for Jefferson was like a republican government. Too much government for a large nation was to be avoided, as liberty would be suffocated. Too little government for a large nation was to be avoided, as it would result in anarchy. Yet among the extremes of surplus and privation of government, the latter was preferable to the former. It was the same with art for the young nation.

Art, if overdone, would be a useless indulgence and an impediment to liberty. It would be difficult, for example, for a nation of mostly farmers to cultivate a large appreciation for sculpture or painting, and if cultivated, it would be a hindrance to industry. Art, if neglected, would stall the engine of liberty. There would never have been an American Revolution, for instance, had the Founders not been skilled in the arts of rhetoric and oratory. And so, Jefferson's critical comments apropos of the fine arts must be seen from the perspective of his republican ideals. William Howard Adams eloquently expresses that notion in the form of a dilemma. "European luxury, overrefinement and effeminacy expressed in much of contemporary art was [*sic*] a threat to the morals and public happiness of the people and their representatives in the new American government. The dilemma was how to establish a foundation of the arts in America without accepting the time-honored conditions of wealth and rank in which they flourished."[5]

As we shall see in chapter 1, Lord Kames and Hugh Blair, whose views on taste Jefferson to some extent appropriated,[6] argued that cultivation and

---

[5] William Howard Adams, *The Eye of Thomas Jefferson* (Washington, D.C.: National Gallery of the Arts, 1976), xxxviii.
[6] M. Andrew Holowchak, *Thomas Jefferson: Moralist* (Jefferson City, NC: McFarland, 2017), chap. 3.

maturation of taste through the fine arts were themselves subject to rational principles. The account Kames gives largely suggests that only those with sufficient leisure, the wealthy and the wellborn, would be capable of that. Were Jefferson's views on the aesthetic sense sufficiently dissimilar in some respect from those of Kames to allow for the democratization of the aesthetic?

That was the problem that artist and philosopher William Hogarth confronted in *The Analysis of Beauty* (1753). Hogarth begins: "For though beauty is seen and confessed by all, yet, from the many fruitless attempts to account for the cause of its being so, inquiries on this head have almost been given up; and the subject generally thought to be a matter of too high and too delicate a nature to admit of any true or intelligible discussion."[7] The reason for the confusion, it seems, is that all expositions of beauty have been highbrow, when the subject admits of a simpler explication. Men of letters, on the "more beaten path of moral beauty," have been "continually discoursing of effects instead of developing causes."[8] All persons have a capacity for aesthetic appreciation, which ought not to be left exclusively to men of letters.

Aesthetic sensibility, Hogarth asserts, is not just for the elite—especially those practiced in the arts. "The more prevailing the notion may be, that painters and connoisseurs are the only competent judges of things of this sort; the more it becomes necessary to clear up and confirm ... that no one may be deterred, by the want of such previous knowledge, from entering into this enquiry."[9] The principles of beauty and grace, like the principles of bodily motion, are in nature and discoverable by all persons, not merely by men of letters. That is a "democratic" point that Jefferson doubtless found appealing. Jefferson owned Hogarth's book and recommended it to Robert Skipwith, brother-in-law of Jefferson's soon-to-be wife Martha, in his suggestions for a private library (3 Aug. 1771), suitable to a pastoral gentleman.

What made an art "fine"? Jefferson writes to granddaughter Ellen Wayles Randolph (10 July 1805), "No perfect *definition* of what is a fine art has ever yet been given." Some say that a fine art allows for manual operations that conjoin "the exercise of the imagination or genius." According to this definition, sculpture, painting, architecture, and gardening are fine arts, but not music, poetry, and oratory. Others say that the fine arts are objects of the senses, while the sciences are objects of the understanding. According to this definition, gardening is a fine art, but not poetry and oratory.

---

[7] William Hogarth, *The Analysis of Beauty: Written with a View of Fixing the Fluctuating Ideas of Taste* (London: J. Reeves, 1753), iii.
[8] William Hogarth, *The Analysis of Beauty*, iii–iv.
[9] William Hogarth, *The Analysis of Beauty*, 3.

Jefferson himself never firmly settled on a definition. It is sufficient to say that "fine" had nothing to do with the quality of a work of art, but instead with the end for which it was created. The fine arts were of such productions that answered merely to aesthetic sensibility—appreciation of beauty only was the aim—not functionality. For Jefferson, all persons were by nature equipped with both a moral sense and an aesthetic sense (*viz.*, taste), and so all persons were at least capable of aesthetic appreciation.

Yet here we return to Kames' notion, shared by most aestheticians of his time, that the cultivation of the fine arts and measured study of its principles required leisure. That militated against their appreciation by the *hoi polloi*. And so, in spite of Hogarth's (and Jefferson's) insistence that the principles of beauty and grace were accessible to all persons, few persons had sufficient leisure to hone their faculty of taste.

That there were fine arts was uncontested in Jefferson's day, but their number was contested. Jefferson continues in his letter to his granddaughter Ellen:

> I must observe that neither the *number* of the fine arts, nor the particular arts entitled to that appellation have been fixed by general consent. Many reckon but five Painting, sculpture, architecture, music & poetry. To these, some have added Oratory, including, within that, Rhetoric which is the art of style & composition. Others again add Gardening as a 7th fine art, not horticulture, but the art of embellishing grounds by fancy.

It is Lord Kames, says Jefferson, who has shown that gardening has its place among the fine arts. Because of the tight alliance with landscape painting, such painters tend to make the best designers of gardens.

The letter commits Jefferson to painting, sculpture, architecture, music, poetry, and gardening—given his comments concerning Kames—in 1805, and suggests that he is open to the inclusion of oratory. In an earlier letter to John Banister (15 Oct. 1785), Jefferson lists painting, sculpture, architecture, and music among those fine arts which can be elegantly cultivated in Rome. In an 1806 letter to John Ogilvie (Jan. 31), he lists gardening, architecture, sculpture, painting, and music in the ninth category for his library at Monticello, thereby intimating that they are among the fine arts, but lists poetry, oratory, and criticism among the ninth (really, tenth), tenth (eleventh), and eleventh (twelfth) categories. It is unclear whether they are to be considered outside the fine arts, given that they are not in the ninth category, or whether they are to be considered as fine arts, with each deserving a separate categorization, for some inexplicable reason.

Yet, Jefferson's 1789 Catalog of Books—separated into History (Memory), Philosophy (Reason), and Fine Arts (Imagination)—lists gardening, architecture, sculpture, painting, music, poetry, oratory, and criticism under Fine Arts. It is the same with his earlier 1783 catalog. In his Retirement Library, he breaks Fine Arts into Beaux Arts (architecture, gardening, painting, sculpture, and music) and Belles Lettres (poetry, oratory, and criticism). So, notwithstanding the fact that Jefferson never settled on a definition of "fine arts," it is clear that Jefferson considered the fine arts to be eight, and I cover all eight in this undertaking.This book—*Thomas Jefferson, Taste, and the Fine Arts*—is an expiscation and critical assessment of Jefferson's views on taste and the fine arts—an incursion into the mind of Thomas Jefferson, more than an attempt, like William Howard Adams' excellent 1986 essay, "The Fine Arts," to recapitulate Jefferson's path over time to the fine arts. Adams' essay, however, disappoints inasmuch as his focus is on painting and sculpture. Adams says nothing about Jefferson's eightfold catalog of the fine arts—their number and what each comprises—and wholly overlooks the three of the four arts in Belles Lettres—poetry, oratory, and rhetoric—and devotes only one sentence to criticism. Of the Beaux Arts, he overpasses gardening and music, and devotes only a few paragraphs to architecture.

Besides the essay by Adams, there is nothing of which I know that offers a sustained discussion of Jefferson and Fine Arts. What is most astonishing is that significant biographies on Jefferson nowise include "fine arts" in their bibliography, though many of the individual fine arts are listed and covered in scattered places throughout the books. That is almost scandalous, given the indispensability of the fine arts, for Jefferson, in the education of Virginian gentlemen and their centrality in the education of Virginian females of refinement, and given that Fine Arts is one of the three axial branches of human learning for Jefferson.

Moreover, other than chapter 2 of my book, *Thomas Jefferson: Moralist,* there has never been a focused critical discussion of Jefferson's view of the aesthetic sense, which, along with reason and the moral sense, is one of the three axial faculties of humans. In this book, *Thomas Jefferson, Taste, and the Fine Arts,* I expand on my prior critical analysis, especially in my discussion in chapter 1 of Jefferson's epistemology of the sublime.

Thus, this book is a preliminary attempt to remedy the defects mentioned in the two prior paragraphs. I write "preliminary," because besides being an expiscation and critical assessment of Jefferson on taste and the fine arts, it is an invitation for other scholars to make a study of Jefferson and taste and Fine Arts as well as those arts subsumable under Fine Arts.

I begin in Part One with Belles Lettres. Chapter 1 covers the art of criticism, which is, to all intents and purposes, a meta-art. In chapter 2, I cover poetry, of which Jefferson was especially found as a youth, but came to disrelish later in life. Next, I examine Jefferson's views of oratory and rhetoric, which might seem to be relatively insignificant arts but are politically two of the most important arts in a thriving Jeffersonian republic. Part Two covers the Beaux Arts. Chapters 4 and 5 cover gardening and architecture—two of the most useful fine arts. In chapter 6, I critically discuss Jefferson's views on painting and sculpture, which as his "gallery" at Monticello shows, Jefferson fully appreciated, though he thought that they were of limited value for a nation, in his vision, comprising mostly farmers. Music is the subject of the final chapter. It has a strange status for Jefferson, as he loved music perhaps as much as he loved architecture, though music might be deemed the least useful of the fine arts—put otherwise, the finest of the fine arts.

In expiscation and critical discussion of Jefferson on taste and the fine arts, I attempt to answer some thorny questions. Was Jefferson's argument against the praxis of criticism merely an argument against its abuses, and thus, a justification of it? Why were women in America almost exclusively to be educated in certain of the fine arts—e.g., poetry, drawing, and music? Could farming, itself concerned mostly with yield, be subsumable in some sense under gardening? Why was music, perhaps the least useful of the fine arts, so important to Jefferson, given his obsession that that beauty is the most beautiful which can be put to aidful human use? If Jefferson thought that too much art was a concern for the jejune nation, why was Monticello almost tawdrily festooned with prints, paintings, busts, drawings, Native American artifacts, and other artistic items? Why did Jefferson, who was much enthusiastic about poetry as a youth, develop a distaste for it in later life?

The most singular question I pose is this. Was Jefferson's obsession that beauty itself be of some use in improving the human condition an albatross to his understanding of the fine arts, which were by definition to be appreciated for reasons other than their use, or was he in effect proposing a redefinition of Fine Arts—at least, for Americans?

My answer is that Jefferson, a man who, like Francis Bacon, was obsessed with the usefulness of knowledge, was interested in the fine arts only inasmuch as beauty could be coupled with utility. That beauty, for Jefferson, was the most beautiful which could be put to human use to better the human condition—e.g., to alleviate human suffering, increase the efficiency of production, and, most significantly, to stimulate moral improvement through reinforcing moral lessons. A tulip poplar, planted in the right location and trimmed of its lower branches, will in time not merely be a beautiful and towering tree, but will offer shade from the oppressive summer heat on a hot Virginian day for those who might wish to sit under it. A painting of a sleeping Ariadne, abandoned by Theseus after she helped him escape from the threat of the Minotaur, offers a lesson concerning the importance of fidelity in human relationships.

Thus, my thesis is that Jefferson's justification and personal cultivation of the fine arts were in effect "redefinitional"—that is, he was proposing a conception of fine arts that not only better fitted the American understanding of beauty, but also suggested a redefinition that better suited the nature of humans, and thus, globally appropriable. In sum, though the moral and aesthetic senses were for him functionally independent of each other, an appreciation of beauty that coupled itself with moral ends, one that was heterotelic, was much preferable to one that viewed beauty as its own end, one that was autotelic. One singular implication of Redefinitional Thesis is that it makes Jefferson through and through a critic of the fine arts—criticism included.

Here I note one oddity of the Redefinitional Thesis. That is Jefferson's Vitruvian tendency (chapter 5) not only to approach architecture but all the fine arts algorithmically—e.g., through principles of geometry or algebra, on especial display in "Thoughts on English Prosody" in chapter 2 and his design of Poplar Forest in chapter 5. Jefferson was fundamentally a mathematician who could see things, natural or artificial, only through the lens of numbers, figures, or equations.

As is my wont when writing on Jefferson, I often show a preference for quoting rather than paraphrasing him, which goes against the scholarly vogue. My reasons for that are two. First, scholars who paraphrase Jefferson often read into his words and wind up ascribing to Jefferson sentiments that he never articulated. That unfortunately happens all too frequently. Second and more importantly, Jefferson was well practiced in belle lettres, and I often consider it to be a signal injustice to place in my own words something Jefferson in his has expressed so eloquently. I shall try to eschew quotations of undue length.

Moreover, I have adopted the convention here, as in other publications, of labeling Jefferson's epistolary writings by reference only to his correspondent and to the date of the letter, if known, thereby giving readers the opportunity to refer to the edition of Jefferson's writings that is most readily available to them.[10] Non-epistolary writings, in contrast, are fully referenced throughout this book.

Before closing, I would like to thank sincerely the two anonymous reviewers whose full and helpful comments have, I am certain, made this book much improved.

---

[10] *The Papers of Thomas Jefferson*, 42 Vols. (to date), ed. Julian Boyd, Charles T. Cullen, John Catanzariti, and Barbara B. Oberg (Princeton: Princeton University Press, 1950–) are readily accessible through *Founders Online*. There are also several one-volume compilations of Jefferson's writings—the best of which is Merrill D. Peterson's *Thomas Jefferson: Writings* (New York: The Library of America, 1984) and M. Andrew Holowchak's *The Scholar's Thomas Jefferson* (Newcastle upon Tyne: Cambridge Scholars, 2021).

Part One
Belles Lettres

Chapter I

The Art of Criticism

"Manifold are the advantages of criticism, when this is studied as a rational science."[1] ~Henry Home (Lord Kames)

Granting that people find pictures "universally delightful" and make them a part of their "ornamental furniture," painter Jonathan Richardson (1667–1745), says in one of the earliest works on criticism, *Essay on a Theory of Painting* (1715)—a book that Jefferson owned early in life[2]—many persons still "consider the art of painting but as a pleasing superfluity," which "holds but a low rank with respect to the usefulness to mankind." Yet even "if it were only one of those sweets that the divine providence has bestowed on us, to render the good of our present being superior to the evil of it, it ought to be considered as a bounty from heaven."[3]

However, painting for Richardson is more than a sweet. First, as one of the means of conveyance of ideas among others, it is "another language," and one with a richness that words cannot express. Language has no name for many colors and figures as well as "an infinity of other ideas" which a painter clearly conveys, "without ambiguity." Second, painting "pours ideas into our minds, [while] words only drop them." A painter expresses much in one scene while a writer can only "lift up the curtain little by little."[4] Moreover, painting has considerable utility. Painters capture models for architects; the texture, form, and parts of the human body for physicians; the faces and figures of famous men for mavens of history; and the phenomena of nature for naturalists. One has only to consider the countless pictures in books without which descriptions would be unavailing.[5]

Yet Richardson is not merely offering an apology for painters. The ambitious aim is much more ambitious: an early rational exposition of the art of

---

[1] Henry Home, *Elements of Criticism* (London, 1824), p. 12.

[2] James Gilreath and Douglas L. Wilson, eds., *Thomas Jefferson's Library: A Catalog with the Entries in His Own Order* (Library of Congress, 1989), http://catdir.loc.gov/catdir/toc/becites/main/jefferson/88607928_forward.html, accessed, 20 May 2020.

[3] Jonathan Richardson, *An Essay on the Theory of Painting* (London: A.C. and A. Bettesworth, [1715] 1725), 1–2.

[4] Jonathan Richardson, *An Essay on the Theory of Painting*, 2–3.

[5] Jonathan Richardson, *An Essay on the Theory of Painting*, 7–8.

painting by expatiating on "the Rules to be observed in the Conduct of a Picture." He says, "The whole ART OF PAINTING consists of these Parts: INVENTION, EXPRESSION, COMPOSITION, DRAWING, COLOURING, and GRACE and GREATNESS."[6] Those "Qualities requisite to the Perfection of the Art" and the uses to which a good painting can be put require that a successful painter "must be a poet, a historian, a mathematician, &c. he [*sic*] must be a mechanic, his hand, and eye, must be as expert as his head is clear, and lively, and well stored with science: he must not only write history, a poem, a description but in a fine character; his brain, his eye, his hand, must be busied at the same time."[7]

Richardson was one of the earliest persons to expose any of the fine arts to rational criticism. Criticism was a fledgling art in Jefferson's day and the fine arts were flourishing in Europe at the time. There was, for instance, no shortage of artists bedecking the streets of Paris in the eighteenth century—"'tis not every *Picture-Maker* that ought to be called a *Painter,*" says Richardson, as "*Painter* ought to be a Title of Dignity, and understood to imply a Person endued with such Excellencies of Mind, and Body, as have ever been the Foundations of Honour amongst Men"[8]—but many artists, as with men of science and letters, found it difficult or impossible to survive without sponsorship and there were not enough sponsors for even the most talented artists. Talent was no guarantee of success, and so networking was necessary, and the more talented painters sought means of distinguishing themselves from the less talented, who, if clever, could peddle second-rank works to dilettantish aristocrats in search of a gallery for their home. Richardson mentions the unscrupulous practice of "the lowest of Face-Painters" who would paint the face of a rakish customer into a social scene of a painting to guarantee a purchase.[9] Thus, criticism was born, as the more talented artists were nowise comfortable with the saw, "Art is what 'artists' do."

This first chapter concerns Jefferson's views of criticism. I begin with a difficulty: Jefferson's avowed distaste for criticism. I then turn to the analysis of two works of criticism that Jefferson owned and read, two of the most significant works on criticism—Francis Hutcheson's *An Inquiry into the Original of Our Ideas of Beauty and Virtue* (1725) and Lord Kames' *Elements of Criticism* (1762)—and assess the extent to which Jefferson might have been influenced by either. I end with a closer look at Jefferson on criticism and at Jefferson as a critic.

---

[6] Jonathan Richardson, *An Essay on the Theory of Painting*, 20.
[7] Jonathan Richardson, *An Essay on the Theory of Painting*, 34–37.
[8] Jonathan Richardson, *An Essay on the Theory of Painting*, 17.
[9] Jonathan Richardson, *An Essay on the Theory of Painting*, 22.

"No man on earth has less taste or talent..."

The Grudging Critic of Criticism

On August 28, 1824, William Munford writes Thomas Jefferson about a "great and bold undertaking" he has completed: a translation of Homer's *Iliad,* without rhyme and with critical notes. Munford seeks "the declaration of a judicious Critic," and "I can find no person as well qualified as yourself to form a *correct* judgment on the subject, and *candidly* to express it." He has endeavored "to express the sense of Homer, more *correctly* & *faithfully* than Pope;—more *elegantly* & *energetically* than Cowper;—to improve the structure of blank verse, by making it more *perspicuous, easy* and *graceful,* than it usually is;—to *imitate* the *harmony,* and beautifully varied modulations, of the Homeric numbers;—the *majestic* simplicity of style, and, above all, the *sublimity* and poetical *fire* of the great father of Poetry." It is an abundantly ambitious project, as new translations of such a master of literature are needed only insofar as they address and improve on defects in older translations.[10] Thus, Munford writes in his preface of the rules of proper translation: "The duty of a translator is that he ought uniformly to express the meaning and spirit of his author with fidelity, in such language as is sanctioned by the use of the best writers and speakers of his own time and country. ... The rule of the translator should be to adhere strictly to the sense of the original; not presuming to omit ideas because he does not like them, nor rashly essaying to embellish or improve his author by additions or variations of his own."[11]

Munford obviously wishes for the patronage of Jefferson for his project, and he is likely aware of Jefferson's distaste for rhymed verse (see chapter 7). Jefferson was no stranger to patronizing projects early in life—e.g., he not only patronized but also translated A.L.C. Destutt de Tracy's *Commentaire sur l'esprit des lois de Montesquieu* and patronized John Baxter's *A New and Impartial History of England* to be used at the University of Virginia as a purgative of David Hume's avowed Tory *History of England*—yet those projects were of the scientific, not the artistic, sort and he seldom patronized

---

[10] For instance, Alexander Pope's translation of Homer's *Iliad* was rightfully much lauded because of his masterful artistry in putting into metered verse with rhyme Homer's elegant Greek prose. Pope's justification for undertaking such a project of unrivaled ambition is nearly as artful as his translation.

[11] Homer, *The Iliad,* trans. William Munford (Boston: Charles Little and James Brown, 1846), vi.

projects later in life, due to the debilitations of age, a desire not to offend others, and a wish for his remaining years to be his.[12]

Thus, Jefferson reply to Munford (6 Sept. 1824) is disobliging. "Of all men living I have the least exercised myself in the office of criticism. I never had the qualifications, the taste or talent of a reviewer," and whatever capabilities he might once have had as a critic have been enfeebled by age. Thus, Jefferson declines Munford's request.

On January 8, 1825, Jefferson receives a letter from Alexander Smyth, who offers the erstwhile president some comments on how to understand the Apocalypse in the Bible and asks for Jefferson's critical assessment.

"From this you must be so good as to excuse me," says Jefferson, "because I make it an invariable rule to decline ever giving opinions on new publications in any case whatever. no man on earth has less taste or talent for criticism than myself," and it has been over 50 years since Jefferson has read the passage.

Having excused himself from commenting, Jefferson adds, "and least and last of all should I undertake to criticise works on the Apocalypse… I then considered it as merely the ravings of a Maniac, no more worthy, nor capable of explanation than the incoherences of our own nightly dreams." Jefferson adds that there is not even sufficient coherence, or sufficient rationality, in such ravings for him to consider them as "an allegorical narrative of events, past or subsequent." Of nonsense, there cannot be an explanation. "What has no meaning admits no explanation." Jefferson adds that Smyth's time is too valuable and his intellect too large for him to waste on deciphering "paralogisms."

Consequently, the pledge to abstain from criticism, Jefferson, here clearly apophatic—he begins by stating his promise to offer no "opinions on new publications," but lapses into criticism of the Apocalypse itself—clearly does not keep. He is here a grudging, remorseful critic, but nonetheless a critic.

On October 7, 1825, Jefferson receives two pamphlets on Greek grammar—ancient and modern, and a subject ever of considerable interest to him—from John Pickering.

> I concur with you in believing that small shades of difference in grammar, are of minor importance, while shifting a student from one school to another, as necessity often obliges us to do, it would be of great importance that he should find the same grammar wherever he

---

[12] The book would not get published until 21 years after the death of Munford in 1825, and it would be well received by critics.

> went, and save the time of learning a new one. I should differ from you perhaps however in chusing between the two systems ancient and modern; because the latter has certainly simplified advantageously the scheme of grammar, and is now the one generally used and established, in this state at least.

There are, Jefferson notes, many useful books on Greek grammar[13]—he mentions those of Valpy, Wettenhall and Hackenberg as the best—but others are best read merely "as works of criticism." He adds: "Grammar, in fact, unconnected with its use in teaching us languages, is not a science of itself. It is a branch of Metaphysics, a region of fog, like that, in which we have neither star nor compass to guide us, nor a harbor of usefulness in which to expect remuneration for the time and labor of our misty pursuit of it."

As the examples above show, Jefferson was no stranger to the art of criticism, though he did, as we have seen, at times profess that he had neither talent nor taste for it.

Yet Jefferson was also a critic of criticism. To William Wirt (12 Nov. 1816), concerning the latter's biography of Patrick Henry, Jefferson states: "I have always very much despised the artificial canons of criticism. When I have read a work in prose or poetry, or seen a painting, a statue, etc. I have only asked myself whether it gives me pleasure, whether it is animating, interesting, attaching? If it is, it is good for these reasons. on these grounds you will be safe." In an earlier letter to Maria Cosway (24 Apr. 1788), he echoes the sentiment as he cites his preference for the paintings for Carlo Dolce and Adriaen van der Werff to Paul Rubens, "I am but a son of nature, loving what I see and feel, without being able to give a reason, nor caring much whether there be one." The notion that criticism is unneeded for works of art takes us beyond criticism and to meta-criticism—a criticism of criticism, or an apprehension of criticism as a fine art above the fine arts. Still, it is significant to note, as we shall see in subsequent chapters, that Jefferson time and again exposed oratory, poetry, painting, sculpture, gardening, architecture, and music to criticism.

"The man who aspires to be a critic in these arts"

The Meta-Art of Criticism

The letter to Wirt also offers a glimpse of Jefferson's view of aesthetic "judgments." If a painting pleases, that is sufficient, without any justification for its pleasantness, because the pleasantness or unpleasantness of a work of art is

[13] Jefferson tended to include analyses on grammar under criticism.

judged by a sensory faculty, taste, not rationality. So, offering an explanation would be as foolish as offering an explanation for why one enjoys macaroni and cheese—a dish that Jefferson imported to North America from France.

Humans, for Jefferson, had three faculties: ratiocination, moral sensitivity, and aesthetic sensitivity. He writes often about the first two, but very little about aesthetic sensitivity. His most elaborate account is in a letter to Thomas Law (13 June 1814). "We have indeed an innate sense of what we call beautiful: but that is exercised chiefly on subjects addressed to the fancy, whether thro' the eye, in visible forms, as landscape, animal figure, dress drapery, architecture, the composition of colours &c. or to the imagination directly, as imagery, style, or measure in prose or poetry, or whatever else constitutes the domain of criticism or taste, a faculty entirely distinct from the moral one."

The letter to Law tells us the aesthetic sensing is "entirely distinct" from the moral sense, and it too is innate. Jefferson says little else about the aesthetic sense, so it is impossible to say just how it works for him, without engagement in some surmise.

In his 1771 letter to Robert Skipwith, Jefferson recommends Lord Kames' *The Elements of Criticism* (1762), which contains an elaborate account of aesthetic sense, as well as Edmund Burke's *A Philosophical Enquiry into the Origin of Our Ideas of the Sublime and Beautiful* (1756), William Hogarth's *Analysis of Beauty* (1753), Thomas Reid's *An Inquiry into the Human Mind* (1764), and Adam Smith's *The Theory of Moral Sentiments* (1759)—each an early work that discusses aesthetic sensibility and all works that influenced Jefferson's own thinking on taste. Jefferson also was likely influenced by Scottish philosopher Francis Hutcheson, Chair of Moral Philosophy at University of Glasgow, whose book *An Inquiry into the Original of Our ideas of Beauty and Virtue* (1725) Jefferson owned.

Of those, Jefferson's moral and aesthetical thinking were likely influenced mostly by Hutcheson and especially Kames, whose views on moral sensing were much like Jefferson's and whose *Elements of Criticism* Jefferson consistently recommended as the main text for Criticism.

Of the works mentioned above, Hutcheson's is the oldest. For him, each person has an "Internal Sense," capable of appreciation of Beauty and Harmony in visible and audible objects. Beauty and Harmony, says he, are essentially matters of the relatively simple formula, "Uniformity amidst Variety."[14] "What we call Beautiful in Objects, to speak in the Mathematical Style, seems to be in a compound Ratio of Uniformity and variety: so that

---

[14] Francis Hutcheson, *An Inquiry into the Original of Our Ideas of Beauty and Virtue* (Indianapolis: Liberty Fund, [1725] 2008), 28.

where the Uniformity of Bodys is equal, the Beauty is as the variety; and where the variety is equal, the Beauty is as the Uniformity."[15]

There is for Hutcheson Absolute Beauty and Comparative or Relative Beauty. "By Absolute Beauty understand only that Beauty, which we perceive in Objects without comparison to any thing external, of which the Object is suppos'd an Imitation, or Picture; such as that Beauty perceiv'd from the Works of Nature, artificial Forms, Figures, Theorems. Comparative or Relative Beauty is that which we perceive in Objects, commonly considered as Imitations or Resemblances of something else."[16] In short, Absolute beauty is the human response, for instance, to the beauty that one sees when observing from a safe distance the Natural Bridge[17] (Figure 1-1) or one experiences when one hears the harmonies of *Hungarian Waltz*[18]; relative beauty is the beauty humans see in humanly crafted imitations: the objects of the various fine arts—e.g., Frederic Edwin Church's 1852 painting, *The Natural Bridge* (Figure 1-2) or a bird lover imitating the sounds of Jefferson's mockingbird, Dick. Both absolute beauty and relative beauty are beautiful from the human perspective, as Hutcheson leaves open the possibility that other sentient animals enjoy perhaps differently beautiful things, though I suspect he thinks that the formula, "Uniformity amidst Variety," still obtains in some visceral sense. Hutcheson acknowledges that different persons will judge uniquely beautiful things. Why is that the case? Each has a different "Association of Ideas," given differences in "Custom, Education, and Example"—by "example," Hutcheson means observing the behavior of others.[19]

There is, one might object, the problem of abstract art, which is recognized today as a viable form of art and which might readily conform to the formula Uniformity amidst Variety, but which is not always meant to be a representation of anything. Consider, for illustration, Wassily Kandinsky's 1923 painting *On White II* (Figure 1-3). Kandinsky uses skillfully lines, shapes, directionality, and colors—the last, of course, cannot be captured in Figure 1-3—to inspire or move an aficionado, but is clearly not working from any one external model. Hutcheson might counter that some of what is today categorized as Modern Art is not really art, because it is not representative in any discernible sense. He might also acknowledge that certain specimens of

---

[15] Francis Hutcheson, *An Inquiry into the Original of Our Ideas of Beauty and Virtue*, 29.
[16] Francis Hutcheson, *An Inquiry into the Original of Our Ideas of Beauty and Virtue*, 27.
[17] Thomas Jefferson, "Travel Journals," in *Thomas Jefferson: Writings*, ed. Merrill D. Peterson (New York: Library of America, 1984), 635.
[18] Harmony, for Hutcheson, is a species of absolute beauty, "because Harmony is not usually conceiv'd as an Imitation of any thing else." Francis Hutcheson, *An Inquiry into the Original of Our Ideas of Beauty and Virtue*, 25.
[19] Francis Hutcheson, *An Inquiry into the Original of Our Ideas of Beauty and Virtue*, 27.

abstract art can be appreciated for their absolute beauty. That is, however, a problem that did not exist in his day.

Fig. 1-1: Natural Bridge (courtesy, author) (left)
Fig. 1-2: Church's *The Natural Bridge* (public domain) (right)

Fig. 1-3: Kandinsky's *On White II* (public domain)

Another problem is artistic idealization or artistic license. Consider Liang Kai's twelfth-century splashed-ink piece *Immortal* (Figure 1-4). Was Kai working from a model or from imagination? If he used a model, one must presume that some of the model's features were exaggerated—e.g., the huge head and shoulders, the protuberant chest and stomach, the thick but short legs, and the heavy cloak and baggy pants—and others neglected by intentional use of broad brushstroke and eschewal of lines or clean lines—e.g., no eyes and upper nose—to give the effect of a deathless being. The overall effect of the broad brushstrokes with few defining features (the ear, mouth and nostrils) is that of a somber being (downturned head and mouth), heavily burdened by immortality and moving forward without any purpose. Kai's exaggerations are what make brilliant, evocative the work, but Hutcheson would likely be inclined to judge the work, if representative, to be some inferior representation, and so inferior in excellence.

Fig. 1-4: Kai's *Immortal* (public domain)

There is an additional problem for Hutcheson. That concerns the degree of uniformity amidst variety. When is there too much uniformity or too much variety in fine art?

Hutcheson never answers that question, very probably because he thinks that it does not admit of a definitive answer. There is no algorithm which one can apply to a portrait let alone a building, garden, or poem. The best poets, for instance, circumspectly use "Resemblances" through the cunning use of "Similitudes, Metaphors and Allegorys" to make a poem beautiful. Poor usage makes a poor poem.[20] Again, the beauty of a garden is not captured through "strict Regularity," for nature is not strictly regular, and strict regularity through symmetrical patterns in gardening is a retreat from imitation of nature; hence it cannot be beautiful.[21] Here we see the theoretical motivation for preference for the natural British style of pleasure gardening that Jefferson so admired in his day in his tour of their gardens with John Adams early in 1786—the subject of chapter 4.

Though Hutcheson does not delve into the art of criticism, we are now in a position to understand the role of early criticism in Hutcheson's day, given Hutcheson's account of the aesthetic sense. Humans have an uncanny penchant for imitation, evident in the process of associating ideas while learning. In the fine arts, "this Beauty is founded on a Conformity, or a kind of Unity between the Original and the Copy."[22] A critic is one who judges the extent to which an imitator has succeeded in his imitation—the extent to which the copy resembles the original. In that, he has a hugely refined sense of the quality of an imitation. There can, however, be no critics of Absolute Beauty, which is simply experienced.

Almost four decades later, Lord Kames (Henry Home) publishes his *Elements of Criticism*. Kames proffers a much richer account of the psychology behind aesthetic approbation or disapprobation and a much more elaborate analysis of taste. His ultimate end, however, is to further our understanding of criticism through disclosure of certain "elements of Criticism," in an effort to show that "the fine arts are a subject of reasoning as well as of taste."[23]

Aesthetic pleasure occupies a "middle place" between the turbulence of organic passion and intellectual pleasures. Organic pleasures are intense, but ephemeral. Attempts to extend them are futile and ever result in disgust. So

---

[20] The "Measures and Cadence," being Harmonies, are instances of Absolute Beauty. Francis Hutcheson, *An Inquiry into the Original of Our Ideas of Beauty and Virtue*, 20.

[21] Francis Hutcheson, *An Inquiry into the Original of Our Ideas of Beauty and Virtue*, 44.

[22] Francis Hutcheson, *An Inquiry into the Original of Our Ideas of Beauty and Virtue*, 42.

[23] Henry Home, *Elements of Criticism* (New York: A.S. Barnes & Burr, 1865 [1762]), 108.

too is it the case with intellectual pleasures, which though not intense, can lead to overstraining, from which cessation offers little relief. Kames sums: "The pleasures of the eye and the ear, ... sweet and moderately exhilarating, ... are in their tone equally distant from the turbulence of passion, and the languor of indolence," and thus mediately situated, they are ideally qualified "to revive the spirits when sunk by sensual gratification" and "to relax them when overstrained in any violent pursuit."[24]

Like moral sensing, appreciation of beauty needs refinement in order for humans to derive the fullest aesthetic enjoyment. "The fine arts are contrived to give pleasure to the eye and ear, disregarding the inferior senses. A taste for these arts is a plant that grows naturally in many soils; but, without culture, scarce to perfection in any soil: it is susceptible of much refinement; and is, by proper care, greatly improved."[25]

Our perception of beauty, distinct from moral sensing, works intimately with the moral sense, so that "it is nearly allied." He continues: "Both of them discover what is right and what is wrong: fashion, temper, and education, have an influence to vitiate both, or to preserve them pure and untainted: neither of them are arbitrary nor local; being rooted in human nature, and governed by principles common to all men." Thus, through cultivation, aesthetic enjoyment finds a link with morally correct action. The transition from "corporeal pleasures" to "the more refined sensual pleasures" and then to the "exalted pleasures of morality and religion" is "sweet and easy."[26] Jefferson says much the same in his 1771 letter to Skipwith (Aug. 3), where he lists Kames' *Elements of Criticism* as recommended reading under criticism.[27]

Kames' aim is to work back from objects "naturally agreeable ... [and] disagreeable" and to uproot for exposure "the principles of the fine arts." That is no easy task. "The man who aspires to be a critic in these arts, must pierce still deeper: he must acquire a clear perception of what objects are lofty, what low, what proper or improper, what manly, and what mean or trivial." Given

---

[24] Henry Home, *Elements of Criticism*, 24–25. One of the difficulties of the work, notes Benjamin Franklin, who befriended Kames, was lack of expatiation on the pleasures of the ear. "I only wish'd that you had examin'd more fully the Subject of Music." Benjamin Franklin to Lord Kames, 2 June 1765. Benjamin Franklin, *The Papers of Benjamin Franklin*, Vol. 12, ed. Leonard W. Labarre, William B. Willcox, and Ellen R. Cohn (New Haven, CT: Yale University Press, 1970), 162.
[25] Henry Home, *Elements of Criticism*, 25–26.
[26] Henry Home, *Elements of Criticism*, 24–26.
[27] See as TJ to John Minor, 30 Aug. 1814.

that there are principles of the fine arts, there can be a "rational science" of them that "may be cultivated to a high degree of refinement."[28]

Kames offers six reasons for practicing criticism. First, "acquaintance with the principles of the fine arts redoubles the pleasure we derive from them." Second, practice of criticism is an exercise of "the most enticing sort of logic," which here is exercised on "subjects so agreeable." Third, the reasoning employed here is exactly that sort of reasoning employed in moral judgments. Fourth, criticism strengthens the moral sense by curbing selfishness, indulgence, pride, and envy. Fifth, criticism engenders social affections by promoting sympathetic interactions with others. Last and most significantly for Kames, criticism "is a great support to morality," as the study of fine arts inclines one to moral duty. "A just relish of what is beautiful, proper, elegant, and ornamental, in writing or painting, in architecture or gardening, is a fine preparation for the same just relish of these qualities in character and behavior." A polished critic will readily see what is beautiful in virtuous activity and what is disgustful in vicious activity. Thus, criticism is a goad to virtue and an obstacle to vice.[29]

Fig. 1-5: Sprawling Texan Oak (author)

Like Hutcheson, Kames posits two species of beauty—relative beauty and intrinsic beauty—though his account differs in significant respects. Intrinsic

[28] Henry Home, *Elements of Criticism*, 26.

[29] It is not clear that the fourth, fifth, and sixth reasons are all that different. Henry Home, *Elements of Criticism*, 27–29.

beauty is "an object of sense merely." One merely sees the beauty of a spreading Texan oak (Figure 1-5). Relative beauty is "founded on the relation of objects." To see the beauty of a machine, say a timepiece, one needs to know much about its function. And so, intrinsic beauty is ultimate and direct; relative beauty is secondary and indirect, and it essentially involves reason and functionality. Both are perceived to belong to objects deemed beautiful. Both can be in the same object. Both can be subjects of rational criticism. A horse is deemed beautiful both from sleekness of figure and ease of motion and from utility—e.g., speed while running in a race.[30]

Like others of his day, Kames thought that there were discoverable "principles" of aesthetic judgments—e.g., principles related to color, figure, size, motion, grandeur, and simplicity. Yet for Kames, beauty is a secondary quality, not a primary quality—i.e., it is not a property of objects, but a property of the mind—and so, the discoverable principles are features of the mind, not features of objects. "*Beauty is not an inherent property or quality of objects at all, but the result of the accidental relations in which they may stand* to our experience of pleasure or emotions." He adds, "The beauty which we impute to outward objects, is nothing more than the reflection of our own inward emotions." He adds, "The *power of taste* is nothing more than the habit of tracing those associations by which almost all objects may be connected with interesting emotions."[31] The subjectivity of beauty, one might thus object, calls into question the worth of refining the aesthetic sense through the discovery of its principles. This objection, of course, applies to all adherents of criticism—e.g., William Hogarth and Hugh Blair as well—who argue for principles of judgments of taste.

Not all forms of subjectivity, however, are damning. Kames, following Hutcheson, believes that humans are so constituted that all are capable of scrutiny of beauty through analysis of elements of color, figure, size, motion, grandeur, and simplicity, which sway human emotions, which for each are uniquely shaped by experiences. I offer some illustrations. Simplicity in art is a desideratum, for too many objects "crowding the mind at once, disturb the attention, and pass without making any impression." Kames cites the move from Doric to Ionian to Corinthian and to the Composite orders as a movement away from beauty and toward complexity. Great artists strive for simplicity; middling artists "supply want of genius by multiplying those that

---

[30] See also Henry Home, *Essays on the Principles of Morality and Natural Religion*, Second Edition (London, 1758), 110.

[31] Henry Home, *Elements of Criticism*, 120. See also Henry Home, *Essays on the Principles of Morality and Natural Religion*, 160.

are inferior."[32] Concerning figure, a circle is more beautiful than a square, as "the attention is divided among the sides and angles of a square," and that is not the case with a circle.[33] Proportion is beautiful insofar as its lack is seen as disgustful, as when a person's head is much too small for his body (e.g., Sully's painting of Jefferson, Fig. 6-11), but it is enhanced by utility, as when "the best proportioned are the strongest and most active."[34] Uniformity, though desirable where there is great variety, "is apt to disgust by excess."[35] Too much uniformity, as in the case of geometrical French gardens, overwhelms and disgusts through boredom. It is too far removed from nature, and incredible.

Kames' psychologizing of kalology, the study of beauty, has no need for an aesthetic faculty. "We thus get rid of all the mystery of a peculiar sense or faculty imagined for the express purpose of perceiving beauty, and discover that the *power of taste* is nothing more than the habit of tracing those associations by which almost all objects may be connected with interesting emotions," says Kames. When we say that some object is beautiful, that beauty is "the reflection of our own inward emotions, ... certain little portions of love, pity, or other affections which have been connected with these objects, and still adhere ... to them." The object calls up in us certain emotions accidentally linked to it by "our own past sensations or sympathies."[36] That is why something can appear beautiful to one person and aversive to another.

How then is the art of criticism possible, if beauty is so protean, so subjective?

Our emotions are very often commonly cultivated through the acquisition of national and natural tastes.

In addition to idiosyncratic ascriptions of "beautiful," there are "national tastes." A Greek has a love of Greece, due to cultural differences that a Native American does not have. An African has a love of his race that an Asian does not have of it.[37] Such "national" differences will appear in their appreciation of the fine arts.

There are also natural tastes—"necessarily and universally connected with the feeling by the law of nature, so that it is always presented to the sense when the feeling is impressed upon the mind." Kames considers laughter linked with gaiety and weeping with distress. Nature's most beautiful object, he adds, is a handsome young woman, inciting youth and health as well as

---

[32] Henry Home, *Elements of Criticism*, 111–12.
[33] Henry Home, *Elements of Criticism*, 113.
[34] Henry Home, *Elements of Criticism*, 112.
[35] Henry Home, *Elements of Criticism*, 114.
[36] Henry Home, *Elements of Criticism*, 120–1.
[37] Henry Home, *Elements of Criticism*, 125.

feelings of innocence, gaiety, sensibility, intelligence, delicacy, or vivacity—e.g., Elisabeth Louise Vigée le Brun's *Self-Portrat in a Straw Hat* (1782, Figure 1-6). Such instances are of natural beauty, in that all persons everywhere, for the most part, are moved in the same way.[38] Kames adds, "The nature of man was originally framed with a relish for them, in order to answer to wise and good purposes,"[39] though it is likely that other species will judge other things naturally beautiful.[40] The addendum is in keeping with Hutcheson, whose notion of beauty is species-specific.

As with Hutcheson, there is also the beauty of things such as poems, theorems, and mechanisms. Poems and other works of prose conjure up beautiful objects or moral/social emotions. Theorems conjure up admiration of the genius of their creators and images of possible uses. Machines also conjure up admiration for the genius of their creators and images of possible uses.[41] Theorems and machines can be universally admired, while written works will generally have more parochial applications.

Fig. 1-6: Brun's *Self-Portrait in Straw Hat* (public domain)

---

[38] Henry Home, *Elements of Criticism*, 121–22.
[39] Henry Home, *Elements of Criticism*, 112.
[40] Henry Home, *Elements of Criticism*, 116.
[41] Henry Home, *Elements of Criticism*, 127.

National and natural tastes make possible the art of criticism, though artwork featuring national tastes will not have appeal to all humans. It might be, for instance, that a Powhatan Native American of Jefferson's time would be perplexed and turned off by the garnishments of European fashion in Brun's painting. For Kames, creators or critics of the greatest and most durable beauty "must be cautious to employ only such objects as are the natural signs, or the inseparable concomitants of emotions of which the greater part of mankind are susceptible."[42] The same holds for grandeur and sublimity, which are serious, not gay.[43] Thus, critics of the fine arts will be students of both national and natural tastes. That implies, à la Richardson, that critics will be knowledgeable vis-à-vis numerous other subjects that have a bearing on bringing their artistic pieces to life.

"The man who aspires to be a critic in these arts"

An Epistemology of the Sublime

Jefferson's views on taste were certainly influenced by Hutcheson, as Hutcheson was perhaps the largest early philosophical influence on Jefferson, and Hutcheson's *An Inquiry into the Original of Our Ideas of Beauty and Virtue* had an enormous influence on the other aestheticians that Jefferson read.

Yet the influence of Kames on taste was likely larger than that of Hutcheson. Kames' views on both morality and aesthetic sensibility were later than Hutcheson's and, given the luxury of time, thus more refined. Moreover, Jefferson, we know, recommended Kames' *Elements of Criticism* in his 1771 letter to Skipwith. He recommended the book among 19 other recommendations in an 1809 enclosure to Samuel R. Demaree. Under "Criticism," he recommended the book, along with Tooke's *Diversions of Purley*, to John Minor in 1814. It was the most significant and germane work on criticism in his possession. And so, it is apposite to ask whether Jefferson's views on the art of criticism were sufficiently similar to those of Kames.

We have seen that Jefferson, unlike Kames, does mention an aesthetic sense in his 1814 letter to Law—"we have indeed an innate sense of what we call beautiful … [which is] a faculty entirely distinct from the moral one"—and so his account might be more Hutchesonian than Kamesian, since Kames does away with a faculty for beauty, which he reduces to associations of ideas. Still, Jefferson, unlike Hutcheson and Kames, never expressly mentions anything like a distinction between relative beauty and absolute beauty, and the

---

[42] Henry Home, *Elements of Criticism*, 128.
[43] Henry Home, *Elements of Criticism*, 131.

suggestion in the 1816 letter to Wirt—where Jefferson mentions the despicableness of the "artificial canons of criticism" and intimates that the pleasure upon reading a poem or seeing a painting is itself proof sufficient of its beauty—is that the aesthetic sense "judges" immediately in the manner of his moral sense.[44] That is why Jefferson disadvises nephew Peter Carr (10 Aug. 1787) to take classes in morality. "I think it lost time to attend lectures in this branch. He who made us would have been a pitiful bungler if he had made the rules of our moral conduct a matter of science." It is likely that Jefferson too believed that there were no principles of kalology, the science of beauty.

Yet Jefferson late in life does include a professorship in moral philosophy at University of Virginia and that professor is to teach, *inter alia*, Ethics and Criticism—strangely enough, two subjects in which no one needs formal schooling. "In the school of Moral philosophy shall be taught, Mental science generally, including ethics, ideology, general grammar, and criticism; and adding rhetoric and Oratory."[45]

What of the influence of two authors that I have overpassed whom Jefferson read and recommended: William Hogarth or Edmund Burke?

If Jefferson did not believe in axial principles of criticism, discoverable by the aid of reason, then he could not have made purchase of Hogarth's six axial principles of beauty—fitness, variety, uniformity, simplicity, intricacy, and quantity—or of Edmund Burke's notions of beauty comprising smallness; smoothness; gradual variation; delicacy; and clean, fair, mild, and diversified colors; and linked with pleasure; and sublimity comprising vastness, greatness, ruggedness, negligence, darkness and gloominess, and solidness and massiveness, and linked with pain.[46]

There were no inviolable rules of morality for Jefferson, though as with the ancient Stoics, there were likely aidful, though not indefeasible, moral guidelines.[47] It was likely the same with rules of aesthetic judgments. Inspection of Jefferson's descriptions of beautiful objects often include smallness, variety, color, and economy, and are linked with pleasure;

---

[44] M. Andrew Holowchak, *Thomas Jefferson: Moralist* (Jefferson, NC: McFarland, 2017), chap. 1.
[45] Thomas Jefferson, "Enactments to Be Proposed to UVa Board of Visitors, 22 Jan. 1824," *Founders Online*, National Archives, https://founders.archives.gov/documents/Jefferson/98-01-02-4003, accessed 18 May 2020.
[46] *William Hogarth, The Analysis of Beauty: Written with a View of Fixing the Fluctuating Ideas of Taste* (London: J. Reeves, 1753), p. 12; and Edmund Burke, *A Philosophical Enquiry into the Origin of Our Ideas of the Sublime and Beautiful* (London, 1757), 115.
[47] M. Andrew Holowchak, *Thomas Jefferson: Moralist* (Jefferson, NC: McFarland, 2017), chap. 1.

inspection of Jefferson's descriptions of sublime objects often include largeness, power, violence, loftiness, fullness, darkness, manliness, and durability, but are not inevasibly linked, as they are with Burke, with dread or fear. For Jefferson, the sublime is often pleasant or leads to what is pleasant. Though in many instances it evokes immediate fear, that fear dissipates and one finds beauty as a distant, finishing impression. One has only to visit his accounts of the violent meeting of the Potomac and Shenandoah Rivers through the Blue Ridge Mountains at Harper's Ferry in Query IV and of the Natural Bridge in Query V of *Notes on Virginia.* In both instances—the first, violent; the second, calm and stunning[48]—one endures the "first glance" of violence and is rewarded by the "distant finishing" of profound beauty.[49]

In Query IV, Jefferson says of the clash of rivers at Harper's Ferry, "The first glance of this scene hurries the senses" to the view that the earth's mountains preceded the rivers, and as the rivers came, their waters swelled until they "have torn the mountain down from its summit to its base." Evidence of the "disrupture and avulsion from their beds from by the most powerful agents of nature" concerns the beds of rocks, especially in the Shenandoah. Then there is the "distant finishing," which is "a true contrast to the fore-ground." The foreground is "wild and tremendous"; the background is "placid and delightful." He continues, "The mountain being cloven asunder, she presents to your eye, through the cleft, a small catch of smooth blue horizon, at an infinite distance in the plain country, inviting you, as it were, from the riot and tumult roaring around, to pass through the breach and participate of the calm below. Here the eye ultimately composes itself."[50]

In Query V, Jefferson states that a peep from the top of the Natural Bridge (Figure 1-1) into the abyss forces one to "fall on your hands and feet." He adds, "The painful sensation is relieved by a short, but pleasing view of the Blue ridge along the fissure downwards, and upwards by that of the Short hills, which, with the Purgatory mountain is a divergence from the North ridge; and, descending then to the valley below, the sensation becomes delightful in the extreme. It is impossible for the emotions, arising from the sublime, to be felt beyond what they are here: so beautiful an arch, so elevated, so light, and springing, as it were, up to heaven, the rapture of the Spectator is really indiscribable! [*sic*]"[51]

---

[48] Thomas Jefferson, *Notes on Virginia,* ed. William Peden (Chapel Hill: University of North Carolina Press, 1954), 24.
[49] Thomas Jefferson, *Notes on Virginia,* 19.
[50] Thomas Jefferson, *Notes on Virginia,* 19.
[51] Thomas Jefferson, *Notes on Virginia,* 24–25.

It is impossible to see these two passages as purely descriptive, as they are suffused with critical commentary. The violent collision of the two rivers in Query IV is attended by what I take to be an *epistemology of the sublime.* The sublime, where it exists in nature, always cloaks the beautiful. The former is an immediate biological response, which must be endured, before its veiled beauty can appear. Thus, for Jefferson, nature, even when it seems most violent, is always and everywhere beautiful and always and everywhere pleasant. That too very likely applies to what is sublime in human productions—e.g., the Cathedral of Notre Dame (Figure 1-7).

Fig. 1-7: Cathedral of Notre Dame (courtesy, Peter K. Burian)

If this reading is correct, then Jefferson might have had something in mind similar to what was said by Hugh Blair, who noted that "the strong emotions of sublimity" were particularly rampant in "the early ages of the world," when so many objects of nature were new and strange."In the progress of society, the genius and manners of men undergo a change more favorable to accuracy, than to strength or sublimity." Blair adds that the sublime, unlike the beautiful, "is an emotion which can never be long protracted. The mind, by no force of genius, can be kept, for any considerable time, so far raised above its common tone; but will, of course, relax into its ordinary situation."[52] Jefferson's account of the epistemology of the sublime is consistent with Blair's evolutionary account of sublimity.

Upshot

Jefferson, I have shown in this chapter, was a grudging critic of the fine arts, and even of criticism, but he was nonetheless a critic, as the passages early in *Notes on Virginia* show. His epistemology of the sublime, based certainly on his own experiences with objects of sublimity, is aesthetically rich and adds a unique contribution to the literature of his day on the aesthetic, if my epistemological reading is correct.

A second feature of Jefferson qua critic was the notion of art capable of being overdone, and underdone.

When Jefferson perambulated the pleasure gardens of England, early in 1786 with John Adam—covered fully in chapter 4—he took with him Thomas Whately's *Observations on Modern Gardening* as a critical guidebook and his "Travel Journals" concerning that experience are fraught with critical insights related to the gardens and to Whately's observations concerning them. At Chiswick, "The garden shows still too much art" and "an obelisk of very ill effect; another in the middle of a pond useless." At Hampton-Court, "Old fashioned." At Esher-Place, "Clumps of trees, the clumps on each hand balance finely—a most lovely mixture of concave and convex." At Claremont, "nothing remarkable." At Paynshill, "The dwelling house by Hopkins, ill-situated" and "its architecture is incorrect." At Caversham, "This straight walks has an ill effect." At Wotton, "much neglected." At Stowe, "The Corinthian arch has a very useless appearance, inasmuch as it has no pretension to any destination." At Leasowes, "This is not even an ornamented farm." At Hagley, "No distinction between park and garden—both blended." At Blenheim, "This garden has no great beauties" and "art appears too much." At Enfield Chase, "The water very fine; would admit of great improvement by extending walks, &c." At Moor Park, "Wants water."[53] His notes are again evidence of Jefferson, here loudly, practicing criticism.

Next, there is Jefferson's remarkable piece, "Thoughts on English Prosody," in an enclosure to Marquis de Chastellux in 1786. As we shall see in the next

---

[52] Hugh Blair, *Lectures on Rhetoric and Belles Lettres* (Philadelphia: Troutman & Hayes, 1853), 39 and 47.

[53] Thomas Jefferson, "Tour of English Gardens," in *Thomas Jefferson: Writings*, ed. Merrill D. Peterson (New York: Library of America, 1984), 623–27.

chapter, where I fully examine it, it is an extraordinary piece of criticism that offers rules for proper poetry. Contravention of those rules is in effect poetry overdone.

In 1788, Jefferson proffers certain sightseeing instructions for Edward Rutledge and William Shippen (June 3), when in a foreign land. He begins with "general observations." "When you are doubting whether a thing is worth the trouble of going to see, recollect that you will never again be so near it, that you may repent the not having seen it, but can never repent having seen it." On the other extreme, there is "seeing too much." He then proffers "objects of attention for an American." Those include, in the order Jefferson gives—and for Jefferson order is seldom discretionary—agriculture, mechanical arts (e.g., forges, stone quarries, boats, and bridges), lighter mechanical arts, gardens, architecture, painting and statuary, politics, and courts. Of gardens, he writes: "peculiarly worth the attention of an American, because it is the country of all others where the noblest gardens may be made without expense. We have only to cut out the superabundant plants." Of architecture, he writes: "Worth great attention. As we double our numbers every twenty years, we must double our houses," and Americans tend to prefer perishable materials, so every 20 years, houses must be rebuilt. Architecture is "among the most important arts: and it is desirable to introduce taste into an art which shows so much." Of painting and sculpture, his verdict is otherwise. "Too expensive for the state of wealth among us. It would be useless, therefore, and preposterous, for us to make ourselves connoisseurs in those arts. They are worth seeing, but not studying."[54] In the words of William Howard Adams, "In a country that was still clearing wilderness and fighting Indians, it was preposterous to consider art among the nation's first priorities."[55]

Such illustrations show plainly, and more can be proffered, that Jefferson might have decried criticism as an unneeded fine art—judging an art fine was a matter of sensing, not reasoning—but he was no stranger to its practice. Hence, we cannot take seriously his comment to Wirt that there is nothing to the art of criticism.

Moreover, criticism, qua fine art, too can be overdone. There are natural and national aspects that have a bearing on criticism, as Kames notes—consider John Trumbull's *Declaration of Independence* (Figure 6.9, below)—and here criticism comes vitally into play. Yet what one finds, say, beautiful is the result of a lifetime of idiosyncratic experiences. One who has never been exposed to

---

[54] Thomas Jefferson, "Travelling Notes for Mr. Rutledge and Mr. Shippen," in *Thomas Jefferson: Writings*, ed. Merrill D. Peterson (New York: Library of America, 1984), 659–60.
[55] William Howard Adams, "The Fine Arts," in *Thomas Jefferson: A Reference Biography*, ed. Merrill D. Peterson (New York: Charles Scribner's Sons, 1986), 204.

the use of octagons in architecture has no inkling of their beauty, and functionality. Still, the aesthetic, unlike Kames, is a sensory faculty for Jefferson, for, say, brightening a room. One sees or feels the beauty of something, and, in many respects, that is enough. As I have noted, no one feels the need to explain his liking of macaroni and cheese. One merely likes it.

Furthermore, artistic expression is, for Jefferson, subject to the same constraints of moral activities. Consistent with Aristotelian virtue ethics, morally correct action is the right person doing the right thing, at the right place, in the right manner, for the right reason, and at the right time—here, the right reason for Jefferson being action in keeping with the feeling of the moral sense.

Again, the fine arts were cultivated chiefly among the gentry in Jefferson's day and they were cultivated for their own sake; they were autotelic. That is why they were construed "fine." Criticism was, thus, some attempt to give a rational account of why something desirable in itself was desirable—a task, in principle, as fruitless as it is futile. Yet Jefferson almost always seems to have had utility in the rear of his mind when it came to any fine art. That beauty which coupled with human utility was the most pleasant, the most beautiful.

Jefferson's insistence that beauty ought to be of some use leads to a final point. Although he says nothing about any distinction between absolute beauty and relative beauty, ascription of such a distinction does some work toward understanding Jefferson qua critic. Jefferson prized enormously that beauty that was heterotelic—*viz.*, that could be put to human betterment, hence, his preference for gardening and architecture to painting and sculpture. Autotelic or absolute beauty, for Jefferson, he misprized, for it was a luxury fit for scobberlotchers, practiced in idleness, not industrious persons.[56] And so, it might be that he too embraced a distinction of absolute and relative beauty—the former being beauty without use (autotelic beauty); the latter being beauty with use (autotelic and heterotelic beauty). That, of course, is not the distinction of Kames or of Hutcheson. However, it just might be that he never gave the notion of distinguishing between absolute and relative beauty much thought, and settled, as I believe, a notion of "Fine Art" best suited for his ideal of American industry.

All fine arts could likely be put to some human use—the right sort of painting was historically availing and a poem or song could be morally uplifting—and so there was, for him, some theoretical space for criticism qua fine art. A Jeffersonian critic of the fine arts was one who speculated about the uses to

---

[56] See M. Andrew Holowchak, *Thomas Jefferson: The Cavernous Mind of an American Savant* (Newcastle upon Tyne: Cambridge Scholars Press, 2019), 189.

which beauty could be put. Beauty without conceivable usefulness was simply to be eschewed as a useless indulgence—a pursuit uniquely unsuited for the sort of citizens needed in a Jeffersonian republic, agrarian-based.

Chapter II

The Art of Poetry

"'Therefore' is a word the poet must not know."[1] ~André Gide

Plato in *Apology* recounts Socrates' trial in Athens as a corrupter of the young. Plato lists three sets of accusers: politicians, poets, and craftsmen. Those groups of men became accusers because Socrates frequented them in search of an answer to a riddle on behalf of the oracle at Delphi. When a friend of Socrates, Chaerephon, once asked the oracle if anyone was wiser than Socrates, the oracle replied, "No one is wiser." Socrates, perplexed because he knew that the oracle was incapable of untruth and because he did not think himself to be wise, went to the politicians, the poets, and the craftsmen to see whether they could help him to unravel the riddle.[2]

When Socrates went to the poets, he asked them also about some of their best-loved poems so that he might learn more about the poems. Yet he found that "all the people present could have discussed those poems better than their authors." It occurred to him that the poets could write such beautiful things only because of a natural or divine inspiration. "They say many fine things, but know nothing about what they speak." And so, their poetic wisdom was mere window dressing.[3]

Plato's view of the ignorance of poets is a view that has been, rightly or wrongly, entertained for centuries. Nonetheless, it is not a view that was prominent in Jefferson's day and not a view shared by Jefferson, as poetry was widely practiced and largely appreciated in the eighteenth and nineteenth centuries. Poems, for instance, were commonly published in the newspapers of the day.

When young, Thomas Jefferson commonplaced numerous fragments of poems in what has come to be called his *Literary Commonplace Book* (*LCB*). Profound interest in proper poetic expression is evident in a 1786 enclosure in a letter to Marquis de Chastellux titled "Thoughts on English Prosody."

---

[1] André Gide, *Journals, 1914–1927,* trans. Justin O'Brien (Urbana: University of Illinois Press, 1948), 448.

[2] Plato, *Apology,* trans. C.D.C. Reeve (Indianapolis: Hackett Publishing Company, Inc., 2012), §§21–22c.

[3] Plato, *Apology,* §§22b–c.

Continued interest in poetry is evident during his presidential years in his composition of two scrapbooks of poems, bound for preservation. Evidence of the significance and power of poetry comes with a poem he crafted for his daughter Martha prior to his passing.

Such things duly noted, there is considerable evidence that the enthusiasm manifest in composition of *LCB* waned as Jefferson matured and aged. What caused his diminution of interest? Did he come to adopt a Socratic attitude concerning poetry and poets, because he thought, perhaps, that it was the "finest" of the fine arts—i.e., the least useful of the fine arts?

In this chapter, I set out to answer those questions. I begin with an inspection of Jefferson's *Literary Commonplace Book*, composed early in life and bound in the 1780s. I then turn to Jefferson's meticulous analysis of English prosody in 1786. The third section concerns Jefferson's passion for the epic poems of a certain "Ossian" through scrutiny of his writings on Ossian. Next, I take a look at his cut-and-paste collection of poems, amassed during his presidential years, which is radically different that the sort of selections he culled for his *LCB*. I end with some thoughts on Jefferson's sea change apropos of the worth of poetry.

"Can make a Heav'n of Hell, a Hell of Heav'n"

Literary Commonplace Book

A fondness for poetry—comprising Narrative, Dramatic, and Didactic—is unmistakable in Jefferson's early life as well as in the period just after he ends his legal practice. Jefferson writes: "I was bred to the law that gave me a view of the dark side of humanity. Then I read poetry to qualify it with a gaze on the bright side."[4]

Jefferson includes in his *Literary Commonplace Book* a surprisingly large number of poets among those authors whom he commonplaces. Commonplacing, the practice of copying down significant passages from favored authors into a booklet for personal use, was widespread in his day, and it is unsurprising that Jefferson practiced it.

Jefferson's *LCB*, a bound manuscript of 123 leaves, was sent to a publisher for binding at some time in the 1780s. The entries comprise five categories; Works in Prose (§§1–84), Classical Poetry (§§85–202), English Poetry (§§203–85), English Dramatic Verse (§§286–341), and Poetic Miscellany (§§342–407).

---

[4] Douglas Wilson, "Thomas Jefferson's Early Notebooks," William and Mary Quarterly, Vol. 42, 1985: 451.

Of them, all categories except the first are poetic, and that makes 323 of the entries of poems or fragments of poems. That number is astonishing, as it shows a profound interest in poetry in Jefferson's formative years. Most selections of the first four categories, says Douglas Wilson, who edited the Princeton version of the book, were entered by 1766, while the last were collected thereafter and sometime prior to binding.[5]

Poets include the Greeks Homer, Euripides, Anacreon, and Smyrnaeus; the Romans Terence, Catullus, Horace, Manilius, Ovid, Seneca, and Virgil; the English Mark Akenside, Samuel Butler, Robert Dodsley, John Dryden, John Langhorne, John Milton, Thomas Moss, Alexander Pope, William Shakespeare, John Sheffield, and Edward Young; the Frenchman John Racine; and the Scotts Ossian (James MacPherson), David Mallet, and James Thomson. Among Classical poets, Jefferson includes selections from the Greek and Roman poets Euripides, Homer, Virgil, Horace, Terence, Livy, Ovid, Seneca, and Pope's Homer.

Among English poets, Jefferson includes selections from Pope, Milton, Young, Shakespeare, Thomson, Dryden, and Butler.

Among Dramatic poets, Jefferson includes selections from Dryden, Johnson, Southerne, Otway, Congreve, Buckingham, Rowe, Mallet, Dodsley, and Milton.

Under miscellanea, Jefferson includes selections from Akenside, Horace, Anacreon,[6] Thomson, Mallet, Moore, Buchanan, Pope, Horace, Seneca, Catullus, Rowe, Dryden, Ossian, Terence, Racine, Langhorne, Moss, an unidentified author, Manilius, and Quintus Smyrnaeus.

Beyond proffering an indication of Jefferson's profound interest in poetry as a youth, the authors he selected for commonplacing and the themes he commonplaced tell us about the turn of his mind, the subjects with which he was preoccupied, in his shaping years. It is worthwhile, thus, to dilate on those authors and themes.

The collection begins with 70 fragments from Euripides and that suggests a strong emotional and cognitive attachment to the somewhat counter-conventional Greek tragedian and perhaps antipathy of Aeschylus and Sophocles, not commonplaced. There are also 28 fragments from Homer, 47 from John Milton, 28 from Edward Young, 16 from William Shakespeare, 14 from "Ossian" (James McPherson), and 11 from Nicholas Rowe.

---

[5] Douglas Wilson, introduction to *Jefferson's Literary Commonplace Book*, ed. Douglas L. Wilson (Princeton: Princeton University Press, 1989), 5.

[6] The works Jefferson cited by Anacreon are not of Anacreon, but were thought to be so during his time.

It is unsurprising that one of the most prominent themes, given 70 selections from Euripides, is *fate* or *misfortune*. Consider §95, which reads in translation from Jefferson's Greek entry: "Egad, nothing is reliable, fair fame is fleeting, and there is no assurance that wealth will not be an encumbrance. The gods confound our fortunes, by tossing them to and from, and birth confusion in us, so that in our ignorance, we might worship them."[7] From Horace (§172), Jefferson commonplaces, "Seize the day and do not trust much tomorrow."[8] There is this fragment from Pope's *Iliad*. "To labour is the lot of man below; / And when Jove gave us life, he gave us woe" (§200).[9] Jefferson quotes from Edward Young (§264): "Misfortune, like a creditor severe, / But rises in demand for her delay; / She makes a scourge of past prosperity, / To sting thee more, and double thy distress."[10] Finally, there is this fragment from John Dryden (§380): "Be juster heaven; such punish'd thus, / Will make us think that Chance rules all above, / And shuffles with a random hand, the lots / Which man is forc'd to draw."[11]

Industry or *hard work*, such an important value in Jefferson's life as is evident abundantly from letters to his daughters and grandchildren, is a common theme. Fragment 110 from Euripides states: "For how can you win a great cause by small efforts? It were senseless even to wish it."[12]

Not unexpected from a young man, *love* is a very prominent theme, but the love of which he writes is conjugal, not lustful. Jefferson commonplaces Thomas Otway: "How vainly would dull Moralists impose / Limits on Love, whose Nature brooks no Laws. / Love is a God, & like a God, should be / Inconstant, with unbounded Liberty; / Rove as he list" (§293).[13] In a fragment from Nicholas Rowe (§307), Jefferson castigates the Lothario: "All the Heav'n they hope for is Variety. / One Lover to another still succeeds, / Another, & another after that, / And the last Fool is welcome as the former, / 'Till, having lov'd his Hour out, he

---

[7] Euripides, *Hecuba*, in *The Plays of Euripides*, trans. Edward P. Coleridge (London, 1910), lines 956–59 (my translation from Jefferson's Greek).

[8] Horace, *The Odes and Epodes*, Vol. 1, ed. C.E. Bennett (New York: 1914), Ode 12.

[9] Homer, *Iliad*, trans. Alexander Pope (London: Casell and Company, 1909), Book X, lines 78–79.

[10] Edward Young, *The Complaint, or Night Thoughts on Life, Death, and Immortality* (New York: Sage & Thompson, 1805), Night Third, lines 320–21.

[11] John Dryden, *All for Love*, Act V, Scene I, lines 1–4, http://public-library.uk/ebooks/10/77.pdf, accessed 14 May 2022.

[12] Euripides, *Orestes*, trans. E. P. Coleridge, http://faculty.fairfield.edu/rosivach/cl109/euripides-orestes.htm, accessed 14 May 2022.

[13] Thomas Otway, *Don Carlos*, Act III, Scene I, lines 1–5, https://quod.lib.umich.edu/e/eebo/A53511.0001.001/1:10?rgn=div1;view=fulltext, accessed 14 May 2022.

gives Place / And mingles with the Herd that goes before him."[14] He commonplaces from James Thomson (§283) to tell of the futility of love: "Even love itself is bitterness of soul, / A pleasing anguish pining at the heart."[15]

In contrast to love, Jefferson commonplaces from Edward Young two lines on *misery*. "Woes cluster; rare are solitary woes; / They love a train, they tread each other's heel" (§252).[16]

There are numerous references to *women*—many, less than flattering, even misogynistic, as many scholars have noted.[17] Euripides (§132) says, "Yea, men should have begotten children from some other source, no female race existing; thus would no evil ever have fallen on mankind."[18] Jefferson commonplaces Thomas Otway's very aggressive language: "The lusty Bull ranges through all the Field, / And from the Herd singling his Female out, / Enjoys her, & abandons her at Will" (§303).[19] It is the only fragment of its sort and atypical of Jefferson.

---

[14] Nicholas Rowe, *The Fair Penitent*, ed. Malcolm Goldstein (Lincoln: University of Nebraska Press, 1969), Act I, lines 401–11.

[15] James Thomson, *Seasons*, ed. Otto Zippel (Berlin: Mayer & Müller, 1908), lines 338–39.

[16] Edward Young, *The Complaint, or Night Thoughts on Life, Death, and Immortality*, Night Third, lines 63–64.

[17] E.g., Merrill D. Peterson, *Thomas Jefferson & the New Nation: A Biography*, (London: Oxford, 1970), p. 20; Douglas L. Wilson, "Thomas Jefferson's Early Notebooks," *William and Mary Quarterly*, Vol. 42, 1985: 442; Jon Kukla, *Mr. Jefferson's Women* (New York: Vintage Books, 2008), 37; and Kenneth Lockridge, *On the Sources of Patriarchal Rage* (New York: NYU Press, 1994), 70; and Jack McLaughlin, *Jefferson and Monticello: The Biography of a Builder* (New York: Henry Holt and Company, 1988), 47–51.

[84] Euripides, *Medea*, trans. E. P. Coleridge, http://classics.mit.edu/Euripides/medea.html, accessed 14 May 2022, lines 516–19 (Douglas Wilson's translation. See also §§117, 236, 238, 241, and 301.

[19] Thomas Otway, *The Orphan, Or, The Unhappy Marriage*, ed. J.C. Ghosh, *The Works of Thomas Otway: Plays, Poems, and Love-letters* (Oxford, 19432). Act I, lines 362–67. See also §§306, 315, and 341. Kukla sees this as evidence of an aggressive posture toward woman after his disastrous episode with Rebecca Burwell, which ended just prior to his twenty-first birthday. Jefferson, clumsy and unassuming with Burwell, turned "bullish," and vigorously pursued close friend John Walker's wife, when Walker was away. Kukla states, "Jefferson's aggressive pursuit of Elizabeth Walker reflected a more predatory sexuality than the adolescent reverence that had characterized his tongue-tied obsession with Rebecca Burwell." Lonely and with many of his friends married, Jefferson was "acting out a role from the angry texts in his notebooks—the playwright Thomas Otway's lusty bull ranging through the fields, singling his female out, and enjoying and abandoning her 'at Will.'" Jon Kukla, *Mr. Jefferson's Women*, 55. That view I have sufficiently refuted. M. Andrew Holowchak, *Thomas Jefferson: Psychobiography of an American Lion* (New York: Nova, 2020), 35–39.

There are other selections on women that are not cynical. From Otway (§309), there is a passage most becoming: "Can there in Women be such glorious Faith? / Sure all ill Stories of thy Sex are false! / O Woman! Lovely Woman! Nature made thee / To temper Man: we had been Brutes without you: / Angels are painted fair to look like you: / There's in you all that we believe of Heav'n, / Amazing Brightness, Purity & Truth, / Eternal joy, & everlasting Love."[20] Another passage (§340) is illustrative of perplexity vis-à-vis women. "It is not Virtue, Wisdom, Valour, Wit, / Strength, Comeliness of Shape, or amplest Merit, / That Woman's Love can win or long inherit; / But what it is, hard is to say, / Harder to hit."[21]

It is best to conclude not that there was a misogynistic phase of Jefferson's life, like many scholars perusing *LCB* state, but that there was a phase of decided ambivalence after his ruinous episode with his first love Rebecca Burwell, which ended prior to his twenty-first birthday. A fine illustration of this ambivalence is §321. "I had beheld ev'n her whole Sex, unmov'd, / Look'd o'er 'em like a Bed of gaudy Flowers, / That lift their painted Heads, & live a Day, / Then shed their trifling Beauties, till she came / With ev'ry Grace that Nature's Hand could give."[22] Fragment 359 empathizes with the fate of women. "Why did leave my tender father's wing, / And venture into love? That maid that loves, / goes out to sea upon a shatter'd plank. / And puts her trust in miracles for safety."[23]

Moral themes are also prevalent and nearly all are Stoic.

From Horace in fragment 177, Jefferson commonplaces a notion of *Stoic wisdom*: "Who then is free? The wise man, who is master of himself, who fears not poverty, death, or chains; who courageously defies his passions, and ignores ambition; who is whole, polished, and rounded in himself so that nothing external to him can settle on his polished surface, and against whom Fortune cannot make a beginning."[24]

---

[20] Thomas Otway, *Venice Preserved, Or, A Plot Discover'd* (London: 1682), Act 1, lines 335–42.

[21] John Milton, *Sampson Agonistes* (London: John Starkey, 1671), lines 1010–17.

[22] Nicholas Rowe, *The Tragedy of the Lady Jane Gray*, Act 3, Scene I.

[23] Edward Young, *The Revenge* (London: 1721), Act. 4, Scene I. The passages on women from §236 to §340 seem to play out psychologically Jefferson's failed affair with Rebecca Burwell. He moves from indignation in the misogynistic poems denial (e.g., §§132, 236, 238, 241, and 301), to praise of women (§309), to resignation (§334), to perplexity (§340), and to empathy (§359).

[24] Horace, *Satires, Epistles, and Art of Poetry of Horace*, trans. John Conington, Book 7, https://www.gutenberg.org/cache/epub/5419/pg5419.html, accessed 14 May 2022.

Fragment 98, again from Euripides, concerns *authenticity*—being one in thought and action. It reads: "Words ought never to count more than actions in this life. When a man's deeds have been good, his words will have been good. Yet when his deeds are wicked, his words will have betrayed insincerity, and it will not have been possible to pay mouth honor to justice. Yet there are clever persons who have gotten away with inauthenticity, but such cleverness cannot last a lifetime. Their end will be bad. No one has ever escaped."[25] From Pope's Homer (§188), we get, "Who dares think one Thing, and another tell, / My heart detests him as the Gates of Hell."[26]

Jefferson also commonplaces passages on *justice*. From Jean Racine (§392), we get: "How much less dire, Heaven, were they victims' plight / If thy bolt crushed the guilty ones outright! / How infinite thy chastisements appear / When thou let'st live those writhing in thy fear!"[27]

Excerpts on *moderation* Jefferson too commonplaces. From Pope (§204), Jefferson writes: "For more Perfection than this State can bear / In vain we sight; Heaven made us as we are. / As Wisely sure a modest Ape might aim / To be like Man."[28] From George Buchanan (§367), Jefferson commonplaces: "Oh happy security of a modest condition! / He is happy indeed who far from disturbances / Spends his years unknown / In a secure obscurity."[29]

One of the most prominent moral themes is *Stoical longanimity*. "It is necessary for humans, being mortal, to bear patiently misfortunes" (§135).[30] Fragment 170 reads, "Through endurance, a burden that the gods refuse to exchange for a good becomes lighter."[31] Fragment 181 says: "We must with lenity bear whatever comes our way. The undeserved penalty [otherwise] comes, and then comes suffering."[32]

---

25 Euripides, *Hecuba*, in *The Plays of Euripides*, trans. Edward P. Coleridge (London, 1910), Book V, line 1187.

26 Homer, *Iliad*, trans. Alexander Pope, Book IX, line 412.

27 Jean Racine, *The Brothers at War*, in *Racine: The Complete Plays*, trans. Samuel Solomon (New York: Random House, 1967), Act I, Scene II.

28 Alexander Pope, *An Essay on Man* (Clarendon Press, Oxford: 1871), Epistle II, lines 19–21.

29 George Buchanan, *Jephtha: A Drama* (London: Alex Gardner Paisley: 1902) (Douglas Wilson's translation).

30 Euripides, *Medea*, trans. E. P. Coleridge, http://classics.mit.edu/Euripides/medea.html, accessed 14 May 2022, line 1018.

31 Horace, *The Odes and Epodes*, Vol. 1, ed. C.E. Bennett (New York: 1914), Ode 24.

32 Ovid, *Heroides and Amores*, trans. Grant Showerman (Cambridge: Loeb, 1925).

There are also references to the Greek conception of *equanimity* (*ataraxia*). "One who brings / A mind not to be chang'd by place or time. / The mind is it's own place, & in itself / Can make a Heav'n of Hell, a Hell of Heav'n" (§229).[33]

Fragment 334 from John Milton concerns *personal responsibility.* "Nothing of all these Evils hath befall'n me / But justly; I myself have brought them on, / Sole Author I, sole Cause; if ought seem vile, / As vile hath been my Folly."[34]

In keeping with the Stoic Seneca's notion that virtue ought frequently to be put to a *test,* Jefferson quotes Dryden (§282): "In struggling with Misfortunes / Lies the true Proof of Virtue. On smooth Seas / How many Bawble Boats dare set their sails, / And make an equal Way with firmer Vessels: / But let the Tempest once enrage the Sea, / And then behold the strong ribb'd Argosie / Bounding between the Ocean & the Air, / like Perseus mounted on his Pegasus / Then where are those weak Rivals of the Main?"[35]

There are also fragments, though not many, with political content.

There are references to *liberty,* though they are surprisingly few. I note two. Jefferson quotes Milton (§224), "Though in this vast Recess, / Free, & to none accountable, preferring / Hard Liberty before the easy Yoke / Of servile Pomp."[36] There is this except from an author unknown (§405): "Sweet are the jasmines breathing flowers / Sweet the soft falling vernal showers / Sweet is the gloom the grove affords / And sweet the note of warbling birds. / But not the grove, nor rain, nor flowers / Nor all the feathered songsters' powers / Can ever sweet & pleasing be / O lovely *Freedom,* without thee."

Fragment 328 from John Milton is about *disdain of birth and wealth*—what Jefferson in a letter to John Adams (28 Oct. 1813) dubs "artificial aristocracy." "For him I reckon not in high Estate / Whom long Descent of Birth / Or the Sphere of Fortune raises."[37]

Fragment 313 concerns the *futility of conformity of thought.* "To subdue th'unconquerable Mind, / To make one Reason have the same Effect / Upon all Apprehensions; to force this, / Or this Man, just to think, as thou & I do; /

---

[33] John Milton, *Paradise Lost* (London, 1667), Book 1, lines 253–55.

[34] John Milton, *Samson Agonistes* (London: John Starkey, 1671), lines 374–77.

[35] John Dryden, *All for Love,* Act V, Scene I, lines 1–4, http://public-library.uk/ebooks/10/77.pdf, accessed 14 May 2022.

[36] From Dryden's William Shakespeare, *Troilus and Cressida,* Act. I, Scene III, lines 55ff., https://www.litcharts.com/shakescleare/shakespeare-translations/troilus-and-cressida/act-1-scene-3, accessed 14 May 2022.

[37] John Milton, *Samson Agonistes* (London: John Starkey, 1671), lines 170–72.

Impossible! unless Souls were alike / In all, which differ now like human Faces."[38]

Given Jefferson's lifelong love of music, it comes as little surprise to find a few selections on *music*. He commonplaces William Shakespeare, William Congreve, and Nicholas Rowe (§294, §295, and §296). "What so hard, so stubborn, or so fierce, / But Music for the Time will change its Nature? / The Man who has not Music in his Soul, / Or is not touch'd with Concord of sweet Sounds, / Is fit for Treasons, Stratagems, & Spoils, / The motions of his Mind are dull as Night, / And his Affections dark as Erebus: / Let no such Man be trusted."[39] Next, "Music has Charms to sooth a savage Beast, / To soften Rocks, or bend a knotted Oak. / I've read that Things inanimate have mov'd, / And, as with living Souls, have been inform'd / By magic Numbers & persuasive Sound."[40] Last, "Let there be Music, let the Master touch / The sprightly String, & softly breathing Lute, / Till Harmony rouse ev'ry gently Passion, / Teach the cold Maid to lose her Fears in Love, / And the fierce Youth to languish at her Feet. / Begin: ev'n Age itself is chear'd with Music, / It wakes a glad Remembrance of our Youth, / Calls back past joys, & warms us into Transport."[41]

There are a very large number of poetic fragments, over 60, which refer or allude to the *finiteness of life* or to *death*. That comes as a surprise, given that the book was composed relatively early in Jefferson's life, and it suggests a preoccupation with death. Fragment 155 states: "One can have cattle and plump sheep just by lifting. One can win tripods and the tawny high heads of horses. Yet a man's life, once ended, cannot return. It cannot be hoisted. It cannot be taken by force, when it has crossed the barrier of teeth."[42] Selections §§347–356 concern death. Finally, there is this oft-quoted except from Book VII of Homer's *Iliad* (§398) "As is the generation of leaves, so is that of humanity, / The wind scatters the leaves on the ground, but the live timber

---

[38] Nicholas Rowe, *Tamerlane: A Tragedy* (London: Sagwan Press, 2015), Act III, Scene II.
[39] William Shakespeare, *The Merchant of Venice*, Act V, Scene I, Lines 90–97, https://shakespeare.folger.edu/downloads/pdf/the-merchant-of-venice_PDF_FolgerShakespeare.pdf, accessed 14 May 2022. Jefferson takes some liberties with the text.
[40] William Congreve, *The Mourning Bride: A Tragedy* (London: John Bell, 1776), Act I, Scene I.
[41] Nicholas Rowe, *The Fair Penitent*, ed. Malcolm Goldstein (Lincoln: University of Nebraska Press, 1969), Act II, Scene I.
[42] Homer, *Iliad*, trans. A.T. Murray (Cambridge: Harvard University Press, 1924), Book IX, lines 406–12 (my translation).

/ Burgeons with leaves again in the season of spring returning. / So one generation of men will grow while another dies."[43]

There is also a selection from John Sheffield on *suicide*, with a Senecan bent. "For noble Life, when weary of itself, / Has always Power to shake it off at Pleasure, / Since I know this, know all the World besides, / That Part of Tyranny prepar'd for me, / I can & will defy. / And so can I. / Thus ev'ry Bondman in his own Hand bears / The Pow'r to cancel his Captivity. / And why should Cæsar be a Tyrant then? / Poor Man! I know he would not be a Wolf, / But that he sees the Romans are but Sheep: / He were no Lion if we were not Lambs."[44]

Last, *domesticity* or a *mal du pay* (homesickness) also occurs. Writes Horace: "Oh country house, when shall I again see you? When shall I be able, first with my books of the ancients and next with sleep and idleness, to drink down the sweet forgetfulness of the troubles of life?" (§175)[45]

What can we conclude from the study of *LCB*?

The many passages commonplaced on fate, resignation, and death shows Jefferson early in life seemed somewhat disposed to dolefulness.

It is unsurprising to find, given Jefferson's age at the time of his commonplacing, so many references to love and women. Yet references to love generally are of the conjugal sort. There is only one crude reference, the lusty-bull fragment (§303), that seems to condone lust. There are more misogynistic passages than there are selections that paint women in a bright light, and that is likely explained by his failed relationship with Rebecca Burwell, which was ended in 1764. It might be that failed relationship which explains also what seems to be a preoccupation with death and the numerous passages on resignation and fate.

Few references to concepts such as liberty, equality, and disdain of wealth and birth, which would form the germ of his robust political philosophy later in life and become themes with which Jefferson would throughout his life be preoccupied, show that thinking about politics was mostly remote from his life early in life, and that is surprising.

---

[43] Homer, *Iliad*, trans. A.T. Murray (Cambridge: Harvard University Press, 1924), Book IX, lines 146–49 (Douglas Wilson's translation).

[44] John Buckingham, *The Tragedy of Julius Caesar, Altered* (Glasgow: Robert and Andrew Foulis, 1752), Act I, Scene V.

[45] Horace, *The Satires, Epistles, and Art of Poetry*, trans. John Conington, Book 6, lines 60–2, https://www.gutenberg.org/cache/epub/5419/pg5419.html, accessed 14 May 2022. See also §378.

Finally, the numerous passages on morality—e.g., virtue, equanimity, forbearance, moderation, and justice—which are themes with which Jefferson was absorbed later in his life, shows a profound interest in morality—an interest that would continue with the same robustness, as I have elsewhere shown,[46] throughout remainder of his life.

"No two persons will accent the same passage alike"

Jefferson on English Prosody

"By industrious examination of the Greek and Latin verse," says Thomas Jefferson in a 1786 enclosure, titled "Thoughts on English Prosody," to Marquis de Chastellux "it has been found that pronouncing certain combinations of vowels and consonants long, and certain others short, the actual arrangement of those long and short syllables, as found in their verse, constitutes a rhythm which is regular and pleasing to the ear, and that pronouncing them with any other measures, the run is unpleasing, and ceases to produce the effect of the verse."[47] This enclosure, neglected by Jeffersonian scholars probably because it is highly esoteric and requires some familiarity with philology, I find to be one of the most fascinating pieces that Jefferson, ever fixed on minutiae, composed.

Jefferson seeks a measure of rhythm—an aesthetic feature of verse—and that measure is quantity, "the length allowed to a syllable," or its accent.[48] He falls upon Samuel Johnson's appropriation of Greek verse. First, an accent can fall on the odd syllable, which Jefferson dubs "imparisyllabic verse" (Gr., "not beside" or trochaic verse). Second, an accent can fall on the even syllable, which he dubs "parisyllabic verse" (Gr., "beside" or iambic verse). Last, an accent can fall on every third syllable: "trisyllabic verse" (Gr., "third" or anapestic verse). "Accent then is ... the basis of English verse; and it leads us to the same threefold distribution of it to which the hypothesis of *quantity* had led Dr. Johnson."[49]

Why are there only those three measures of accent?

It is a matter of the nature of sounds of which the English language is composed—though Jefferson means any language—and of "the construction

---

[46] M. Andrew Holowchak, *Thomas Jefferson: Moralist* (Jefferson, NC: McFarland, 2017).

[47] Thomas Jefferson, *Writings*, ed. Merrill D. Peterson (New York: The Library of America, 1984), 594.

[48] Thomas Jefferson, *Writings*, 595.

[49] Thomas Jefferson, *Writings*, 598.

of the human ear," as "it has pleased God to make us so."[50] There are, it seems, objective criteria, or at least, species-specific criteria, for euphony, and aesthetic sensitivity.

An English poet, then, is constrained in arrangement of words so that lines accord with one of the three arrangements, and they present grave difficulties for aspiring poets.

Yet a poet is not without resources—poetic license. "To aid him in this he has at his command the whole army of monosyllables in which the English language is a very numerous one." A poet may choose to accent or leave unaccented a monosyllable.[51] Jefferson has us consider "with" in lines from Milton and Hopkins:

> The témpted *wíth* dishónor fóul, suppósed. –Milton
> Attémpt *with* cónfidénce, the work is dóne. –Hopkins

One can also make a syllable long or short by positioning. Jefferson has us consider "αγες" in the line from the *Iliad:*

> Ἄγες, Ἄγες βροτολοιγὲ, μιαι φόνε τει χεσιπλητα. –Homer

In the first instance, "αγες," bisyllabic, is long in the first syllable and short in the second and then short in the first and long in the second.

Yet there are limits to such license vis-à-vis euphony. Jefferson has us consider:

> Thróugh the dárk póstern óf time lóng eláps'd. –Young

Jefferson asserts, "It is impossible to read this without throwing the accent on the monosyllable *of* and yet the ear is shocked and revolts at this."[52]

There follows certain "observations" on the three measures, which illustrate conformity, and also disconformity, to the threefold distribution, some of which are due to poetic license in the service of euphony. I offer two illustrations. Parisyllabic verse, says Jefferson, should be completely iambic. Yet it is not uncommon for the first foot to be a trochaic. For instance:

---

[50] Thomas Jefferson, *Writings*, 596.

[51] Thomas Jefferson, *Writings*, 596.

[52] The point is understood, though Jefferson's parsing of the line might seem to be strange. A more reasonable rendering might seem to be, "Thróugh the dárk postérn of tíme long eláps'd," but "postern" has its entrenched accent on the first syllable and the fragment, from Young's *The Ruin*, is in imparisyllabic verse.

Yé who (imparisyllabic) e'er lóst an ángel, píty mé! (parisyllabic)[53] –Young

Again, the trisyllabic verse should admit no exceptions, but poets take liberty, as does Shenstone in the third line, below.

I have foúnd out a gíft for my faír;
I have foúnd where the woód-pigeons breéd;
But lét me that plúnder forbeár,
She will sáy 'twas a bárbarous deéd.[54] –Shenstone

Then there are lines such as, "Gód save great Wáshington," which completely baffle him.[55]

Jefferson next turns to use of elision, synecphonesis, rules for accent, and the length of verse.

Synecphonesis through diphthongs is sometimes obvious, but "vowels belonging to different syllables are sometimes forced to coalesce into a diphthong if the measure requires it."

And wish th*e a*venging fight
B*e i*t so, for I submit, his doom is fair.
When wint'ry winds deform the plent*eo*us year
Droop'd their fair leaves, nor knew th*e u*nfriendly soil...[56]

In line one, *e* and *a* are run together; line two, *e* and *i*; line three, *eo*; and line four, *e* and *u*.

Concerning rules for accent, Jefferson asserts that it is best for one unfamiliar with a language to learn the accent of each word either by reference to a dictionary, not by rules, for rules are too often broken to be of help, or by reading poetry and knowing the three measures, which will demonstrate accent of a multisyllabic word, given that the poet does not deviate too freely from the measures.[57]

Yet accentuation is not simple; it admits degrees. Jefferson illustrates through some lines from Armstrong—numbers in parentheses being indicative of the relative strength of an accent for the italicized syllable.

---

[53] Thomas Jefferson, *Writings*, 602.
[54] Thomas Jefferson, *Writings*, 603.
[55] Thomas Jefferson, *Writings*, 604.
[56] Thomas Jefferson, *Writings*, 605.
[57] Thomas Jefferson, *Writings*, 603.

> *Oh* (4) when the *grow*ling (3) *winds* (3) con*tend* (3) and all
> The *sound*ing (3) *fo*rest (2) *fluc*tuates (3) in the *storm* (2)
> To *sink* (2) in *warm* (2) re*pose* (2), and *hear* (1) the *din* (1)
> *Howl* (2) o'er the *stea*dy (2) *bat*tlements (2), de*lights* (2)
> A*bove* (2) the *lu*xury (2) of *vul*gar (2) *sleep* (1).

He adds, "No two persons will accent the same passage alike."[58]

How long should a line be?

Jefferson answers by offering a passage from Homer in which the lines are thrown together so that they are fitted to the sides of the page and not as customarily offered in feet per line. Even in such an instance, the passage "would still immortalize its author," for a good poet "has studied the human ear," which if aesthetically stimulated, naturally pauses at regular intervals. "He who can read it without pausing at every sixth foot, like him who is insensible to the charm of music, who is insensible of love or of gratitude, is an unfavored son of nature to whom she has given a faculty fewer than to others of her children, one source of pleasure the less in a world where there are none to spare. A well-organized ear makes the pause regularly whether it be printed as verse or as prose."[59]

The English language tolerates lines as long as six feet, but only rarely lines that are longer. He offers Psalm 15 as an instance of lines of seven feet.

> 'Tis he whose ev'ry thought and deed by rules of virtue moves;
> Whose gen'rous tongue disdains to speak the thing his heart disproves.

Yet Jefferson notes that we read it and naturally pause at the fourth foot as well as the seventh. In effect, we thus parse it:

> 'Tis he whose ev'ry thought and deed
> By rules of virtue moves;
> Whose gen'rous tongue disdains to speak
> The thing his heart disproves.[60]

Jefferson then offers an argument for his preference of blank verse to rhymed verse. While passion for rhyme is fleeting, that of blank verse lasts longer. "The fondness for the jingle leaves us with that for the rattles and baubles of childhood," says Jefferson, "and if we continue to read rhymed verse at a later

---

[58] Thomas Jefferson, *Writings*, 611.
[59] Thomas Jefferson, *Writings*, 614.
[60] Thomas Jefferson, *Writings*, 617.

period of life it is such only where the poet has had force enough to bring great beauties of thought and diction into this form. When young, any composition pleases which unites a little sense, some imagination, and some rhythm." When mature, one naturally turns to blank verse, unless a poet is extraordinarily dexterous and inventive. Yet even appreciation of blank verse is mitigated over time. "As we advance in life these things fall off one by one, and I suspect we are left at last with only Homer and Virgil, perhaps with Homer alone."[61]

Much of Jefferson's thinking on the merit of poetry is in keeping with Hugh Blair's thoughts on poetry in *Lectures on Rhetoric and Belle Lettres,* which Jefferson much lauded.

Blair argues that "poetry is more ancient than prose," in that early linguistic expression was highly enthusiastic and fraught with metaphors as early humans found themselves in a new and dangerous world. Over time, as humans became more comfortable in the world, linguistic expression has become more precise and simpler, denuded of its poetry.[62] It follows that appreciation for poetry is appreciation for humans' archaic part.

Like Jefferson, Blair too argues for the superiority of blank verse to rhymed verse. Blank verse is "infinitely more favourable than rhyme," as it is bold, free, and varied.[63] The main defect of rhyme is the close that it forces on the ear at the end of each couplet. Blank forces no such closure. Its lines "run into each other with as great liberty as the Latin suited to subjects of dignity and force, which demands more free and manly numbers than rhyme." Rhyme is also "unfavourable to the sublime." Rhyme fetters, even degrades, epic poetry and tragedy. In sum, "rhyme finds its proper place in the middle, but not in the higher regions of poetry. Yet that is not wholesale condemnation, as Blair refuses to "join in the invectives which some have poured out against it, as if it were a mere barbarous jingling of sound, fit only for children and owing to nothing but the corruption of taste in the monkish ages."[64]

"Book and bowl carried us far into the night"

The Epic Poetry of Ossian

Marquis de Chastellux, on a visit to Monticello in 1782, writes that he at first found Jefferson "grave and even cold"—a response typifying those who first

---

[61] Thomas Jefferson, *Writings,* 619.

[62] Hugh Blair, *Lectures on Rhetoric and Belle Lettres* (Philadelphia: Troutman & Hayes, 1853), 67.

[63] Hugh Blair, *Lectures on Rhetoric and Belles Lettres,* 44.

[64] Hugh Blair, *Lectures on Rhetoric and Belles Lettres,* 431–32.

met Jefferson. Yet after spending some two hours with him, "I felt as if we had spent our whole lives together." One evening, over a bowl of punch, their conversation turned to the poetry of Ossian. "It was a spark of electricity which passed rapidly from one to the other; we recalled the passages of those sublime poems which had particularly struck us.... Soon the book was called for, to share in our 'toasts': it was brought forth and placed beside the bowl of punch. And, before we realized it, book and bowl carried us far into the night."

It is well known that Jefferson was under the spell of the epic poems of Ossian. What he did not know is that James McPherson, who claimed to have discovered manuscripts with Ossian's poems, was an impostor—at least, that is the verdict of a consensus of critics today. In 1760, Macpherson published *Fragments of Ancient Poetry, Collected in the Highlands of Scotland, and Translated from the Gaelic or Erse Language.* Those fragments were said to be collected by word of mouth. Later in the same year, he claimed to have found an epic concerning Fingal (Fionnghall), composed by Ossian. The popular poem *Fingal* was composed in 1762. By 1765, Macpherson published *The Works of Ossian.*

Ossian is said to be an old, blind poet in the manner of the Greek Homer and the poems are to be for those persons of Gaelic ancestry what Homer's two epics are for Greeks. Ossian came from the character Oisin, son of Fionn mac Cumhaill, a legendary bard of Irish mythology. Macpherson claimed to have collected word-of-mouth fragments in the original Gaelic and later a Gaelic manuscript with an epic, and then translated them into English.

In spite of the likelihood of Macpherson's duplicity, the poems were translated into several languages—e.g., Danish, French, German, Hungarian, Italian, Polish, Russian, Spanish, and Swedish—from Macpherson's presumed English translation, and they became internationally popular. Celebrities such as William Wordsworth, Walter Scott, Henry David Thoreau, Johann Wolfgang von Goethe, Denis Diderot, Voltaire, and even Napoleon Bonaparte read and enjoyed the poems.

Writer and critic Dr. Samuel Johnson, however, was immediately convinced that Macpherson was "a mountebank, a liar, and a fraud."[65] Gaelic scholar Charles O'Connor formally challenged the authenticity of the poems in an additional chapter, titled "Remarks on Mr. Mac Pherson's Translation of Fingal and Temora," to his previously published manuscript, *Dissertations on the Ancient History of Ireland.*[66] Other scholars, e.g., Derick Thomson and Hugh

---

[65] See Thomas M. Curley, *Samuel Johnson, the Ossian Fraud and the Celtic Revival in Great Britain and Ireland* (Cambridge: Cambridge University Press, 2009).

[66] James McPherson, *Dissertations on the History of Ireland* (Dublin: G. Faulkner, 1766).

Blair, defended Macpherson. Most persons at the time, however, merely ignored the fray, assumed no duplicity, and enjoyed the poems.

Jefferson showed no signs of concern over the controversy that followed publication, though he did own Blair's *A Critical Dissertation on the Poems of Ossian, Son of Fingal.* Perhaps on the authority of Blair, he never entertained doubts about the authorship of Ossian. Jefferson wrote to Charles Macpherson (25 Feb. 1773), the brother of the avowed collector and translator, James Macpherson with refulgent praise. "These pieces have been and will, I think, during my life, continue to be to me the sources of daily pleasures. The tender and the sublime emotions of the mind were never before so wrought up by the human hand. I am not ashamed to own that I think this rude bard of the north the greatest poet that has ever existed." Jefferson adds that he has become anxious to learn Gaelic, if only to read the poems in the language in which they were originally sung.

Jefferson then asks Macpherson for a manuscript copy of his brother's work on Ossian, if it has not already gone to print. "I would chuse it in a fair, round, hand, on fine paper, with a good margin, bound in parchment as elegantly as possible, lettered on the back and marbled or gilt on the edges of the leaves. I should not regard expence in doing this." He also asks Macpherson for "a catalogue of books written in that language," with a dictionary and a book on Gaelic grammar, so that he might learn Gaelic. He finally asks if there are further poems to be published—any "manuscript copies of any which are not in print." He adds, "The glow of one warm thought is to me worth more than money."

Macpherson answers on August 12, 1773, after he receives a reply, dated August 7, 1773, from his brother, James. Charles regrets to note that the poems were never printed in Gaelic and that he cannot procure a copy of his brother's Gaelic text. The task, said James in his letter to Charles, would prove to be too onerous. Charles thanks Jefferson for the praise, "and the praise is due," as "if to melt, to transport the soul be an excellence, as sure it is, our venerable Bard possesses it in an eminent, a superlative degree." Charles then apologizes for not being able to procure a Gaelic dictionary or book of Gaelic grammar. He does send to Jefferson with the letter a Gaelic New Testament. He ends by stating that though there are doubtless "a number of Ossian's Poems, abounding equally in the tender and sublime with those with which Mr. Macpherson has favored the public" in the "remote Highlands," they are merely "chanted away, with a wildness [and] a sweetness of enthusiasm, in the true spirit of Song."

There would be no further letters.

Beyond the letter to Macpherson, there are scattered references to Ossian in Jefferson's correspondence,[67] but nothing of consequence. There are also a few letters with catalogs of books that include Ossian's poems.[68]

In spite of the controversy concerning Ossian's authorship of the Gaelic epics, Chastellux's visit to Jefferson at Monticello and their bonding over punch and the "Ossianic" poems shows the power of poetry to promote conviviality.[69]

"Fly from the crowd, and be to virtue true"

Jefferson's Scrap Books of Poems

Given the thoughtfulness, circumspection, and acuity with which he crafted his "Thoughts on English Prosody" and given the selections in his *LCB*, one would expect that any collection of poems, gleaned by Jefferson later in life, would be from some of the world's finest poetic minds: e.g., Homer, Virgil, Dante, Chaucer, Coleridge, Blake, Donne, and Wordsworth. Yet Jefferson did collect poems—he did so during his presidency—yet not by commonplacing, but instead by cutting and pasting poems. He created two volumes with poets not so widely celebrated: John "Peter Pindar" Wolcot, William Ray, Anna Barbauld, Samuel Jackson Pratt, Elizabeth Ferguson, John Braham, Robert Anderson, and a political poem by a certain "Rusticus." Each volume was bound by boards that are 9.25 by 6.25 inches and each volume included poems cut and pasted mostly on gray papers of varied thickness and on old envelopes that are 8.75 by 5.75 inches.[70]

The scrapbooks, with volume one having 407 poems and volume two having 477 poems, might have begun as early as November 10, 1801, and the collection seems to have come from publically available verses, especially those published in newspapers. It was not uncommon in his day for newspapers—in the

---

[67] E.g., TJ to John Adams, 25 May 1785; TJ to William Short, 21 May 1787; TJ to Maria Eppes, 7 Feb. 1799; TJ to Cornelia Jefferson Randolph, 25 Dec. 1808; and TJ to Lafayette, 4 Nov. 1823.

[68] E.g., TJ to Robert Skipwith, 4 Aug. 1773, and TJ to Peter Carr, 19 Aug. 1785 and 10 Aug. 1787.

[69] I have to thank one of the reviewer's for this excellent point. Whatever the demerits of poetry, because it is such a "fine" fine art, its capacity for convivial intercourse is evident in this entertaining episode.

[70] Thomas Jefferson, *Thomas Jefferson's Scrapbooks*, ed. Jonathan Gross (Hanover, NH: Steerforth Press, 2006), 465–66.

businesses of information, advertising, and entertaining—to publish poems, especially topical poems, and not uncommon that the poems were anonymous.[71]

It has long been assumed that the two books were not composed by Thomas Jefferson, but by his grandchildren. Yet recently scholars such as Lee Smith, Robert McDonald, James Horn, and Jonathan Gross have argued convincingly that the work was compiled by Jefferson and in a manner similar to his 1804 and 1820 bibles.[72]

John Wayland says that each volume "is a scrap book in a double sense; for not only is it filled with clippings, but it is itself constructed from a number of miscellaneous scraps of paper. ... The materials used in constructing the book were old letters, letter wrappers, printed sheets, and a few blank sheets of paper, varying much in hue, quality, and weight."[73] Paper, of great significance to a person such as Jefferson, was in his day costly, and not, as in our time, to be cavalierly discarded.

The poems were not haphazardly thrown together. Since they were bound, there was some effort to arrange them thematically. For instance, a prevalent theme in the first 100 poems is liberty. Death is the prevailing theme from I: 113 to II: 135. From II: 135 to II: 197, nature is a recurrent theme.

The most common themes, in keeping with his *LCB*, are morality, love, and death. Yet, *pace* his *LCB*, poems with political content are rife. Liberty, which was nearly absent in *LCB*, is an especially common theme. There are also many patriotic poems and several poems in celebration of July 4 and about Jefferson's second-term embargo, manqué. Ancillary themes are religion, science, nature, husbandry, domesticity, and even Jefferson himself, sometimes in a self-effacing manner.

Inspection of the collection readily reveals that Jefferson's purpose was not scholarly. It is also apparent that the aim, unlike *LCB*, was neither self-edification nor edification pertinent to any bookish young man. For instance, to nephew Peter Carr (19 Aug. 1785), Jefferson enjoins the young man to read and study Virgil, Terence, Horace, Anacreon, Theocritus, Homer, Euripides, and Sophocles, among the Greek and Latin poets, and Milton, Shakespeare, Ossian, Pope, and Swift, among contemporary poets, "in order to form your style in your own language." Again, in an 1814 letter to General John Minor (Aug. 14), he advises any aspiring lawyer to read "the best of the poets, epic, didactic, dramatic, pastoral, lyric &c," and to pay special attention to

---

[71] Thomas Jefferson, *Thomas Jefferson's Scrapbooks*, 467–80.

[72] Thomas Jefferson, *Thomas Jefferson's Scrapbooks*, 2.

[73] John W. Wayland, "The Poetical Tastes of Thomas Jefferson," *The Sewanee Review*, Vol. XVIII, 1910: 285–91.

Shakespeare "to learn the full powers of the English language." Instead, the motivation for the two volumes was edification and entertainment of his granddaughters, from whom he was away as president. His granddaughters at the time were Ann Cary (1791–1826), Ellen Wayles (1796–1876), Cornelia Jefferson (1799–1871), Virginia Jefferson (1801–1882), and Mary Jefferson (1803–1876)—all Randolphs. Ann Cary and Ellen Wayles Randolph were of an age during his presidency—the latter toward the end of his second term—to glean instruction from or be entertained by the right sort of poetry.

I offer a small, but representative, sample of the poems. Because many of the poems are lengthy, I offer only excerpts.

I begin with poems with political content.

Here there is the first stanza from an anonymous poem in praise of Jefferson and liberty (I: 2)[74] the latter being an especially prominent theme of the first book.

> Well met, fellow freemen! let's cheerfully greet,
> The return of *this* day, with a copious libation.
> For freedom this day in her chosen retreat,
> Hailed her favourite JEFFERSON Chief of our nation.
> A chief in whose mind Republicans find,
> Wisdom, probity, honor and firmness combined.
> Let our wine sparkle high, whilst we gratefully give,
> The health of our Sachem, and long may he live.

The following two verses of the untitled and anonymous poem on republicanism (I: 25) is self-effacing and shows Jefferson's unpretentiousness as well as his sense of humor.

> A republican's picture is easy to draw,
> He can't bear to *obey*, but will *govern* the law;
> His manners unsocial, his temper unkind,
> He's a rebel in conduct, a tyrant in mind.
>
> He's envious of these, who have riches or pow'r,
> Discontented, malignant, implacable, sour!
> Never happy himself, he would wish to destroy
> The comfort and blessings, which others enjoy.

---

[74] Volume I, page 2. There is frequently more than one poem per page.

Consider also stanza six of Henry Mellen's poem *The Embargo* (I: 47–48), which pokes fun at Jefferson's embargo during his second term as president.

Our ships all in motion,
Once whiten'd the ocean,
The sail'd and return'd with a Cargo;
Now doom'd to decay
They have fallen a prey
To Jefferson, worms and Embargo.

Jefferson too collected poems in praise of others, like George Washington, but also adversaries like King George III and Alexander Hamilton. Consider stanza seven of the poem *To the Memory of Gen. Hamilton* by a certain "PATRIOTICUS" (I: 26):

Great Hamilton! Thy country's story
To latest time will clearly prove,
How great thy worth and martial glory,
Embalm'd with all Columbia's love.

R. Anderson's *The Slave* (2: 191) is indicative of Jefferson's lifelong abhorrence of slavery. I include the first and last stanzas.

Torn from every dear connection,
Forc'd across the yielding wave,
The Negro, stung by keen reflection,
May exclaim, man's but a slave! …

Thus dup'd by fancy, pride or folly,
Ne'er content with what we have;
Toss'd 'twixt hope and melancholy,
Death at last sets *free* the slave.

In keeping with Jefferson's lifelong interest in morality, I offer a sample of poems with moral content—perhaps the most prominent theme in the collection.

The poem *In Praise of Content* (I: 136) is indicative of Stoic happiness.

No glory I covet, no riches I want,
    Ambition is nothing to me;
The one thing I beg of kind heaven to grant,
    Is a mind independent and free. …

How vainly, thro' infinite trouble and strife,
    Do many their labours employ;
Since all that is truly delightful in life,
    Is what all, if they will, may enjoy.

The poem *The Bottle* by Hugh Kelly (I: 127/124) lambently begins as a paean to the carefreeness of drinking in the manner of Omar Khayyam.

WHILE the bottle to humour and social delight
The smallest assistance can lend,
While it happily keeps up the laugh of the night,
Or enlivens the mind of a friend;
O let me enjoy it, thou bountiful pow'r!
That my time may deliciously pass!
And should care ever think to intrude on the heart,
Scare the haggard away with a glass. ...

Yet the third and final stanza is with a bold declamation on insobriety, suggestive of Jefferson's own detestation of drunkenness.

From my lips dash the poison, O merciful Pow'r!
    Where the madness or blasphemy hung,
And let ev'ry word, at which Virtue should low'r,
    Parch quick on my infamous tongue—
From my sight let the cause be eternally driv'n,
    Where my reason so fatally stray'd,
That no more I may offer an insult to Heav'n,
    Or give man a cause to upbraid.

There are also many poems that concern friendship. Consider stanzas one and six of the poem *Lines of Friendship* by a certain "Freeman's Friend":

WHAT warms the soul, what cheers the heart,
Is FRIENDSHIP'S renovating tie;
Yes, this can social joy impart,
And wipe the tear from sorrow's eye. ...

Thus private friends who dwell in love,
Are taught to feel another's woe,
To raise their thoughts on things above,
And live in friendship here below.

The lines are indicative of Jefferson's own sentiments on the value and beauty of friendship through the mouth of Heart while controverting with Head in his *billet doux* to Maria Cosway (12 Oct. 1786).

Jefferson draws from *The Monthly Anthology* to procure the poem *Ode to Modesty* (I: 163). I include the opening and sixth stanza.

NYMPH of the downcast eye,
Sweet blushing MODESTY,
Whose mien supplies the music of the tongue;
Thy charms were still delay'd,
Thy beauties unportray'd,
Though Fancy pencil'd while the Muses sung! ...

Come, sweet nymph, and bring with thee
Thy sister, dear SIMPLICITY.

The Poet's Last Advice (I: 18), a poem about virtue and the danger of overreaching, is by Geoffrey Chaucer (1328–1400) and was put into modern English by a certain Dr. Kippia. I include selections from the first and third stanzas.

Fly from the crowd, and be to virtue true,
Content with what thou hast, tho' it be small.
To hoard brings hate; nor lofty thoughts pursue,
He who climbs high, endangers many a fall. ...

Whatever happens, happy in thy mind
Be thou, nor at thy lot in life repine,
He 'scapes all ill, whose bosom is resigned,
Nor way, nor weather will be always fine.

There are also a large number of poems that concern love and are in praise of women. Here is the final stanza of an anonymous poem *Song in Praise of Women* (I: 109).

Form'd from nature's choicest treasures,
Virtues all in her unite;
Life's short path she strews with pleasures,
Goddess of supreme delight!
Homely fare to me be given,
Sweet the limpid stream will prove,
Earth will be a little heaven,
With the woman that I love.

There are also many poems that focus on nature or have strong naturalistic language. I list the first stanza from *Lines* (I: 201).

HAIL, beauteous stream that smoothly glides along,
With pleasure oft upon thy banks I've stray'd
Oft, separated from the world's gay throng,
Reclin'd my limbs beneath thy yew trees' shade.

Jefferson also includes a few poems that are silly or humorous. *Potatoes* is one. I include the second, fourth, and seventh stanzas.

O thou honest Irish sirloin!
How I chuckle when I see
Social on the table smoking,
Hot Potatoes stand by thee! ...

Here, ye nauseous frog destroyers,
Here the feasts of health behold;
Feed on these, ye wiser Irish,
If ye covet to be old. ...

These, in bread, in pie, or pudding,
Scallop'd, roasted, boil'd excel;
All their uses, all their value,
Not the Muse herself can tell.

Address to My Segar (Cigar; II: 41) is another.

Companion of my leisure hours,
Sweet softner of my care;
I court thy kind solacing aid,
Thou fragrant sweet Segar.

Finally, there is a large number of poems with the theme or mention of death. The anonymous poem *To Virtue* (II: 163) ends:

Yet, VIRTUE! thou shalt make me blest,
Thy hand shalt lead, thy arm sustain;
And *life*, with thee shall lack no rest,
And *death*, with thee shall give no pain!

One surprising finding is the number of poems, 18, that have Irish themes. In addition, there are 10 poems from the Irish poet Thomas Moore and several other poems by Irish poets. As an official of the British government, Moore traveled to the United States during Jefferson's first term as president and his poems were popular in America. Moore was openly critical of Jefferson and the United States, and when Moore's *Irish Melodies* was published in 1804, Jefferson exclaimed astonishingly, "Why this is the little man who satirized me so!" Upon reading the book, he added, "He is a poet after all," and took a liking to the diminutive Irishman.

John Wayland maintains that Jefferson's fondness of Irish poetry went beyond his fancy for Moore. He fancied Moore because Moore was Irish, as he indentified with the Irish struggle for liberty. "All struggles for liberty and the hardships resulting from the failure of such struggles found a ready response at all times in Jefferson's nature; and the sorrows of the Irish patriots affected him deeply." Wayland cites the Wexford uprising of 1798, the defeat of the insurgents at Vinegar Hill and thereafter the reign of terror, and Emmet's outbreak in 1803 and its suppression. In addition to the uprisings of the Irish, Besides, there were the sons of Fingal and Ossian.[75] Also, it is significant to add that Jefferson considered his roots were Welch, not British.[76]

There are very few poems in the collection that can be said to be true gems—masterpieces of masterful poets. Unlike the pieces he commonplaces in *LCB*, these selections are meant to be light and fun, and they are selected with his granddaughters in mind for their practicality, not their fineness—for their moral lessons for life, to teach them euphony, and at times to put smiles on their faces. However, some poems—e.g., *The Embargo* and *Address to My Segar*—were selected because Jefferson himself found them entertaining.

"America's first romantic president"

Did Jefferson's Passion for Poetry Fade over Time?

Early in life, as we have seen, Jefferson was very fond of poetry of all sorts. His *Literary Commonplace Book*, which offers a visual illustration of Jefferson's early-life reading interests, lists 10 authors of prose and over 30 poets. That by itself speaks to a profound interest in poetry as a fount of edification and especially "moral and philosophical content." Douglas Wilson notes, "The study of poetry [early on] he regarded not only as a

---

[75] John W. Wayland, "The Poetical Tastes of Thomas Jefferson," p. 293.

[76] Thomas Jefferson, "Autobiography", in *Thomas Jefferson: Writings*, ed. Merrill D. Peterson (New York: Library of America, 1984), 3.

pleasurable but as a useful undertaking, affording instructive examples in both morality and composition."[77]

Yet by the time of his presidency, his fondness abates. He writes to John D. Burke (21 June 1801) concerning some comments on Joel Barlow's epic "The Columbiad," which Burke had sent to him in a prior communication. After giving the poem a "hasty perusal," he adds that the office of presidency affords him little leisure to read poetry, though he adds that the moments he has spared to read through the poem were "agreeable." He adds: "Of all men living I am the last who should undertake to decide as to the merits of poetry. In earlier life I was fond of it, and easily pleased. But as age and cares advanced, the powers of fancy have declined. Every year seems to have plucked a feather from her wings till she can no longer waft one to those sublime heights to which it is necessary to accompany the poet." So much has his relish for poetry declined that he even finds Virgil unpleasant. "I am consequently utterly incapable to decide on the merits of poetry. The very feelings to which it is addressed are among those I have lost." It is as much as to ask a blind man to examine a painting or a deaf man to critique a musical composition.

It has customarily been asserted that, as the letter to Burke shows, Jefferson's passion for poetry grayed as he grayed.

Jonathan Gross, who, as we have seen, has made a study of Jefferson's scrapbook of poems, has recently challenged that view, received. He cites the "rhetorical occasion" of the letter to Burke as a reason for his "self-effacing remarks concerning his knowledge of poetry." Gross writes: "Barlow was a propagandist for the Republican cause, too useful to risk alienating." If the letter is evidence of Jefferson's "growing insusceptibility to the beauty of poetry," he did not remain mortified by it for long. "This letter may well have been the catalyst for Jefferson to assemble two volumes of newspaper verse. He did so that same year, judging from the dates of the earliest entries; interestingly, Barlow's poem appears in volume one."[78]

Jefferson, according to Gross, never lost his love of poetry. It was an important "means of communicating with those he loved." He sums,

---

[77] Thomas Jefferson, *Jefferson's Literary Commonplace Book,* ed. Douglas L. Wilson (Princeton: Princeton University Press, 1989), 14.

[78] Jonathan Gross, introduction to *Thomas Jefferson's* Scrapbooks: *Poems of Nation, Family & Romantic Love Collected by America's Third President,* ed. Jonathan Gross (Hanover, NH: Steerforth Press, 2006), 5.

"Jefferson was not only America's third president, but America's first romantic president."[79]

Gross' First-Romantic-President Thesis cannot be sustained, as it is at least much too strongly stated. The reasons go beyond the letter to Burke. Jefferson over time developed a general disdain of fiction of all sorts.

Why is that the case?

First, except for very early in life, poetry never had that pride of place that had other arts. In his schoolmasterist letter to nephew Peter Carr (19 Aug. 1785), Jefferson it comes as no surprise recommends highly the poetry of Greek and Latin authors such as "Virgil, Terence, Horace, Anacreon, Theocritus, Homer, Euripides, [and] Sophocles. Read also Milton's Paradise Lost, Shakspeare [*sic*], Ossian, Pope's and Swift's works, in order to form your style in your own language." He enjoins Carr to devote his "vacant hours" to history, philosophy, and poetry. "Divide what remains (I mean of your vacant hours) into three portions. Give the principal to History, the other two, which should be shorter, to Philosophy and Poetry."

Jefferson, we know, always had a profound appreciation for history, for the right sort of history—that of Thucydides, Xenophon, Quintus Curtius, Diodorus Siculus, Arrian, Livy, and Plutarch—as a proper goad to morally correct activity. The prescription to spend more time on history than on philosophy or poetry is indicative of the greater utility of history.

Is that also the case with fiction—both novels and poetry?

An early letter to Robert Skipwith (3 Aug. 1771) suggests high praise of works of fiction. Jefferson begins. "A little attention however to the nature of the human mind evinces that the entertainments of fiction are useful as well as pleasant."

Wherein is the utility of fiction? Are we to assume "all" or "some" as the implicit qualifier to "the entertainments of fiction"?

"Everything is useful which contributes to fix in the principles and practices of virtue," answers Jefferson, and he lapses into a paean to the merits of fiction of the right sort.

Whenever we view or imagine an act of charity or gratitude, he continues to Skipwith, "we are deeply impressed with its beauty and feel a strong desire in ourselves of doing charitable and grateful acts also." Whenever we view or imagine an act of enormity or ingratitude, "we are disgusted with it's deformity, and conceive an abhorence [*sic*] of vice."

---

[79] Jonathan Gross, "Introduction," 6 and 10.

Acts of virtue or vice, whether real or imagined, exercise each person's moral sense, which acquires strength through exercise. Exercise leads then to habit—a tendency more frequently to act virtuously and eschew vicious activity. In literature, it is immaterial whether what we read is truth or fiction. Jefferson illustrates by reference to Lawrence Sterne's *A Sentimental Traveller:*

> We neither know nor care whether Lawrence Sterne really went to France, whether he was there accosted by the Franciscan, at first rebuked him unkindly, and then gave him a peace offering: or whether the whole be not fiction. In either case we equally are sorrowful at the rebuke, and secretly resolve we will never do so: we are pleased with the subsequent atonement, and view with emulation a soul candidly acknowleging it's fault and making a just reparation.

In offering moral lessons, fiction has a decided advantage over history. "Considering history as a moral exercise, her lessons would be too infrequent if confined to real life." There are too few instances in history of events depicted "with such circumstances as to excite in any high degree this sympathetic emotion of virtue." Thus, for moral inspiration, fiction trumps history. Jefferson sums, "This is my idea of well-written Romance, of Tragedy, Comedy and Epic poetry."

It is manifest that Jefferson is acknowledging that some fiction, "well written" fiction, is morally inspiring. The early letter to Skipwith, however, settles little. It merely indicates that Jefferson believes that fiction has a capacity to exceed history in being morally stirring. Jefferson says nothing about fiction actually exceeding history in being morally stirring. Thus, the letter cannot be taken as confirmatory evidence of the First-Romantic-President Thesis—a presidency that occurred 30 years after the letter to Skipwith.

An 1818 letter to Nathaniel Burwell (Apr. 9) is also relevant, as it offers confirmatory evidence of the sentiment in Jefferson's letter to Burke. Burwell in a prior letter has asked Jefferson about female education. Jefferson replies that he has only given the matter thought insofar as it relates to his own daughters. Jefferson then rails against the time wasted in reading novels—"the time lost in that reading which should be instructively employed." He continues: "When this poison infects the mind, it destroys its tone and revolts it against wholesome reading. Reason and fact, plain and unadorned, are rejected" until "nothing can engage attention unless dressed in all the figments of fancy, and nothing so bedecked comes amiss. The result is a bloated imagination, sickly judgment, and disgust towards all the real businesses of life."

"This mass of trash," Jefferson continues, "is not without some distinction; some few modelling their narratives, although fictitious, on the incidents of real life, have been able to make them interesting and useful vehicles of a sound morality." He cites the writings of the female authors Marmontel, Edgeworth, and Genlis.

Jefferson then adds: "For a like reason, too, much poetry should not be indulged. Some is useful for forming style and taste. Pope, Dryden, Thomson, Shakespeare, and of the French Molière, Racine, the Corneilles, may be read with pleasure and improvement." The merits are style, taste, pleasure, and improvement—taste and improvement relating to exercising the aesthetic and moral senses.

Moreover, Jefferson's "Thoughts on English Prosody" comes into play. Recall his (possibly Blair-inspired) sentiment that as we age, our taste for poetry wanes, until we are left "perhaps with Homer alone."[80] That was written in 1786—to wit, 15 years after his letter to Skipwith.

Finally, there is the testimony of granddaughter Ellen Randolph Coolidge, who writes in a missive to early biographer Henry S. Randall: "In his youth he had loved poetry, but by the time I was old enough to observe, he had lost his taste for it, except for Homer and the great Athenian tragics, which he continued to the last to enjoy. He went over the works of [A]eschylus, Sophocles and Euripides, not very long before I left him."[81]

In sum, there is no reason to downplay Jefferson's 1801 letter to Burke, as does Gross, who explains away the letter as a whimsical instance of the "rhetorical occasion"—a sentiment, unfortunately, given no amplification, when amplification is sorely needed.

That Jefferson kept a scrapbook of poems, mostly fashioned in his years as president, does strongly suggest, as Gross notes, Jefferson did throughout his life value largely poetry. Yet the poems he collected were all with application for political, moral, or aesthetic reflection, though some, but few—*Ham & Turkey, Satire on Snuff,* and *On a Long Nose,* the latter certainly picked because of the references in Lawrence Sterne's *Tristram Shandy* to long noses—are evidence of Jefferson's delitescent, dry sense of humor. Every indication suggests that the book's poems were collected to share with his granddaughters, as means of familial communication and of moral, aesthetical, and even political instruction, while he was away. The authors whom he valued in *LCB* are absent in his scrapbook. He selected themes that were educative for and befitting the young ladies of high society, his granddaughters.

---

[80] Thomas Jefferson, *Writings,* 619.

[81] Henry Stephens Randall, *The Life of Thomas Jefferson,* Vol. 3 (Philadelphia: J.B. Lippincott & Co., 1871), 346.

Upshot

Even though Jefferson's taste for poetry abated much in life, it was never extinguished. First, poetry was such a prevalent part of everyday life in his time, unlike ours, that no one of proper education could neglect it. Next, poetry was always a vehicle of communication for him and a means of intimate expression. He commonly turned to poetry as a means of communication when friends or intimates died, and when he acquiesced to his own impending death, he crafted a poem titled *A Death-Bed Adieu* as a keepsake for his beloved daughter Martha, whom he told of the poem two days prior to his passing. Lines two and four of each stanza contain rhymes or quasi-rhymes.

Life's visions are vanished,
It's dreams are no more.
Dear friends of my bosom,
Why bathed in tears?

I go to my fathers;
I welcome the shore,
Which crowns all my hopes,
Or which buries my cares.

Then farewell my dear,
My lov'd daughter, Adieu!
The last pang in life
Is in parting from you.

Two Seraphs await me,
Long shrouded in death;
I will bear them your love
On my last parting breath.[82]

The poem, though moving, is far from polished, but Jefferson likely composed it while he was sickly and not in full command of his faculties.

Overall, Jefferson's dissatisfaction for poetry as he matured concerned not only its inutility—it truly was a "fine" art—but also its potential for harm, especially for females, because it was so fine. He cognized that many poems were instructive—e.g., morally or politically—but those poems were too few and often not widely read. The majority of poems, he came to realize later in

---

[82] TJ to Martha Jefferson Randolph, 2 July 1826.

life, put false or delusive ideals in the heads of readers, hence, not only the inutility of poetry, but also its danger.

Yet Jefferson also recognized that women, given their restrictive domestic role in a Virginian household, were ineluctably drawn to fiction. It was a way to pass the idle hours of each day, especially during the cold, wintry months—those hours that Jefferson would pass typically with a Greek or Latin text. He wished that females, if drawn to poetry, should focus on the sort of poems that would fill their heads with both notions of virtuous ideas and of industry vis-à-vis a woman's proper domestic role, lest they should be carried away in the manner of Don Quixote of La Mancha by windmills, seen as giants, or be seduced by slothfulness.

In sum, that Jefferson's interest in poetry waned as he aged was not too surprising. As American adolescents of his day became men, they naturally shifted their attention from things lofty to more practical concerns—e.g., for Jefferson, to law, politics, science, and his plantation. Absorption in poetry would not only have been impossible for such any busy man, but also a botheration—an impediment to engagement and advancement in his affairs.

Yet as I show in this chapter, there is more to note than Jefferson's iminution of interest due to preoccupation with other, more practical concerns. Jefferson, it is clear, came to feel some degree of dislike for poetry, because of its general inutility and potential for harm, through neglect of human industry. Preoccupation with poetry meant lack of engagement with more pressing concerns. Thus, he no longer found enjoyment in the celebrated poets whom he much loved in his youth, and turned to an appreciation for poetry merely as a means for communicating significant lessons, mostly of the moral sort, to his grandchildren. During that process of communication through poems, he found some enjoyment in light, satirical poems.

Chapter III

The Arts of Rhetoric and Oratory

"I am no Ennemy [*sic*] to Elegance. but I Say no Man has a right to think of Elegance, till he has secured Substance—nor then to Seek more of it, than he can afford."[1] ~John Adams

Query VI of Thomas Jefferson's *Notes on the State of Virginia*, titled "Productions Mineral, Vegetable and Animal" and the largest query of the 23 queries in the book, contains an account of North American "aborigines" in an attempt to address Comte de Buffon's, and others', claim that all forms of life in North America—"all living nature has become smaller on that continent"[2]—are deficient, because of coldness and wetness of the New World.

Much of Jefferson's critique of Buffon concerns those persons native to the continent. As part of his defense of the Native Americans, Jefferson appeals to their "eloquence in council [and] bravery and address in war." Instances of bravery and address in war are numerous—"we have multiplied proofs"—but there are fewer illustrations of their "eminence in oratory ... because it is displayed chiefly in their own councils."[3]

Jefferson then turns to an instance of what he takes to be the unexampled brilliancy of the indigenes' oratorical eloquence: the speech of Mingo chief Logan to then-governor of Virginia, Lord Dunmore, which challenges "the whole orations of Demosthenes and Cicero, and of any more eminent orator."[4]

Jefferson begins with an incident in spring 1774. Two Shawnees committed a theft and murder, which outraged the neighboring Whites, who vowed to seek vengeance. And so, Colonel Cresap, "a man infamous for the many murders

---

[1] John Adams to Richard Cranch, 15 Jan. 1787, *The Adams Papers, Papers of John Adams, Vol. 18, December 1785–January 1787*, ed. Gregg L. Lint, Sara Martin, C. James Taylor, Sara Georgini, Hobson Woodward, Sara B. Sikes, and Amanda M. Norton (Cambridge, MA: Harvard University Press, 2016), 543.

[2] Buffon's comments have scope over both Americas, but Jefferson, much ignorant of South America, restricts his investigation to North America. Thomas Jefferson, *Notes on Virginia*, ed. William Peden (Chapel Hill: University of North Carolina Press, 54), 58.

[3] Thomas Jefferson, *Notes on the State of Virginia*, ed. William Peden (Chapel Hill: University of North Carolina Press, 1954), 62.

[4] Thomas Jefferson, *Notes on Virginia*, 62.

he had committed on those much injured people," gathered a group of men, who canoed down the Kanawha River, and hid themselves in boscage near the river. They there espied a canoe with one man and several women, and children, all Shawnees and members of the family of Logan, "who had long been distinguished as a friend of the whites." The man, women, and children were slaughtered. Logan considered that massacre an "unworthy return" for the crime of the two Shawnees, thus an army of Shawnees, Mingos, and Delawares was formed and there was a great battle with the Whites at the mouth of the Kanawha River. The Virginian militia won the battle and the Natives sued for peace.[5]

It was beneath Logan, who consented to the peace, to be present at the meeting, given what had happened to his family. He, thus, sent an emissary to deliver a speech to Gov. Dunmore.

> I appeal to any white man to say, if ever he entered Logan's cabin hungry, and he gave him not meat; if ever he came cold and naked, and he cloathed him not. During the course of the last long and bloody war Logan remained idle in his cabin an advocate for peace. Such was my love for the whites, that my countrymen pointed as they passed, and said, "Logan is the friend of white men." I had even thought to have lived with you, but for the injuries of one man. Colonel Cresap, the last spring, in cold blood, and unprovoked, murdered all the relations of Logan, not sparing even my women and children. There runs not a drop of my blood in the veins of any living creature. This called on me for revenge. I have sought it: I have killed many: I have fully glutted my vengeance: for my country I rejoice at the beams of peace. But do not harbour a thought that mine is the joy of fear. Logan never felt fear. He will not turn on his heel to save his life. Who is there to mourn for Logan?—Not one.[6]

Jefferson's inclusion of the speech of Logan was his sockdolager—a decisive blow as a striking illustration of eminence in oratory, which was a skill, requiring both ample uses of reason and of imagination, and a skill, Buffon likely thought, of which Native Americans were eminently incapable.

Jefferson himself was limited in his oratorical skills. He was unassuming in presence and of soft voice. Yet he had unexampled preparatory or rhetorical skills, as he employed reason and imagination to their fullest in speeches.

---

[5] Thomas Jefferson, *Notes on Virginia*, 62.
[6] Thomas Jefferson, *Notes on Virginia*, 63.

Nonetheless, he more than compensated for what he lacked in in-presence command in oratory by extraordinary dominion with his pen.

This chapter covers Jefferson on the arts of fineness of speaking and fineness of writing. I begin with Jefferson's thoughts on oratory as preparation for practice of law, turn to Jefferson's thoughts on Patrick Henry's oratorical skills, move to Jefferson's patronage of Hugh Blair's book on rhetoric and belle lettres, and end with Jefferson on the need of fineness of speaking and writing in a sound republican government.

"Suit your arguments to the audience..."

Oratory as Preparation for Law

When he left William and Mary in 1762, Jefferson took to the study of law under the guidance of George Wythe (Figure 3-1).[7] He, however, tells us nothing of his apprenticeship. He merely writes, "In 1767, he led me into the practice of the law at the bar of the General court, at which I continued until the revolution shut up the courts of justice" in 1774.[8]

Fig. 3-1: George Wythe (public domain)

---

[7] Wythe would take the chair of the School of Law at College of William and Mary. Dumas Malone, *Jefferson and His Time*, vol. 1, *Jefferson the Virginian* (Boston: Little, Brown & Company, 1948), 66.

[8] Thomas Jefferson, "Autobiography", in *Thomas Jefferson: Writings*, ed. Merrill D. Peterson (New York: Library of America, 1984), 5.

Yet a 1790 letter of Jefferson to fellow Virginian John Garland Jefferson (June 11), concerning a course of study for a would-be lawyer, is suggestive. "It is a general practice to study the law in the office of some lawyer. This indeed gives to the student the advantage of his instruction. But I have ever seen that the services expected in return have been more than the instructions have been worth. All that is necessary for a student is access to a library, and directions in what order the books are to be read." The letter intimates that Jefferson did not depend much on Wythe, or anyone else, for his education in practice of the law. Moreover, there was little need of Wythe to take Jefferson by the hand, as it were, and to show him the ins and outs of the profession. Jefferson was a self-starter and likely appealed to Wythe only for answers to questions that he could not get from books.[9]

Jefferson's tenure as lawyer was unquestionably successful, and his success was due to uncommon preparation through laborious study and practice in rhetoric, for Jefferson, the art of "style and composition."[10] It was an art needed for effective public speaking. It was an art especially desirable for lawyers and politicians, for those were professions in which public speaking was needed. And so, it was typical for a lawyer-in-training to spend much time learning how to speak persuasively. A lawyer could not reach the pinnacle of his career without a commanding courtroom presence.

Tall, of light complexion, and gangly, it is well-known that Jefferson did not have a commanding presence. Jefferson also did not have the sort of voice that resonated.[11] William Wirt—lawyer, politician, and friend of Thomas Jefferson—said of Jefferson in a eulogy on Jefferson and Adams a few years after their death. "It is true he was not distinguished in popular debate.... He had all the attributes of the mind, and the heart, and the soul, which are essential to the eloquence of the highest order. The only defect was a physical one; he wanted volume and compass of voice for a large deliberative assembly; and his voice, from the excess of his sensibility, instead of rising with his feelings and conceptions, sunk under their pressure, and became guttural and inarticulate."[12]

---

[9] M. Andrew Holowchak, *The Cavernous Mind of Thomas Jefferson, An American Savant* (Newcastle upon Tyne: Cambridge Scholars, 2019), 6–7.

[10] TJ to Ellen Wayles Randolph Coolidge, 10 July 1805.

[11] When he gave his First Inaugural Address as president, many could not hear his speech. In anticipation of that, he had printed copies of the address passed out to all in attendance.

[12] Frank Moore, *American Eloquence: A Collection of Speeches and Addresses by the Most Eminent Orators of America* (New York: D. Appleton and Company, 1857), 449–50.

Given such things, Jefferson's choice of law as a profession seems mystifying. Nevertheless, there were not many feasible options for a rural gentleman of Virginia. Most grew up on plantations, so they were born into husbandry. Outside of practice of the law—there was a large need for lawyers in Virginia to settle claims of property—there were few viable options for a gentleman. There were no professional architects at the time, and it would have been beneath the dignity of one of the gentry to accept money for performance of music (chapter 7). Thus, it is probable that Jefferson, as a youth, never seriously thought of any other career than that of lawyer.

In possession neither of a booming voice nor of an authoritative visage, Jefferson's plan for success at law entailed omnilegency—that any aspiring lawyer be fully studies in any subject of practical significance—or nearly so, and matchless preparation.

That is best illustrated by an advisory letter to Gen. John Minor[13] (30 Aug. 1814) in which Jefferson offers Minor detailed instructions for preparation study of law. It is a copy of a letter, with new suggested books added, that Jefferson had sent to Bernard Moore early in the 1770s.

The course of study was brutal, even inhumane, for that course required that a lawyer be knowledgeable about all matters of any practical significant. One wonders how anyone, except Jefferson or a simpatico bibliophile, could have kept to it. All waking hours of the day were devoted to study, and the meaty hours of the day were dedicated to those subjects most pertinent and useful to a lawyer.[14]

Jefferson does not neglect rhetoric and oratory. It is to be studied from dark till bedtime. He elaborates: "Criticise the style of any books whatever, committing your criticisms to writing. Translate into the different styles, to wit, the elevated, the middling and the familiar": orators and poets for the first, historians for the second, letter and comic writers for the last. "Undertake, at first, short compositions, as themes, letters &c., paying great attention to the correctness and elegance of your language." Minor is to pay special attention to the orations of Demosthenes and Cicero. "Analyse these orations and examine the correctness of the disposition, language, figures, states of the cases, arguments &c." He can then turn to "good samples of English eloquence": e.g., Small's *American Speaker* and Carey's *Criminal Recorder*.

Jefferson adds that Minor should even make up cases, and practice with another, as if one were in a real courtroom, as the "last and most important exercise" of the day. Minor is to take up one side of a cause, while his friend,

---

[13] Minor writes on behalf of his son (Moore to TJ, 8 Sept. 1814).

[14] M. Andrew Holowchak, *The Cavernous Mind of Thomas Jefferson*, 10–14.

the other; but later, he is to take up the other side, while his friend takes up the one. "Adapt your language & figures to the several parts of the oration, and suit your arguments to the audience before whom it is supposed to be spoken. Practice just as is the custom of the bar, where the plaintiff opens, the defense attorney answers, and then the plaintiff replies. "It would farther be of great service to pronounce your orations (having before you only short notes to assist the memory) in the presence of some person who may be considered as your judge."

The letter to Minor suggests that oratory is not of significance to politics, law, or history, as it can be practiced at night, after a grueling day of study, or during the unoccupied intervals of the day. As I show by the chapter's end, however, that is not the case. Oratory is a crucial art in a thriving Jeffersonian republic, for when used rightly, it allows for the possibility of open, respectful, and intelligent discussion of contentious issues, which often require conciliation on behalf of the discussants.

Compared to others of his day, Jefferson proved to be a very successful lawyer. Nonetheless, he relinquished his practice in 1774 and he turned to politics.

Why was that the case?

The letter to Minor gives part of the answer. Jefferson thought that a lawyer ought to be logical, laconic, and authentic—*viz.*, he ought to plead rationally, not emotionally; he ought to make his argument in plain language and with the fewest possible words; and he ought to practice his discipline with the utmost integrity. Such things doubtless were taught or reinforced in his apprenticeship with Wythe. It is no stretch to assert that few other lawyers practiced logically, laconically, and authentically. That could only have frustrated Jefferson, who was already handicapped by his weedy presence and forceless voice.

"The laziest man in reading I ever knew"

The Fiery Oratory of Patrick Henry

A Virginian lawyer with a stout presence and forceful voice was Patrick Henry (1736–1799, Figure 3-2). Jefferson's view of Henry is neatly summed in a letter to Leavit Harris (11 Oct. 1824): "I never heard anything that deserved to be called by the same name with what flowed from him, and where he got that torrent of language is unconceivable. I have frequently shut my eyes while he spoke, and, when he was done, asked myself what he had said, without being able to recollect a word of it. He was no logician. He was truly a great man, however—one of enlarged views."

It is tempting to take the last sentence, given the two sentences prior to it, as a contradiction, or at least as irony, yet it is not. Henry to Jefferson was a man of heart, not of head. The passage, however, suggests confusion, tergiversation.

Henry studied law on his own and began practice of law in 1760. He won oratorical fame in the "Parson's Cause" (1763). The Anglican clergy at the time were to be paid, for their services, 16,000 pounds of tobacco per year—a sum that amounted to two pennies per pound or some 320 dollars. After a poor crop in 1758, the price of tobacco rose threefold, hence inflating clerics' salary threefold. Virginia's House of Burgesses responded with the Two Penny Act, which fixed a clergyman's salary at two pennies per pound. King George III subsequently vetoed the law, which caused tumult in Virginia because the king was intervening in colonial matters and essaying to coerce citizens to triple the salaries of clergymen.

Fig. 3-2: Patrick Henry (public domain)

Rev. James Maury, Jefferson's mentor after the death of his father, Peter, sued Hanover County Court on April 1, 1762, for back wages. In doing so, he was representing all the Anglican clergymen who had not received their inflated salary, and in effect representing the king and the interests of Britain. The court ruled in favor of Maury, but there was a need of a jury to decide the amount of back wages owed. A jury assembled two months later. A young Patrick Henry argued against remuneration and presumably stated traitorously that the king, by his veto and intervention in colonial matters, "degenerated into a Tyrant and forfeits all right to his subjects' obedience."[15] So persuasively did Henry speak that the jury awarded Maury reparation of only one penny and the effect was nullification of King George's veto, an act that certainly did not sit well with the king. Biographer Henry Mayer writes that Henry "defined the prerogatives of the local elite by the unorthodox means of mobilizing the emotions of the lower ranks of religious and political outsiders."[16]

Jefferson tells in his *Autobiography* of witnessing Henry's oratorical skills when the Stamp Act was debated in 1765. Jefferson was 22 and certainly impressionable. At the door of the House of Burgesses, he heard Henry speak. "When the famous Resolutions of 1765, against the Stamp-act, were proposed, I was yet a student of law in Wmsbg. I attended the debate however at the door of the lobby of the H. of Burgesses, & heard the splendid display of Mr. Henry's talents as a popular orator. They were great indeed; such as I have never heard from any other man. He appeared to me to speak as Homer wrote."[17] That was indeed praise of the highest sort.

The Stamp Act was passed in 1765 as a means of collecting revenue from colonists for British purposes—most notably, for some 10,000 British troops to be stationed in North America avowedly to guard the American frontier. It mandated that many printed materials—e.g., legal papers, newspapers, magazines, and even playing cards—in the colonies were to be made from paper, stamped and produced in London.

While the actual cost of the tax on colonists was minimal, most colonists vigorously objected to a tax, made law, without colonial consent, because of its precedent. Thus, Henry, newly elected to the House of Burgesses, put forth several Stamp Act Resolves to the house, which passed the first four, which maintained in gist that colonists have "all the liberties, privileges, franchises, and immunities that have at any time been held, enjoyed, and possessed by the people of Great Britain," that the only legitimate means of taxation is "of the people by themselves, or by persons chosen by themselves to represent them" (as others cannot "know what taxes the people are able to bear"), and that every law wins legitimacy only by consent of the people. Henry went so far as to assert in Resolve 7, not passed, that anyone, through speaking or

---

[15] "Patrick Henry Arguing the Parson's Cause," Virginia Museum of History & Culture, https://www.virginiahistory.org/node/2294, accessed 1 June 2020.
[16] Henry Mayer, *A Son of Thunder: Patrick Henry and the American Republic* (New York: Grove Press, 1986), 66.
[17] Thomas Jefferson, "Autobiography", 5–6.

writing, asserting that any tax can be imposed on the people without approbation of the general assembly "shall be deemed an enemy to this his majesty's colony."[18]

Yet Henry is best known to posterity for his clamorous speech at St. John's Church in Richmond, VA, on March 23, 1775. In it, Henry pushed fellow Virginians to take up arms against the British, whose interventions in colonial matters and large military presence posed a genuine threat to colonists' liberty. Henry supposedly said: "If we were base enough to desire it, it is now too late to retire from the contest. There is no retreat but in submission and slavery! Our chains are forged! Their clanking may be heard on the plains of Boston! The war is inevitable and let it come! I repeat it, sir, let it come. ... I know not what course others may take, but as for me, give me liberty or give me death!"[19]

As a youth, Jefferson was always moved by Henry's fiery speechcraft. Yet he soon came to discover that Henry's capacity to inspire men—"his sublime imagination, his lofty and overwhelming diction," says Jefferson in his *Autobiography*[20]—came not from a vast storehouse of knowledge, linguistic fluency, and command of language, but instead from a knack for moving men through intonation and bulk of presence. There was potency, even ferocity, in his words, but according to Jefferson, neither logic nor eloquence. Though he had an expansive imagination, it was hazy, unlearned, and wooly. Henry was, said Jefferson, "the laziest man in reading I ever knew."

Is Jefferson's assessment of Henry correct or is it due to jealousy or even execration,[21] because Jefferson believed that the investigation into his possible misconduct during his final term as governor (1781) was incited by

---

[18] Thomas Jefferson, "Enclosure: Patrick Henry's Stamp Act Resolves, 30 May 1765," in *The Papers of Thomas Jefferson, Retirement Series, Vol. 7, 28 November 1813 to 30 September 1814*, ed. J. Jefferson Looney (Princeton: Princeton University Press, 2010), 496–497.

[19] Thomas S. Kidd, *Patrick Henry: First Among Patriots* (New York: Basic Books, 2011), 55. Henry's actual words were not transcribed and lost to posterity. The prose comes from the biography of William Wirt, who was three when Henry gave the speech.

[20] Thomas Jefferson, "Autobiography", 33.

[21] Ragosta, for instance, maintains that Jefferson "over time developed a deep loathing of Henry." John Ragosta, "Patrick Henry: Forgotten Founder," https://www.coursera.org/lecture/henry/conclusion-thomas-jefferson-versus-patrick-henry-x0Eyj, accessed 1 June 2020.

Henry and because Henry enjoyed a reputation and success in law and politics through oratory of which Jefferson was incapable?[22]

Concerning the latter, much of what we ascribe to Henry in his incendiary speeches has come down to us through William Wirt, who corresponded with Jefferson concerning particulars of the first biography of Henry, *Sketches of the Life and Character of Patrick Henry* (1817), prior to its publication. The work is generally regarded by historians as unrepresentative of Henry because it smacks of hero-worship, and we know what Jefferson thought about the work, as he shelved his copy of the book in his library under "Fiction."

While writing his biography, Wirt relied often on Jefferson for details. Jefferson replied with often lengthy letters to Wirt about what he knew, what he did not know, and what could be reconstructed from written records of events. These letters offer us a vivid depiction of what Jefferson thought of Henry.

On August 4, 1805, Jefferson writes: "In matters of law it [Henry's opinion] was not worth a copper: he was avaritious & rotten hearted. His two great passions were love of money & fame: but when these came into competition the former predominated."

Some seven years later, Jefferson says (12 Apr. 1812) that Henry was a very ineffective politician and unclear thinker. In the House of Burgesses, "he could not draw a bill on the most simple subject which would bear legal criticism, or even the ordinary criticism which looks to correctness of style and ideas, for indeed there was no accuracy of idea in his head. His imagination was copious, poetical, sublime, but vague also. He said the strongest things in the finest language, but without logic, without arrangement, desultorily."

Two years later (14 Aug. 1814), Jefferson tells of Henry's "first remarkable exhibition" in the House of Burgesses in May 1765 and of the debate concerning his Stamp Act Resolves. Jefferson says of the former:

> I can never forget a particular exclamation of his in the debate in which he electrified his hearers. It had been urged that from certain unhappy circumstances of the Colony, men of substantial property had contracted debts, which, if exacted suddenly, must ruin them and their families, but, with a little indulgence of time, might be paid with ease. 'What, Sir!' exclaimed Mr. Henry in animadverting on this, 'is it proposed then to reclaim the spendthrift from his dissipation and extravagance, by filling his pockets with money?

---

[22] See Michael Kranish, *Flight from Monticello: Thomas Jefferson at War* (Oxford: Oxford University Press, 2010), 312.

Jefferson adds that his recollection of that event has been "indelibly impressed on my memory. He laid open with so much energy the spirit of favoritism on which the proposition was founded, and the abuses to which it would lead, that it was crushed in its birth." That is certainly not the recollection of a man, fraught with nothing but hatred and contempt.

Of Henry's Resolves, Jefferson has much to say to Wirt, and does what he can to help any biographer to decide unsettled issues. Jefferson's account of Henry throughout is fair. He has no ax to grind. He wishes merely to get right the history. Though distrustful of Henry's oratorical means, he compliments Henry for having taken "the lead out of the hands of those who had heretofore guided the proceedings of the House"—the "honest and able" Pendleton, Wythe, Bland, Randolph, and Nicholas.

On May 12, 1815, Jefferson tells Wirt of the years of his first acquaintance with Henry in 1759. Jefferson was 16 at the time. He met Henry in his town of Hanover at Nathan Dandridge's and the time was around Christmas. Jefferson recalled Henry's coarse manners, and his passion for fiddling, dancing and pleasantry, which made his a favorite of all. Yet he avoided "any conversation which might give the measure either of his mind or information," though there was ample opportunity for that. When his store had "broken him up," he soon came to Williamsburg for his license to practice law, after having "read law not more than six weeks."

Over one year later (4 Sept. 1816), Jefferson objects to Wirt's exaggerated account of Henry's vast learning. "The study and learning ascribed to him, in this passage, would be inconsistent with the excellent and just picture given of his indolence through the rest of the work." Jefferson elaborates: "A first reading of a book he could accomplish sometimes and on some subjects, but never a second. He knew well the geography of his own country, but certainly never made any other a study. So, as to our ancient charters; he had probably read those in Stith's history; but no man ever more undervalued chartered titles than himself." Henry was cautious and selective in conversation. "He never, in conversation or debate, mentioned a hero, a worthy, or a fact in Greek or Roman history, but so vaguely and loosely as to leave room to back out, if he found he had blundered." Yet Henry's intentions were unadulterated—that is, morally grounded. "He drew all natural rights from a purer source—the feelings of his own breast"—a clear reference to Jefferson's notion of the moral sense, acting instinctively.

Allowing for some jealousy on Jefferson's part—he was a soft-spoken, perhaps even clumsy speaker, while Henry had the attention of all in an audience and the respect of most—Jefferson railed against Henry's oratorical "artistry" because of it was a verbal cosmetic. Languages were rich, diverse, historically entrenched, and ever evolving. They offered irrefutable proof of the fertility and complexity of human ideas, as well as the stark commonalities among humans, long separated by time and circumstances. Jefferson, his writings on language show definitively (e.g., "Thoughts on English Prosody"), that he had a full grasp of such things. He could only have considered someone like Henry, who pretended to have an understanding of language he could not have had, as a vulgarian. That said, it is also clear, from scattered comments, that in spite of Henry's uncouth and earthy catachresis, Jefferson fully respected Henry as a man of sound moral instincts. Jefferson knew that without such men, the American Revolution would not have been successful.

Thus, it is best not to ascribe ambivalence to Jefferson concerning Henry. The depiction Jefferson gives in writings on Henry is not a matter of conflicted feelings. It is about essaying to leave behind a correct picture of Patrick Henry, the man. Though Henry had numerous intellectual shortcomings, he was also proudly patriotic and was possessed of morally correct intuitions concerning the just path for colonists to take concerning the British, interloping in American affairs. Those intuitions drove his impassioned oratory.

"They strew flowers in the path of science"

Blair on Rhetoric (and Belle Lettres)

Jefferson's analysis of Patrick Henry qua man is evocative. Jefferson and Henry were in key respects polar figures. Jefferson was measured, studied, precise, and economical in verbal linguistic displays. Yet he was also taciturn and unassuming, and so he lacked command of his audience. Delivery of his First Inaugural Address—few could make out what Jefferson was saying—is an illustration. Henry was impetuous, underprepared, often imprecise, and generally verbose. Yet he was also boisterous and ostentatious, and so he had command of his audience. His perfervid speech at St. John's Church in 1775 is an illustration. Jefferson aimed to move men by virtue of reason; Henry, by emotional vitality. One might say that the ideal orator had Henry's presence and Jefferson's preparation.

Rhetoric and belle lettres—fineness of speech and of writing—were important arts in Jefferson's day, because in part speeches and literature were frequent topics of critical discussion in polite society. "We can hardly mingle in polite society without bearing some share in such discussions," writes Rev. Hugh Blair (1718–1800, Figure 3-3) in his popular *Lectures on Rhetoric and Bell Lettres*. Taste through sound criticism is "one of the most improving employments of the understanding," he adds. "To apply the principles of good sense to composition and discourse; to examine what is beautiful, and why it is so; to employ ourselves in distinguishing accurately between the specious and the solid, between affected and natural ornament, must certainly improve us not a little in the most valuable part of all philosophy, the philosophy of human nature." We learn self-understanding and improve morally, through the study of the imagination.[23]

Fig. 3-3: Hugh Blair (public domain)

Lectures on Rhetoric and Belle Lettres, published relatively late in Blair's life (1783), would become Jefferson's go-to book on rhetoric, and so we can assume that Jefferson's views on rhetoric were very similar to Blair's. On February 20, 1784, Jefferson writes to James Madison, "I shall take care to get Blair's Lectures for you as soon as published." Jefferson's statement is in reply to a request from Madison (11 Feb. 1784) for a copy of the book, which Jefferson would thereafter heartily recommend to others for rhetoric.[24]

---

[23] Hugh Blair, *Lectures on Rhetoric and Belles Lettres* (Philadelphia: Troutman & Hayes, 1853), 13.

[24] E.g., John Garland Jefferson, 11 June 1790; TJ to John Garland Jefferson, 14 pr. 1793; TJ to William G. Munford, 5 Dec. 1798; TJ to Joseph C. Cabell, Sept. 1800; and TJ to Francis Eppes, 13 Dec. 1820.

Jefferson certainly was on tenterhooks, while waiting for the book, as he was familiar with the Scotsman from two other works that earned Blair celebrity.

In his recommended list of books for a young gentleman's library to Robert Skipwith (3 Aug. 1771), Jefferson lists Blair's *A Critical Dissertation on the Poems of Ossian* (1763). Recommendation of that book comes as no surprise, given Jefferson's especial fondness for the epics of Ossian (chapter 2), presumably gathered by James Macpherson, who scholars today recognize was the true author of the poems. Blair directly addresses claims that the poems were crafted by Macpherson and not by the old poet Ossian—Samuel Johnson was the loudest proponent of Macpherson's fraud—and defends the authorship of Ossian. As I have already mentioned, there is no evidence that Jefferson ever questioned the authorship of Ossian.

From 1777 to 1801, Blair also published five volumes of his sermons, titled *Sermons.* On July 7, 1792, Jefferson writes in his Memoranda Book, "Pd. on sbscribg. to Blair's sermons 25."[25] Though he was anti-sectarian when it came to religion—true religion was a matter between a man and his god[26]—Jefferson often found moral inspiration in sermons, and it was the custom of his day that inspiring sermons of the most eloquent sermonizers be published for public consumption. Jefferson would sometimes recommend collections of sermons from sermonizers under "Morality" for morality-motivating reading.[27] Though he was noted to be poor at delivering a sermon, Blair's style was cordial and his sermons were intelligent and logically written, and he was considered the most popular sermonizer in Scotland. Jefferson certainly found attractive Blair's anti-Calvinism as well as Blair's focus on virtue, not revelation. Blair preached trust in the goodness of God, industry, Stoic resignation, and disdain of indolency.

As an illustration of Blair's easy manner of composition, there is his commentary of 2 Peter 3:10 in his sermon "On the Dissolution of the World." The verse reads, "But the day of the Lord will come as a thief in the night; in which the heavens shall pass away with a great noise, and the elements shall melt with fervent heat, the earth also and the works that are therein shall be burned up."

---

[25] Thomas Jefferson, "Memorandum Books, 1792," *Founders Online,* National Archives, https://founders.archives.gov/documents/Jefferson/02-02-02-0002, accessed 3 June 2020.
[26] See M. Andrew Holowchak, *American Messiah: The Surprisingly Simple Religious Views of Thomas Jefferson* (Abilene: Abilene Christian University Press, 2020).
[27] M. Andrew Holowchak, *Thomas Jefferson: Moralist* (Jefferson, NC: McFarland, 2017), chap. 4.

Blair comments on the passage, from which I proffer a lengthy quote to give readers an estimate of Blair's elegance of composition and clarity of style in defense of elegance of composition and clarity of style:

> The dissolution of the material system is an article of our faith, often alluded to in the Old Testament, clearly predicted in the New. It is an article of faith so far from being incredible, that many appearances in nature lead to the belief of it. We see all terrestrial substances changing their form. Nothing that consists of matter, is formed for perpetual duration. Everything around us, is impaired and consumed by time; waxes old by degrees, and tends to decay. There is reason, therefore, to believe, that a structure so complex as the world must be liable to the same law; and shall, at some period, undergo the same fate. Through many changes, the earth has already passed; many shocks it has received, and still is often receiving. A great portion of what is now dry land appears, from various tokens, to have been once covered with water. Continents bear the marks of having been violently rent, and torn asunder from one another. New islands have risen from the bottom of the ocean; thrown up by the force of subterraneous fire. Formidable earthquakes have, in divers' quarters, shaken the globe; and at this hour terrify, with their alarms, many parts of it. Burning mountains have, for ages, been discharging torrents of flame; and from time to time renew their explosions, in various regions. All these circumstances show that in the bowels of the earth, the instruments of its dissolution are formed. To our view, who behold only its surface, it may appear firm and unshaken; while its destruction is preparing in secret. The ground on which we tread is undermined. Combustible materials are stored. The train is laid. When the mine is to spring, none of us can foresee.[28]

Blair's commentary aims to reconcile revelation with reason. The verse in Peter is not incredible, and once we go beyond the surface appearance of things, it even seems inevitable. What is true of the parts is true of the whole, because the natural laws that govern the parts also govern the whole. The globe itself has given, over the centuries, abundancy of evidence of combustion. The earth is drying, decaying over time, like all living bodies dry, decay over time. Blair betrays a scholar's grasp of natural history, and he puts that expressively into his sermon. Jefferson could only have found Blair alluring.

---

[28] Hugh Blair, "On the Dissolution of the World," *Sermons*, Vol. 2 (Philadelphia: Hickman & Hazzard, 1822), 74–75.

Lectures on Rhetoric and Belles Lettres was perhaps Blair's most significant work. It was a collection of 47 lectures, given while he was a professor at the University of Edinburgh. Though it is a collection of lectures, the book is no grab bag. It is remarkably structured—each lecture follows another in a logical manner—and marks him as the most significant early theorist on oratory and belles lettres.

The significance of the book comprises its comprehensiveness, structural integrity, and its scope. First, Blair draws from the early history of oratory—Demosthenes, Cicero, and Quintilian—as well as from contemporaries such as Edmund Burke, Joseph Addison, and Lord Kames. Next, the 47 lectures are neatly and soundly structured and the manner of composition, elegant yet plain, is illustrative of points enumerated throughout the work.[29] Last, Blair focuses not merely on fineness of speaking, but also fineness of writing—that is, not just oratory, but also on belle lettres—and he does so through examination not only of celebrated orations, but also of history and poetry. Belles Lettres and criticism, says Blair, consider man as naturally endowed with taste and imagination, "to embellish his mind, and to supply him with rational and useful entertainment." He continues: "All that relates to beauty, harmony, grandeur, and elegance; all that can soothe the mind, gratify the fancy, or move the affections, belongs to their province." Moreover, those arts "bring to light various springs of action, which, without their aid, might have passed unobserved; and which, though of a delicate nature, frequently exert a powerful influence on several departments of human life." Yet they also offer repose to a mind, strained by excessive activity. "They strew flowers in the path of science; and while they keep the mind bent, in some degrees, and active, they relieve it at the same time from that more toilsome labour to which it must submit in the acquisition of necessary erudition, or the investigation of abstract truth."[30]

Fineness of speech and writing, says Blair, is thought by many to be a sham art. "When the arts of speech and writing are mentioned … a sort of art is immediately thought of, that is ostentatious and deceitful; the minute and trifling study of words alone; the pomp of expression; the studied fallacies of rhetoric; ornament substituted in the room of use." He admits that rhetoric

[29] Blair acknowledged that his *Lectures* would itself be subject the points he made apropos of fineness of writing. "It, after the liberties which it was necessary for him to take, in criticizing the style of the most eminent writers in our language, his own style shall be thought open to reprehension, all that he can say, is, that this book will add one to the many proofs already afforded to the world, of its being much easier to give instruction, than to set example." Hugh Blair, *Lectures on Rhetoric and Belles Lettres,* 3.

[30] Hugh Blair, *Lectures on Rhetoric and Belles Lettres,* 13–14.

and belles lettres have been often misused "to the corruption, rather than to the improvement, of good taste and true eloquence." That has been noted since the time of Plato.

Blair continues with his *modus operandi:* "It is equally possible to apply the principles of reason and good sense to this art, as to any other that is cultivated among men. If the following Lectures have any merit, it will consist in an endeavour to substitute the application of these principles in the place of artificial and scholastic rhetoric; in an endeavour to explode false ornament, to direct attention more towards substance than show, to recommend good sense as the foundation of all good composition, and simplicity as essential to all true ornament."[31]

One aspiring to excellence in speaking and writing, for Blair, must have large acquaintance with the other fine arts—even the sciences. "The orator ought to be an accomplished scholar, and conversant in every part of learning." There can be no art, "rich or splendid in expression," but empty of thought. Grace cannot compensate for want of matter.[32] Thus, beauty of expression, without meaning, without knowledge, is gibberish.

The aims of fineness in speaking and writing are perspicuity, agreeableness, purity, grace, and strength. Yet conformance to rules of right speaking and writing is insufficient for right speaking and writing. There are also "private application and study," as rules alone cannot inspire genius, but they can direct and assist it. Rules cannot remedy barrenness; but they may correct redundancy. Rules point out proper models for imitation. Rules bring into view the beauty that ought to be examined, and the imperfections that ought to be avoided. Consequently, while rules might be insufficient for genius, they are sufficient for keeping an aspirant from being a fool. "What would not avail for the production of great excellencies, may at least serve to prevent the commission of considerable errors."[33]

Blair lapses into an apology for the fine arts: a defense of criticism. The study of rhetoric and belles lettres, criticism, is allied with "sound logic." He elaborates, "The study of arranging and expressing our thoughts with propriety, teaches us to think, as well as to speak, accurately."[34] "True criticism is a liberal and humane art. It is the offspring of good sense and refined taste. It aims at acquiring a just discernment of the real merit of authors. It promotes a lively relish of their beauties, while it preserves us from that blind

---

[31] Hugh Blair, *Lectures on Rhetoric and Belles Lettres,* 10.
[32] Hugh Blair, *Lectures on Rhetoric and Belles Lettres,* 10.
[33] Hugh Blair, *Lectures on Rhetoric and Belles Lettres,* 12–13.
[34] Hugh Blair, *Lectures on Rhetoric and Belles Lettres,* 12.

and implicit veneration which would confound their beauties and faults in our esteem. It teaches us, in a word, to admire and to blame with judgment, and not to follow the crowd blindly."[35]

Outside of the rejuvinative effects of cultivation of the fine arts, one of the strongest arguments in their favor is that they are a diversion from the vices which to many are enticements. "He is so happy as to have acquired a relish for these, has always at hand an innocent and irreproachable amusement for his leisure hours, to save him from the danger of many a pernicious passion. He is not in hazard of being a burden to himself. He is not obliged to fly to low company, or to court the riot of loose pleasures, in order to cure the tediousness of existence." Thus, à la Kames (chapter 1), the pleasures of taste have been placed by providence "in a middle station between the pleasures of sense, and those of pure intellect. We were not designed to grovel always among objects so low as the former; nor are we capable of dwelling constantly in so high a region as the latter. The pleasures of taste refresh the mind after the toils of the intellect, and the labours of abstract study; and they gradually raise it above the enjoyments of virtue."[36]

A person introduced to the pleasures of taste—"the power of receiving pleasure from the beauties of nature and art"—transitions readily to virtue. "To be entirely devoid of relish for eloquence, poetry, or any of the fine arts, is justly construed to be an unpromising symptom of youth; and release suspicions of their being prone to low gratifications, or destined to drudge in the more vulgar and illiberal pursuits of life." Taste exercises tenderness and humaneness, and weakens the grip of the barbaric and violent emotions. "The elevated sentiments and high examples which poetry, eloquence and history are often bringing under our view, naturally tend to nourish in our minds public spirit, the love of glory, contempt of external fortune, and the admiration of what is truly illustrious and great."[37] The sentiment is again consistent with Kames on the benefits of cultivation of the fine arts.

The "characters" of taste are two: delicacy and correctness. Delicacy concerns the perfection of "that natural sensibility on which taste is founded." Correctness concerns the improvement of taste through understanding. "The power of delicacy is chiefly seen in discerning the true merit of a work; the power of correctness, in rejecting false pretensions to merit." While delicacy leans toward feeling, correctness leans toward reason.[38]

---

[35] Hugh Blair, *Lectures on Rhetoric and Belles Lettres*, 11–12.
[36] Hugh Blair, *Lectures on Rhetoric and Belles Lettres*, 13–14.
[37] Hugh Blair, *Lectures on Rhetoric and Belles Lettres*, 15–16.
[38] Hugh Blair, *Lectures on Rhetoric and Belles Lettres*, 20–1.

Finally, Blair, certainly following Aristotle's notions of *dunamis* (potentiality) and *energeia* (actuality), proffers a distinction between taste and genius. "Taste consists in the power of judging; genius, in the power of executing."[39] And so, genius is a "higher power of mind than taste," for genius is in some sense the actualization of taste.

"To be led by reason and persuasion, and not by force"

Status of Oratory as a Fine Art

Like Blair, Jefferson thought that the best models of excellence in oratory were from antiquity, and as we saw from his letter to Minor, he considered the Greek Demosthenes and the Roman Cicero to be the two foremost models from antiquity.[40] Here Jefferson and Blair follow Plutarch, who wrote on and compared the two in his *The Lives of the Noble Greeks and Romans.* While the former overcame severe deficiencies—soft voice, shortness of breath, and poor enunciation—to become a formidable orator, the latter was a prodigy as a youth.

Jefferson always considered oratory—comprising in his 1789 catalog of books logic, rhetoric, and oration—as an indispensible fine art. He says to son-in-law Thomas Mann Randolph (6 July 1787) of its importance in his education for law and politics. He advises Randolph, who is at William and Mary at the time, to begin with a foundation—to wit, languages and math—and then proceed to politics, law, rhetoric, and history. "As to these, the place where you study them is absolutely indifferent. I should except Rhetoric, a very essential member of them, and which I suppose must be taught to advantage where you are: you would do well therefore to attend the public exercises in this branch also, and to do it with very particular diligence."

To son-in-law John Wayles Eppes (17 Jan. 1810), Jefferson writes of "the ill effect of the long speeches in the House of Representatives" in vogue at the time. The effect on the citizenry is to "transfer their confidence from the legislative to the Executive branch," which is a recipe for autocracy—the end of representative government. Again, Jefferson turns to antiquity for "the models for that oratory which is to produce the greatest effect." He cites Livy, Tacitus, and Sallust, but "most assuredly not ... Cicero," whose imaginative prose is best left for the courts.

---

[39] Hugh Blair, *Lectures on Rhetoric and Belles Lettres,* 29.

[40] See also TJ to Francis Eppes, 6 Oct. 1820.

To Jason Chamberlain (1 July 1814), Jefferson writes of Cicero, Demosthenes, Aeschynes and the other Grecian orators as the finest verbal specimens and of Homer, Anacreon, Theocritus, Virgil, Horace, Terence and the Greek tragedians as the finest examples of belle lettres. Four days later, he says of Cicero's patronage of the eloquence of Plato: "altho' Cicero did not wield the dense logic of Demosthenes, yet he was able, learned, laborious, practised in the business of the world, & honest. he could not be the dupe of mere style, of which he was himself the first master in the world."

Once he involved himself in birthing the University of Virginia, Jefferson's thoughts turned much more frequently to oratory, since he had to establish a curriculum for the institution. I offer several illustrations.

One of Jefferson's most significant passages on the value of oratory is in a letter to John Garland (27 Feb. 1822). In a government where politicians are elected by the public to represent their interest, eloquence is powerful and necessary. Yet models of "chaste and classical oratory" are rare in the United States, as well as in England. Nevertheless, they can be found in antiquity—in, for instance, Livy, Sallust and Tacitus. "Their pith and brevity constitute perfection itself for an audience of sages, on whom froth and fancy would be lost in air." In America, however, there are no audiences of sages, but still there is a need for eloquence in politics and law. "for Senatorial eloquence Demosthenes is the finest model; for the bar Cicero.[41] the former had more logic, the latter more imagination." Yet the English do offer singular instances of eloquence of the pen: Robertson, Sterne,[42] and Addison in composition, and Hume, "in the circumstance of style."[43]

Jefferson advises Creed Taylor (27 Mar. 1823) of the utility of the rhetoric. "it gives opportunities to Students of practising their lessons in Rhetoric, of habituating themselves to think and to speak with method, and lessens the shock of a premier debut at the bar, so terrible in a first essay of strength before the public."

To David Harding (20 Apr. 1824), Jefferson writes, "Antiquity has left us the finest models for imitation; and he who studies and imitates them most nearly will nearest approach the perfection of the art." He again picks out Livy,

---

[41] Cf. Blair, who writes, "Of orators, Cicero has more of the beautiful than Demosthenes, whose genius led him wholly towards vehemence and strength." Hugh Blair, *Lectures on Rhetoric and Belles Lettres*, 55.

[42] He is likely referring both the Sterne's fiction as well as his sermons. Sterne took great liberties with the English language in his fiction and Jefferson doubtless found that intoxicating.

[43] See also TJ to John Carr, 28 Apr. 1807; TJ to Tobias Lear, 19 June 1813; TJ to Dabney Carr Terrell, 26 Feb. 1821; and TJ to Francis Terrell, 16 Sept. 1821.

Sallust, and Tacitus. He sums, "Amplification is the vice of modern oratory. It is an insult to an assembly of reasonable men, disgusting and revolting instead of persuading. Speeches measured by the hour, die with the hour."

From the letters to Eppes, Chamberlain, Garland, Taylor, and Harding, fine speaking for Jefferson is both logical (Demosthenes) and imaginative (Cicero). Pith and brevity are critical for effective argumentation; amplification through long speeches fraught with redundancies and blatherskite, empty talk, is disgustful to men of reason and refined taste. So too is discretionary employment of language, without substance, for effect.

With his experience in law and in politics, Jefferson was keenly aware of the significance of oratory and belles lettres for a republican nation. In the 1824 letter to Harding, he says: "in a republican nation whose citizens are to be led by reason and persuasion and not by force, the art of reasoning becomes of first importance." As Blair notes, the aim of oratory in law differs from that of politics. The former aims at conviction, which "affects the understanding only"; the latter, at persuasion, which concerns the will and is meant to inspire action.[44]

So the key was oratory for Jefferson that the first professorship at the University of Virginia would be of "languages, history, rhetoric, oratory & belles lettres."[45] On September 1, 1817, he says of the first professorship: "the first called for, as first wanting, will be a professor of languages, to wit Greek & Latin essentially, history, Rhetoric, Oratory, belles letters, to which if he adds modern languages so much the better, to wit French, Spanish, Italian and German. as his school will be the most numerous, we give him only 500.D. fixed, and 20.D. tuition fees for every scholar."[46] The University of Virginia, Jefferson thought, would be the premier academic institution in the Southern states and perhaps eventually even in the country. It was uniquely to churn out, *inter alii*, those politicians would govern the state and even the country—those persons who imbibed freely and adequately the principles of liberty and equality and those persons whose inclinations were toward husbandry and not manufacture.

---

[44] Hugh Blair, *Lectures on Rhetoric and Belles Lettres*, 262.
[45] Thomas Jefferson, "Anonymous to the Richmond Enquirer, [ca. 29] August 1817," *The Papers of Thomas Jefferson*, ed. J. Jefferson Looney (Princeton: Princeton University Press, 2014), 665.
[46] See also TJ to William Russell, 1 May 1824.

Upshot

Toward the end of his unfinished *Autobiography,* Thomas Jefferson writes of a signal dinner party at his residence, while minister plenipotentiary to France. The occasion was the early stages of the French Revolution and the need to discuss a constitution for France. Writes Jefferson: "in this uneasy state of things, I recieved one day a note from the Marquis de la Fayette, informing me he should bring a party of six or eight friends to ask a dinner of me." In addition to Lafayette, there were Dupont, Barnave, La Meth, Blacon, Mounier, Maubourg, and Dagout. Jefferson continues: "these were leading patriots, of honest but differing opinions sensible of the necessity of effecting a coalition by mutual sacrifices, knowing each other, and not afraid therefore to unbosom themselves mutually."

After dinner was finished, the tablecloth was removed. Wine was put on the table "after the American manner," in readiness for political conversation. The time was critical, for if there were to be no action toward republicanism, "the Aristocracy would carry everything."

Lafayette opened the discussion, which began at 4 p.m. and continued till 10 p.m. Jefferson relates that he was "a silent witness to a coolness and candor of argument unusual in the conflicts of political opinion; to a logical reasoning, and chaste eloquence, disfigured by no gaudy tinsel of rhetoric or declamation, and truly worthy of being placed in parallel with the finest dialogues of antiquity, as handed to us by Xenophon, by Plato, and Cicero."[47]

How well did Jefferson follow the discourse? He, of course, had command of French, but it was far from full, and it is likely from his comments that he paid as much attention to the how of the conversation as he did to the what. The overall bent of the discussion was action, and action demanded coolness, chasteness, logic, and perhaps most significantly conciliation, which, it seems, was achieved by the discussants.

Jefferson ended his autobiography shortly after his time in France. His reason for failing to continue the book, undertaken in 1821, is a matter of contention among scholars. The French Revolution, if its aim was to establish a republic like the United States, was a failure, as Jefferson would come to discover.

Yet Jefferson's account of the success of his dinner party, given the utmost urgency of the scenario, is one of the political highlights of his autobiography. It underscores the message that republican government can only succeed when its leaders, elected by the citizenry as *primus inter pares,* debate contentious issues with civility, *sang froid,* respect, integrity, and regard for

---

[47] Thomas Jefferson, "Autobiography", in *Thomas Jefferson: Writings,* 95–96.

reason, not with "gaudy tinsel." Because of the indispensability of "the art of reason" in republican government, fineness of speaking and writing—substantive prose that is elegantly crafted—must be politically an art second to none, given that concinnity is partnered with substance. Moreover, in keeping with one of the key themes of this book, there must be pith and brevity to good speaking and writing. They too can be overdone, and when overdone, they lose their effect.

Part Two
Beaux Arts

Chapter IV

The Art of Gardening

"It [gardening] is the purest of human pleasures; it is the greatest refreshment to the spirits of man; without which buildings and palaces are but gross handyworks; and a man shall ever see that, when ages grow to civility and elegancy, men come to build stately, sooner than to garden finely; as if gardening were the greater perfection."[1] ~Francis Bacon

Writes Jean-Jacques Rousseau, who was exiled in 1762 in Neuchâtel near the Swiss border and came to acquire a love of botany: "L'étude de la nature nous détache de nous-même et nous élève a son auteur. C'est en ce sens qu' on deviant vraiment philosophe; c'est ainsi que l'histoire naturelle et la botanique ont un usage pour la sagesse et pour la vertue."[2] William Bartram, the son of John Bartram, Quaker and botanist, expresses a sentiment similar in *Travels*: "THIS world, as a glorious apartment of the boundless places of the sovereign Creator, is furnished with an infinite variety of animated scenes, inexpressibly beautiful and pleasing, equally free to the inspection and enjoyment of all his creatures. PERHAPS there is not any part of creation, within the reach of our observations, which exhibits a more glorious display of the Almighty hand, than the vegetable world. Such a variety of pleasing scenes, ever-changing, throughout the seasons, arising from various causes and assigned each to the purpose and use."[3]

Jefferson, like Rousseau and Bartram, had a deep love of nature and an unslakable desire to study it, when time allowed. One way, of the most profitable ways, of studying nature was through growing things, which necessitated knowledge of climate, soil, and plants, *inter alia.*

---

[1] Francis Bacon, *Bacon's Essays* (Boston: Little, Brown, & Company, 1900), 249–50.

[2] "Study of nature detaches us from ourselves and elevates us to our Author. It is in this sense that one becomes truly a philosopher; it is thus that natural history and botany conduce toward wisdom and virtue" (my translation). "Jean-Jacques Rousseau botaniste...," *Botanique,* 19 Apr. 2020, https://www.botanique-jardins-paysages.com/jean-jacques-rousseau-lettres-elementaires-sur-la-botanique-1771/, accessed 13 May 2022.

[3] William Bartram, *Travels through North & South Carolina, Georgia, East & West Florida, the Cherokee country, the extensive Territories of the Muscogulges, or Creek Confederacy, and the Country of the Chactaws; Containing an Account of the Soil and natural Production of those regions, Together with Observations on the Manners of the Indians* (Philadelphia: James Johnson, 1791), xiv.

Jefferson enjoyed growing things, useful things chiefly, and applied mathematics to growing just as he did to architecture, human labor, and study of other aspects of nature. He loved order, symmetry, and beauty, and few occupations allowed for human expression of that triad more than gardening.

In this chapter, I cover Jefferson on gardening. In doing so, I treat husbandry as a species of gardening, given that Jefferson, like Lord Kames, had both practical and aesthetic approaches to husbandry and given Jefferson's uptake of Englishman Philip Southcote's notion that a gentlemanly estate should itself be treated as a garden. I begin with Jefferson's views on the praxis and theory of husbandry, move to an expiscation of Jefferson's vegetable and fruit gardens, and end with some thoughts on Jefferson's many pleasure gardens and Monticello's numerous acres themselves as a large pleasure garden.

I offer two caveats, before proceeding. Throughout this chapter, I am loathed to make too much of the distinction between husbandry and gardening—only the latter, strictly speaking, was among the fine arts, as only the latter had beauty as its aim, while the former was concerned with yield—because Jefferson had a heartfelt love for growing things, and when he grew things, even crops, beauty was never absent from his thoughts. Moreover, it is perhaps artificial to proffer a sharp distinction between architecture, the topic of the next chapter, and gardening, what is often called landscape architecture. A building of a certain type, like Richmond's Capitol, cannot be fitted into any landscape, and the garden(s) around a particular estate, like Jefferson's Monticello, must be carefully designed to complement the estate. And so, the architects of Jefferson's day needed to know much about landscapes, and gardeners needed to know much about architecture. The difference between the two "artists" is that the latter worked with living materials.

"It is nature that makes this so"

Praxis & Theory of Growing Things

In *The Gentleman Farmer*, Lord Kames remonstrates that husbandry has a just claim to being not only a fine art, but the most important of the fine arts. "Agriculture justly claims to be the chief of the arts: it enjoys beside the signal pre-eminence of combining deep philosophy with useful practice." It is the most productive of contentment, the sweetest sort of happiness and it is unrivaled for linking private interest with public wellbeing. "How appealing to think, that every step a man makes for his own good, promotes that of his country!"[4] Jefferson, I maintain, appropriated that view.

Kames distinguishes between the practice and the theory of farming. The former, concerning only effects, is rightly a branch of Natural History. The latter, concerning causes, is rightly a branch of Natural Philosophy. Most writers treat husbandry as Natural History, because they treat only of the practice of farming.

Kames aims to delve also into the causes of husbandry. While praxis deals with tools, farm offices, types of plants cultivated (whether for fruit, roots, or leaves), types of grass, and rotation of crops, fencing, and the proper size of a farm, theory deals with chemical principles apposite to agriculture, the plasticity of plants, the need of variability in procreation of animals, and quality of soils.

As Jefferson owned Kames' book and was much influenced by Kames on numerous issues—the moral sense, the aesthetic sense, theory of criticism, theory of social evolution, law, natural religion, and education—we might profitably assume that he made ample use of Kames' thoughts on farming fields and gardens in a gentlemanly manner. A letter to President George Washington (14 May 1794), for illustration, on the use of dung in fields is clearly drawn from chapter 11, titled "Manures," from Kames' book.

Husbandry had an especial place in Jefferson's political philosophy—his notion of thriving republican government.[5] The life of a farmer, he thought, was suited superlatively to promote large-scale human flourishing by enhancing independency of all citizens, by allowing both for some measure of political participation through the leisure provided by scientific farming, and by cultivating virtue through labor, both honest and necessary. Jefferson's ideal society, says Robert Shalhope, was "the middle landscape [which] served as a guide or a model: a constant reminder of what was possible." He aimed to ground his republicanism on "ordinary farmers," whom he considered to be "superior citizens."[6]

Early in his political career, Jefferson considered the life of agriculture and the life of manufacture in some sense as competing alternatives—that is, a

---

[4] Henry Home, *The Gentleman Farmer: Being an Attempt to Improve Agriculture, By Subjecting It to the Test of Rational Principles*, ed. 4 (Edinburgh: Bell & Bradfute, 1798), v and xvii–xviii.

[5] M. Andrew Holowchak, "Jefferson's Moral Agrarianism: Poetic Fiction or Moral Vision?" *Agriculture and Human Values*, Vol. 28, 2011, 497–506.

[6] Robert Shalhope, "Agriculture," in *Thomas Jefferson: A Reference Biography*, ed. Merrill D. Peterson (New York: Charles Scribner's Sons, 1986), 396.

society could be predominantly one of manufacture or one of agriculture—and while the former was life-affirming, the latter was life-mephitic. The life of a husbandman was a beautiful life.

That sentiment comes out neatly in Query XIX of Jefferson's *Notes on Virginia*, published while he was minister plenipotentiary to France (1784–1789). Virginians have been largely wedded to agriculture but only to the manufacture of such items, clothing especially, that are "most necessary." They appeal to foreign manufacture for unneeded finer items, often worthless gewgaws.[7]

Yet Europe's political economists, Jefferson adds, have mandated that each nation should engage in its own manufacture. Jefferson accepts the principle, but adds a caveat: Different circumstances often produce different results. In Europe, "manufacture must ... be resorted to of necessity not of choice, to support the surplus of people" and dearth of land.

Farmed goods are to be mostly imported. In America, "we have an immensity of land courting the industry of the husbandman."[8]

Jefferson then offers two options for Americans in the form of a dilemma. All citizens can be involved in improving the land or half can be involved in its improvement and half can be involved in manufacture.[9]

The dilemma is flimsy, however. Jefferson nowise genuinely considers the viability of having half of America's citizens engaged in manufacture. He counters with two arguments for the worth of farming: The argument of virtue and the argument from independency. He offers, in an oft-quoted passage, an account of the sacrosanctity, the beauty, of the agricultural lifestyle. "Those who labor the earth are the chosen people of God, if ever he had a chosen people, whose breasts he has made his peculiar deposit for substantial and genuine virtue. It is the focus in which he keeps alive that sacred fire, which otherwise might escape from the face of the earth." Husbandry is the most virtuous profession. History has failed to record an instance of a facinorous husbandman. Moreover, farmers are independent. They need not depend on the "casualties and caprice of customers," whose wants are unpredictable, as do manufacturers, who must look up to heaven for help. "Dependence begets subservience and venality, suffocates the germ of virtue, and prepares fit tools

---

[7] Thomas Jefferson, *Notes on the State of Virginia*, ed. William Peden (Chapel Hill, NC: University of North Carolina Press, 1954), 164.

[8] Thomas Jefferson, *Notes on Virginia*, 164.

[9] Thomas Jefferson, *Notes on Virginia*, 164.

for the designs of ambition."[10] In short, independency makes husbandmen champions and lovers of liberty, and thus, the fittest republican citizens.

With reference to the subservience and venality that it engenders, manufacture is not for Jefferson a viable option. Farmers, preoccupied with their land and crops, have not the time to occupy themselves with seedy ventures and get-rich-at-the-expense-of-others schemes. Instead, they work, and in Jefferson's eyes, improve the land, and so their livelihood contributes immensely to human betterment and happiness. There is no reason for scheming when their goods come to market. Food is not an extravagance; it is needed. Manufacturers, in contrast, make an abundancy of products: some, genuine goods (clothes and tools); most, unneeded furbelows. Consequently, they must scheme or consort with schemers to market and sell most of their manufacture—hence, subservience and venality. Success in scheming creates motivation for greater, ever clever scheming. Much schooled in algorithms, Jefferson sums, "The proportion which the aggregate of the other classes of citizens bears in any state to that of its husbandmen, is the proportion of its unsound to its healthy parts, and is a good-enough barometer whereby to measure its degree of corruption."[11] Americans ought never to occupy a work-bench or twirl a distaff, but ought to farm while there are plenty of fields.[12]

Jefferson is certainly moved by an economic vision of a stable and thriving country, but agrarianism, for him, is chiefly a moral and aesthetic, not an economic or political ideal: The more a husbandman benefits himself, the more he benefits others. That is consistent with the sentiment of others of his day—e.g., Lord Kames, who says: "Agriculture justly claims to be the chief of the arts: it enjoys beside the signal pre-eminence of combining deep philosophy with useful practice." It is the most productive of contentment, the sweetest sort of happiness and it is unrivaled for linking private interest with public wellbeing. "How appealing to think, that every step a man makes for his own good, promotes that of his country!"[13] Benjamin Franklin states that agriculture is "the only honest way" to acquire wealth, for a "man receives a real increase of the seed thrown into the ground, in a kind of continual miracle, wrought by the hand of God in his favor, as a regard for his innocent life and his virtuous industry."[14] Working the land, Jefferson says in Query XIX

---

[10] Thomas Jefferson, *Notes on Virginia*, 164–65.
[11] Thomas Jefferson, *Notes on Virginia*, 165.
[12] Thomas Jefferson, *Notes on Virginia*, 165.
[13] Henry Home, *The Gentleman Farmer*, v and xvii–xviii.
[14] Peter Loewer, *Thomas Jefferson's Garden* (Mechanicksburg, PA: Stackpole Books, 2004), 1.

of *Notes on Virginia* and in numerous letters,[15] conduces to virtue and human happiness. Virtue and happiness are the first rewards, and immeasurable, and the secondary rewards of economic and political stability are a consequence of working within the frame of human nature, not against it.

In a letter to Benjamin Austin (9 Jan. 1816), Jefferson gives what might be dubbed the *argumentum sequi natura* (follow-nature argument) for the preferability of husbandry to manufacture. Manufacture is fruitless, while husbandry is cornucopian. He writes, "Agriculture is productive, manufacturing is sterile, and it is nature that makes this so." He explains, "To the labor of the husbandman, a vast addition is made by the spontaneous energies of the earth on which it is employed: for one grain of wheat committed to the earth, she renders twenty, thirty, and even fifty-fold, whereas to the labor of the manufacturer nothing is added." Thus, American citizens ought to pursue careers that are by nature cornucopian and ought to eschew occupations that are by nature sterile.

Furthermore, husbandmen have a link to the land that manufacturers, tradesmen, and merchants do not. In times of economic distress or war, the latter can liquidate their assets and abandon the state; husbandmen cannot. Husbandmen have an investment in the land, and thus, an investment in their state and country that others cannot have. In times of war, a husbandman readily marches to defend his motherland—"every man being at his ease, feels an interest in the preservation of order, and comes forth to preserve it at the first call of the magistrate"[16]—for invaders threaten to take away his land and his way of life.

We must not think of Jefferson's arguments as being only provincial. They are catholic. Husbandry for Jefferson is not just an American ideal, but ought to be a global ideal. The manufacture that predominates in parts of Europe comes at the expense of human happiness.[17] He writes John Jay (23 Aug. 1785): "I consider the class of artificers as the panders of vice & the instruments by which the liberties of a country are generally overturned." He adds: "Cultivators of the earth are the most valuable citizens. They are the most vigorous, the most independent, the most virtuous, & they are tied to their country & wedded to its liberty & interests by the most lasting bonds." Jefferson's arguments relate to the human condition, not just to the American

---

[15] 4. See, for example, TJ to John Jay, 23 Aug. 1785; TJ to John Blair, 13 Aug. 1787; TJ to George Washington, 14 Aug. 1787; TJ to James Madison, 20 Dec. 1787; TJ to Jean Nicholas Démeunier, 29 Apr. 1795; TJ to Jean Baptiste Say, 1 Feb. 1804; and TJ to Caspar Wistar, 21 June 1807.

[16] TJ to Marc Auguste, 5 Feb. 1803.

[17] TJ to James Madison, 20 Dec. 1787.

scenario of abundancy of unemployed land, and it is the same, as I argue throughout, with Jefferson's American aesthetic ideal.

The key to successful husbandry Jefferson, ever arithmetizing, also reduces to an algorithm. He says to Charles Willson Peale (17 Apr. 1813) and in agreement with him that a small farm properly manned and worked, can be more productive than one larger, not so properly worked and manned. Yet there are extremes, and a medium must be had.

> The true medium may really be considered and stated as a mathematical problem. 'Given the quantum of labor within our command, and land ad libitum offering its spontaneous contributions: Required the proportion [*sic*] in which these two elements should be employed to produce a Maximum?' it is a difficult problem, varying probably in every country according to the relative value of land and labor. The spontaneous energies of the earth are a gift of nature, but they require the labor of man to direct their operation, and the question is, so to husband his labor as to turn the greatest quantity of this useful action of the earth to his benefit.

The essence of sound farming for Jefferson is aesthetic: a matter of proportioning labor to yield. A good husbandman will know how to maximize yield with a minimum of labor, and part of his labor is planning through knowledge of land and climate, and agricultural techniques. Though the algorithm is simple, the problem is complex, as there are many variables that need to be plugged into the algorithm and it is not trouble-free to ascertain numbers for them.

In Query IV of *Notes on Virginia*, Jefferson turns to Virginia's native vegetables and proffers a fourfold classification—medicinal. esculent, ornamental, and useful. He lists 24 Medicinals (e.g., Arsmart or *Cassia ligustrina*, Virginia Marshmallow or *Napæa* hermaphrodita, and Virginia Snake-root or *Aristolochia serpentaria*), 35 Esculents (e.g., Jerusalem artichoke or *Helianthustuberosus*, Sugar Maple or *Acer saccharinum*, and Black Raspberries or *Robus occidentalis*), 44 Ornamentals (e.g., Poplar or *Liriodendron tulipifera*, catalpa or *Bignonia catalpa*, and Candleberry Myrtle or *Myrica cerifera*), and 28 Usefuls (e.g., Cypress or *Cupressus disticha*, Juniper or *Juniperus virginica*, and Black Jack Oak or *Quercus aquatica*).[18]

Jefferson's approach to his land was overall metempirical or theoretical, more than practical. That is because he had spent so many decades of his life in legal

[18] Thomas Jefferson, *Notes on Virginia*, 38–43.

and political duties that have kept him from Monticello. Thus, he never acquired an intimate knowledge of his fields, but was reduced to management of them from afar via letters by means of knowledge gleaned through books and maps, and by advice from neighbors. Indirect management would prove disastrous not only for his fields at Monticello but also for them at other places like Poplar Forest in Bedford County and Pantops in Albemarle County.

Jefferson had some 5,000 acres of land around Monticello, says Duc de la Rouchefoucauld-Liancourt after a visit to Monticello in 1796. Of those, 1,120 were cultivated. Of the cultivatable, he has fashioned four farms, "every farm into six [*sic*] fields of forty acres," for a total of two hundred and eighty acres" per farm. "His system of rotation embraces seven years, and this is the reason why each farm has been divided into seven fields."[19] Wheat is cultivated in the first, Indian corn in the second, peas or potatoes in the third, vetches in the fourth, wheat in the fifth, clover in the sixth and seventh. With each year, there is a rotation of crops to use the soil most efficiently.[20]

Each farm, continues the duke, is directed by a steward, who oversees four male slaves, four female slaves, four oxen, and four horses. Each farm, because of the hilliness of the land, has its own barn to make easy transport of crops.[21]

The duke's account and numerous entries in Jefferson's Farm Book, begun in 1774 and ended just prior to his death, betray Jefferson's obsession with mathematics—specifically arithmetic and geometry—when it came to farming. Most calculations, derived from personal observations or the testimonies of friends, seem to make no concessions to hands-on experience.

Jefferson often and meticulously observed the work one, two, or a few persons did to measure with precision just how much work should be expected of any laborer in similar circumstances. In reference to threshing wheat in 1772, he states: "it would take 4. men & a girl to work, and they would get out about 4. bushels in 12 hours, when the [threshing] machine comes to work glib and smooth. one may say on the whole that it gets out double of what the same men could thresh. but infinitely cleaner. there did not appear

---

[19] "Six," above, being an obvious mistake by the duke, as 280 acres for each of four farms yields 1,120 cultivated acres and six fields of 40 acres yields 240 acres per farm, not 280. Seven is the proper number of fields.

[20] Duc de la Rochefoucauld-Liancourt, "A Frenchman Views Jefferson the Farmer," in *Visitors to Monticello*, ed. Merrill D. Peterson (Charlottesville: University Press of Virginia, 1989), 23–24. Kames recommends wheat, peas/beans, barley, oats, and fallow, when manure is abundant, and posits as a general rule culmiferous crops should be rotated with leguminous. Henry Home, *The Gentleman Farmer: Being an Attempt to Improve Agriculture by Subjecting it to the Test of Rational Principles* (Edinburgh: 1776), 141–42.

[21] Duc de la Rochefoucauld-Liancourt, "A Frenchman Views Jefferson the Farmer," 25.

to be 1. grain in 100. or 150. left in the straw."[22] On July 7, 1796, he writes, "13. cutters x 12 day = 156. which gives near 2a^{s}. a day for each cutters, supposing 300. acres."[23] On July 2, 1796—and here we have an illustration of lack of hands-on experience—Jefferson writes with frustration, "we stopped our ploughs; the pickers up not keeping up the cutters." Yet he adds that the wheat that year was especially heavy.[24] With his love of technology, Jefferson was ever interested in machines which could offer similar or greater yield with less human labor.

Jefferson frequently thought that if agricultural matters could be worked out mathematically, and beautifully, on paper, they must work out in reality, and sometimes they did. His design of a plow moldboard which curves gradually from the vertical end of a right angle to the horizontal end is a fine illustration, and one that worked not only beautifully on paper, but also neatly in praxis.[25]

At other times—especially when Jefferson was away from his lands—he was content that matters worked beautifully on paper, and only addressed the practical difficulties as they arose after implementation of theoretical designs.

"Laid off ground to be leveled for a future garden"

Jefferson's Vegetable & Fruit Gardens

In 1811, Jefferson writes Charles Willson Peale (Aug. 20): "No occupation is so delightful to me as the culture of the earth, and no culture comparable to that of the garden. Such a variety of subjects, someone always coming to perfection, the failure of one thing repaired by the success of another, and instead of one harvest a continued one through the year." Jefferson here writes not only of pleasure gardening, but vegetable and fruit gardens. There is for him an art to growing edibles, and that art includes assurance that different foods would be table-ready at different times of a year.

Jefferson had a scientific approach to gardening that was axially aesthetical. As we have seen, he divided trees, plants, fruits, and vegetables in four classes: the medicinal, the esculent, the useful, and the ornamental. "I have always thought that if in the experiments to introduce or to communicate new plants," he writes to Samuel Vaughan 27 Nov. 1790), "one species in an

---

[22] Thomas Jefferson, The Garden and Farm Books of Thomas Jefferson, 311.

[23] Thomas Jefferson, The Garden and Farm Books of Thomas Jefferson, 293.

[24] Thomas Jefferson, The Garden and Farm Books of Thomas Jefferson, 293.

[25] M. Andrew Holowchak, *Thomas Jefferson: Psychobiography of an American Lion* (New York: Nova, 2019), 247.

hundred if found useful and succeeds, the ninety nine found otherwise are more than paid for."

On March 31, 1774, Jefferson writes in his Garden Book of his first vegetable garden at Monticello: "laid off ground to be levelled for a future garden. the upper side is 44. f. below the upper edge of the Round-about and parallel thereto. it is 668 feet long, 80 f. wide, and at each end forms a triangle, rectangular & isosceles, of which the legs are 80. f. wide, & the hypotenuse 113. feet."[26] The garden, today a showpiece at Monticello, would come to be 1,000-foot long and grow some 330 varieties of vegetables and some 170 types of fruit in the garden and in orchards over the over the years (Figure 4-1): "fruits" such as a variety of peas, beans, melons, peppers, berries, cucumbers, gerkins, tomatoes, okra, asparagus, artichokes, and squashes; "roots" such as carrots, beets, salsify, scallion, garlic, onion, leeks, shallots, chives, parsnip, and potatoes; and other, mostly leafy vegetables such as spinaches, lettuces, nasturtium, endive, tarragon, celery, sorrel, mustard, cauliflower, broccoli, sprout kale, and cabbages. He especially enjoyed peas and beans, as he planted over 50 types of peas and 44 types of beans over the years.

Fig. 4-1: Monticello's Vegetable Garden (courtesy, Vivienne Kelley)

Monticello's kitchen garden and fruit trees displayed plants from various parts of the world. He grew "mammoth cucumbers" (4′ 6″ in length),[27] flowering currant and snowberry bushes from Lewis and Clark's westward

---

[26] 80 x 80 = 6400, and the square root of 6400 is roughly 113. Thomas Jefferson, *The Garden and Farm Books of Thomas Jefferson*, p. 62.
[27] TJ to Thomas Worthington, 29 Nov. 1825.

expedition, and peaches and grapes from Italy. Having exchanged plants and seeds with husbandmen and natural scientists from many parts of the world, he had very likely the most diverse garden in America in his day.

Jefferson corresponded and traded seeds and plants with farmers and some of the foremost horticulturalists of his day.[28] He stole and smuggled Piedmont rice into America by illegally filling "as much as my coat & surtout pockets would hold,"[29] thereby risking the penalty of death, and brought olive trees to America, though he was never successful in establishing the trees.[30] He scoured not only Virginia for plants rare or unknown, and also other states.[31]

A letter to Lynchburger and businessman John Hollins (19 Feb. 1809) is illustrative of the spirit behind such mutually beneficial agricultural exchanges. In it, Jefferson writes of his membership in the Agricultural Society of Paris and his subsequent capacity to trade plants and seeds with other scientific societies.

> The correspondence ... is carried on between societies instituted for the benevolent purpose of communicating to all parts of the world whatever useful is discovered in any one of them. these societies are always in peace, however their nations may be at war. like the republic of letters they form a great fraternity spreading over the whole earth, & their correspondence is never interrupted by any civilized nation.

Jefferson also had a vineyard (Figure 4-2) and cellar for the wine he made and he grew hops for his in-house ales. While in France, he writes to James Madison (28 Oct. 1785) of French statesman Guillaume-Chrétien de Lamoignon de Malsherbes, "who is making for me a collection of the vines from which the Burgundy, Champagne, Bourdeaux, Frontingnac, and other the most valuable wines of the country are made."[32] He would later tour

---

[28] E.g., TJ to John Hollins, 19 Feb. 1809; TJ to George Divers, 10 Mar. 1812; TJ to Andre Thouin, 14 Dec. 1813; TJ to Thomas Leiper, 31 May 1823; and TJ to Dr. John Emmet, 27 Apr. 1826.

[29] TJ to Edward Rutledge, 14 July 1787.

[30] He writes to Washington (1 May 1791) that he brought 40 olive trees "of the best kind" for Charleston from Marseilles along with "a box of the seed"—"the latter to raise stocks, & the former cuttings to engraft on the stocks"—and commissioned for another cargo of trees from Bordeaux. One year later, he again writes Washington (16 May 1792) that he has sent 100 more olive trees to Charleston. For Jefferson's account of the failure of the olive trees in America, see TJ to James Ronaldson, 12 Jan. 1813.

[31] TJ to Thomas Mann Randolph, Jr., 5 June 1791.

[32] *Thomas Jefferson: Writings*, ed. Merrill D. Peterson (New York: Library of America: 1984), p. 178.

Southern France and Northern Italy in while minister to France—with the object of visiting the seaports "where we have trade ... to hunt up all the inconveniencies under which it labours, in order to get them rectified"—and visit Champagne, Burgundy, Dijon, Beaujolais,[33] and Bordeaux and sample their wines, inspect their soils, study the vines and grapes, scrutinize the method of planting, and compare prices.[34] On September 3, 1814, he writes, "began to malt wheat. a bushel will make 8. or 10. gallons of strong beer such as will keep for years, taking ¾ lb of hops for every bushel of wheat."[35]

Fig. 4-2: Jefferson's Vineyard (courtesy, Vivienne Kelley)

Jefferson started his Garden Book in 1766. Jefferson, almost 23 and still at Shadwell, begins the book somewhat inconspicuously. He notes on March 30—"Purple hyacinth [Figure 4-3] begins to bloom"—and ends on May 4—"The purple flag, Dwarf flag, Violet & wild Honeysuckle still in bloom. Went journey to Maryland, Pennsylvā, New York. So observations cease." The

[33] "This is the richest country I ever beheld," said Jefferson, while traveling through Southern France, in 1787.

[34] Thomas Jefferson, "Notes of a Tour into the Southern Parts of France," in *The Papers of Thomas Jefferson, Vol. 11, 1 January–6 August 1787*, ed. Julian P. Boyd (Princeton: Princeton University Press, 1955), 415–464. See also M. Andrew Holowchak, *Thomas Jefferson in France: The Ministry of a Virginian "Looker on"* (Wilmington, DE: Vernon Press, 2022), chap. 21.

[35] Thomas Jefferson, *The Garden and Farm Books of Thomas Jefferson*, 362.

following year, he began vegetable and landscape gardens. "Feb. 20. Sowed a bed of forwardest and a bed of middling peas." The peas were up on March 9. He then planted asparagus (Mar. 15); more peas (Mar. 17); celery, lettuce, and Spanish onions (Mar. 23); carnations, Indian pink, marigold, globe amaranth, auricular, double balsam, tricolor, Dutch violet, sensitive plant, cockscomb, a quasi-Prince's feather, lathyrus, lilac, Spanish broom, umbrella, laurel, almonds, muscle plumbs, and cayenne pepper (Apr. 2). The entries—the sowing, opening, and coming to the table of fruits and vegetables, and the blooming and vanishing of flowers—continue till November 22, when he notes, "9 bundles x 130. days = 1170. for the winter."[36] Entries would continue till 1783, then resume in 1790, end in 1795, continue from 1802 to 1806 (no entry for 1805), resume in 1809 and continue till 1822.

Fig. 4-3: Purple Hyacinth (courtesy, Peter Loewer)

With the passing of years, Jefferson's Garden Book began to become more of a journal, in which he recorded his successes and failures with plants as well as miscellanea, such as observations, suggestions from neighbors, and things learned from books. I offer some illustrations, which show he had an aesthetician's approach to gardening.

On May, 20, 1767, Jefferson notes that strawberries have come to the table. Jefferson being Jefferson, he begins to arithmetize, presumably based on personal observations. "this is the first year of their bearing having been planted in the spring of 1766. and on an average, the plants bear 20. strawberries each.

[36] Thomas Jefferson, *The Garden and Farm Books of Thomas Jefferson,* 49–51.

100 fill half a pint."[37] He writes on July 27, 1769, and here he draws from one of his books: "Millar's Gard's dict. sais that 50. hills of Cucumbers will yeild 400. cucumbers a week during the time they are in season, which he sais is 5 weeks. so that 50 hills will yeild 2000, or 1. hill yeild 40. cucumbers."[38] The "Millar" to whom Jefferson refers was Philip Miller (1691–1771)—a Scotch gardener, well-known because he published *Gardener's Dictionary* in 1731. Like many other serious gardeners and husbandmen of his time, Jefferson owned the work, a 1768 edition, "succinctly" titled *The Gardeners Dictionary: Containing the Best and Newest Methods of Improving the Kitchen, Fruit, Flower Garden, and Nursery; As also for Performing the Practical Parts of Agriculture: Including the Management of Vineyards, with the Methods of Making and Preserving Wine, According to the Present Practice of the Most Skilful Vignerons in the Several Wine Countries in Europe, Together with Directions for Propagating and Improving, From Real Practice and Experience, All Sorts of Timber Trees*—and a French edition (1785). Jefferson also owned Miller's *The Gardeners Kalendar; Directing What Works Are Necessary to Be Done Every Month in the Kitchen, Fruit, and Pleasure-Gardens, and in the Conversatory: With an Account of the Particular Seasons for Propagating and Use of All Sorts of Esculent Plants and Fruits Proper for the Table, and All Sorts of Flowers, Plants and Trees, that Flower in Every Month* (1731).[39]

On May 26, 1771, Jefferson writes, "the greatest flood ever known in Virginia."[40] On September of the same year, he includes suggestions from Harrison, Willis, and Sharpe. "Cart. H. Harrison tells me it is generally allowed that 250 lb green pork makes 220. lb pickled." "Stephen Willis sais it takes 15. Bushels of lime to lay 1000. Bricks." "Old Sharpe sais a bushel of Lime-stone will weight 114 lb and if well burnt will make 2. bushels of slacked lime."[41]

On September 30, 1771, he lists "Shrubs not exceeding 10. F. in height," "Trees," "Climbing shrubby plants," "Evergreens," and Hardy perennial flowers."[42]

On July 31, 1772, he writes of certain observations concerning the efficiency of the two-wheeled barrow when compared to the one-wheeled barrow. His tendency to arithmetize his observations is once again on display. Mechanical

---

[37] Thomas Jefferson, *The Garden and Farm Books of Thomas Jefferson*, 50.
[38] Thomas Jefferson, *The Garden and Farm Books of Thomas Jefferson*, 53.
[39] Other books Jefferson owned were Dexallier d'Argentville's *The Theory and Practice of Gardening* (1728), William Chambers *Views at Kew* (1763), Joseph Heely's *Letters on the Beauties of Hagley, Envil, and the Leasowes* (1777), and B. Steeley's *Stowe: A Description* (1783). The final three betray a preoccupation with English gardens.
[40] Thomas Jefferson, *The Garden and Farm Books of Thomas Jefferson*, 54.
[41] Thomas Jefferson, *The Garden and Farm Books of Thomas Jefferson*, 55.
[42] Thomas Jefferson, *The Garden and Farm Books of Thomas Jefferson*, 55.

efficiency was for him, as it was for Stoic philosophers, was efficiency of living, which had approbation of both the moral and aesthetic senses.

> Julius Shard fills the two-wheeled barrow in 3. minutes and carries it 30. yds. in 1½ minutes more. now this is four loads of the common barrow with one wheel. so that suppose the 4. loads put in in the same time viz. 3. minutes, 4. trips will take 4 x 1½ minutes = 6′ which added to 3′ filling is = 9′ to fill and carry the same earth which was filled & carried in the two-wheeled barrow in 4½′. from a trial I made with the same two-wheeled barrow I found that a man would dig & carry to the distance of 50. yds 5. cubical yds of earth in a day of 12. hours length.[43]

On March 10, 1774, Jefferson sows "a bed of Early & a bed of Marrow-fat peas," and notes on the twenty-first that all the peas are up. He lists numerous other vegetables—he lived principally on vegetables and used meats much like garnishments[44]—and mentions for the first time his use of "numbered sticks in the beds" for distinguishing the various beds. The vegetables listed here and elsewhere are many—e.g., cabbages, peas of various sorts, parsley, beans of various sorts, carrots, onions, beets, parsnips, spinach, asparagus, and lentils—and offer a window into Jefferson's culinary tastes and his preferences for experimenting with certain vegetables—e.g., white, purple, and green broccoli.[45]

Jefferson also records extremes of temperature. In March 1790, after having returned from France, Jefferson notes, "a cold wind in this month killed all the peaches at Monticello. the other species of fruit escaped tolerably well."[46] Reference is presumably only to fruit trees. In July 1792, he writes: "Sunday. The thermometer at D^{r}. Walker's was this day at 96°, which he says is 3 higher than he ever know it since he lived at the mountains. There was no thermometer at Monticello; but I have observed when I had one here, that it was generally about 2.º below D^{r}. Walker's. & mr Maury's. so we may suppose it would have been 94.º"

Jefferson waxes systematically in 1814. He begins a table of vegetables with six columns. He lists in the first the vegetables, where they are planted in the second, when they are planted in the third, when they come to the table in the

---

[43] Thomas Jefferson, *The Garden and Farm Books of Thomas Jefferson*, 56.

[44] He writes to physician, Vine Utley (21 Mar. 1819), "*I have lived temperately, eating little animal food, and that not as an aliment, so much as a condiment for the vegetables, which constitute my principal diet.*"

[45] Thomas Jefferson, *The Garden and Farm Books of Thomas Jefferson*, 60–1.

[46] Thomas Jefferson, *The Garden and Farm Books of Thomas Jefferson*, 82.

fourth, when they are gone[47] in the fifth, and leaves a sixth column for miscellaneous comments such as: "Kalendar [following Miller]. 1814. Where. When. Come to table. Gone. Miscellaneous." For example, frame peas were planted in fields D.1 and E.1 on February 8, they came to the table on May 9, he lists nothing under "gone," and under miscellaneous he adds, "Feb. 22. up. Apr. 13. Blossom. Apr. 26. pod."[48]

Jefferson would continue to observe, measure, record, and comment in his Garden Book till 1824, with no recordings from 1796 to 1801—the years roughly of his vice-presidency. Observing, measuring, recording, and commenting—the last, a form of criticism applied to gardening—were for him reducible to a way of life.

"What a joy it was"

Jefferson's Late-in-Life Pleasure Gardens

Jefferson's aesthetic views on landscape gardening contrasted much with his aesthetic views on architecture. In architecture, Jefferson usually expressed buckram—a sort of stiff formality through strict adherence to geometric patterns and arithmetic ratios dictated by Palladian standards, derived from Vitruvian antiquity. When it came to the beauty of pleasure gardens, however, he inclined not to the strict geometric patterns that predominated in many French pleasure gardens, but to the relatively relaxed and flowing patterns of the modern English gardens, following nature, of his day. By following nature, he was guided by Thomas Whately, who said: "Architecture requires symmetry; the object of nature freedom; and the properties of the one, cannot be with justice transferred to the other."[49]

Those patterns were dictated much by philosophers William Hogarth, Edmund Burke, and Lord Kames. Burke published *A Philosophical Enquiry into the Origin of Our Ideas of the Sublime and Beautiful* (1756). He maintains that "another principal property of beautiful objects is that the line of their parts is

---

[47] Presumably, when a plant no longer offers food.

[48] Thomas Jefferson, *The Garden and Farm Books of Thomas Jefferson*, 144–45.

[49] Thomas Whately, *Observations of Modern Gardening*, 120. In a letter to François de Paule Latapie, who translated Whately's *Observations* into French. "I readily confess that I am an enemy to symmetry [in gardens] and that no one admits more sincerely the new taste that reigns in the gardens of England." Thomas Whately, "Whately's Letter," in *Observations of Modern Gardening*, p. 218.

continually varying."[50] Kames, as we note in chapter 1, published *Elements of Criticism* (1762) and argued that beauty, following nature, takes a middle, Bolingbrokean path between uniformity and variety.[51] Hogarth published *The Analysis of Beauty* in 1770 and argued that winding lines were essential for beauty. "There is scarce an Egyptian, Greek, or Roman deity, but hath a twisted serpent, twisted cornucopia, or some symbol winding in this manner to accompany it."[52] His view of the beauty of winding lines was popular in Jefferson's day and was much put to use in crafting Jefferson's garidens.

To pander to his beloved granddaughters, Jefferson in the spring of 1807, drew up 20 floral beds to bedeck Monticello. They were laid out on April 11 and by April 13, were planted with trees, shrubs, and flowers—many of which he got from Bernard McMahon, author of *The American Gardener's Calendar.* Thirteen paper mulberries, six-horse chestnuts, two tacamahac poplars, four purple beeches, two robinias, two chokecherries, three mountain ashes, two zanthoxylums, one redbud, one fraxinella, and two guelder roses were planted in the circular beds at the corners of the residence. The oval beds were festooned with numerous types of flowers from China pink, yellow-horned poppies, and dianthuses to single carnations, yellow lillies, and Jeffersonia diphylla.[53]

The last, commonly called Twinleaf, was named after Jefferson on account of horticulturalist Benjamin Smith Barton. In a paper to the American Philosophical Society (18 May 1792), Barton said: "In imposing upon this genus the name of Mr. Jefferson, I have had no reference to his political character, or to his repuation for general science and for literature. My business was with his knowledge of natural history. In the various departments of this science, but especially in botany and zoology, the information of this gentleman is equalled by that of few persons in the Unites States."[54]

---

50 Edmund Burke, *A Philosophical Enquiry into the Origin of Our Ideas of the Sublime and Beautiful* (London: R. and J. Dodsley, 1757), 158.

51 Henry Home, *Elements of Criticism* (New York: A.S. Barnes & Burr, 1865), 178.

52 William Hogarth, *The Analysis of Beauty: Written with a View of Fixing the Fluctuating Ideas of Taste* (London: J. Reeves, 1753), xviii.

53 Edwin M. Betts and Hazlehurst Bolton Perkins, *Thomas Jefferson's Flower Garden at Monticello* (Charlottesville: University of Virginia Press, [1971] 1986), 26–27. For an account of the flowers, shrubs, trees, and vines that Jefferson planted at Monticello, see Peter Loewer, *Jefferson's Garden.*

54 Edwin M. Betts and Hazlehurst Bolton Perkins, *Thomas Jefferson's Flower Garden at Monticello,* 145–47.

Fig. 4-4: Jeffersonia diphylla (courtesy, Peter Loewer)

To accent the oval beds, he put in a winding walkway (Figure 4-5)—following Hogarth's "serpentinism" and the current English vogue, he preferred ambages to straight walkways—on the West Lawn of Monticello. To granddaughter Anne Cary Randolph (7 June 1807), Jefferson writes: "I find that the limited number of our flower beds will too much restrain the variety of flowers in which we might wish to indulge, & therefore I have resumed an idea, which I had formerly entertained, but had laid by, of a winding walk surrounding the lawn before the house, with a narrow border of flowers on each side. this would give us abundant room for a great variety." The walkway was implemented in spring 1808.

Jefferson's daughter and granddaughters, often under the direction of slave Wormly Hughes, or Jefferson, would upkeep the flower gardens, each 10-foot bed featuring a different flower.

Jefferson was decidedly a great lover of flowers—an anthophile. "Of flowers … he was very fond," writes granddaughter Ellen Randolph Coolidge. She continues: "I remember the planting of the first hyacinths and tulips, and their subsequent growth. The roots arrived, labelled each one with a fancy name. There was Marcus Aurelius, and the King of the Gold Mine, the Roman Empress, and the Queen of the Amazons, Psyche, God of Love." She and her sisters then waited for spring. "What joy it was for one of us to discover the tender green breaking through the mould, and run to grandpapa to announce, that we really believed Marcus Aurelius was coming up, or the

Queen of the Amazons was above ground!"[55] The letter, characteristic of many other writings on Jefferson by his grandchildren, betrays profundity of love by them for him. Jefferson make anthophilism fun.

Fig. 4-5: Monticello's Winding Walkway (courtesy, Vivienne Kelley)

"Shade is our Elysium"

Monticello as a Pleasure Garden

Husbandry, *pace* Kames, was generally not considered to be a fine art, because husbandry did not aim at beauty, but yield. Nonetheless, the gentleman farmer could aim for beauty as well as yield and also could make his entire estate—its buildings, fields, woods, rivers, hills, valleys, and even its laborers considered as an efficient (or inefficient) system on the estate[56]—to be a garden. Hence, there is justification for insistence on including husbandry as a species of gardening, since for an estate to be beautiful, there must be some beauty in all its parts, farmed fields included, and beauty in the whole, as measured by its uniformity proportioned to its variety. As Philip Southcote, designer of an estate at Woburn in Surrey, England, said, "Why may

---

[55] Henry Stephens Randall, *The Life of Thomas Jefferson*, Vol. 3 (Philadelphia: J.B. Lippincott & Co., 1871), 346–47.

[56] Consider his thoughts above on preferability of the two-wheeled barrow to the one-wheeled barrow.

not a whole estate be thrown into a kind of Garden? If the natural Embroidery of the meadows were [*sic*] Additions of Art, and the several rows of Hedges set off by Trees and flowers, a man might make a pretty landskip of his own Possessions."[57] Jefferson, who visited Woburn while touring the gardens of England with Adams, wrote coolly of its gardens: "Four people to the farm, four to the pleasure garden, four to the kitchen garden. All are intermixed, the pleasure garden being merely a highly-ornamented walk through and round the divisions of the highly ornamented garden."[58]

Fig. 4-6: Landscape at Monticello (courtesy, Vivienne Kelley)

Jefferson grappled with beautification of his lands at Monticello (Figure 4-6). As early as 1771, he wrote up a plan in his Account Book for elaborates on an account for the site of "a burying place" for "an unfrequented vale in the park" where there are "antient and venerable oaks."[59] Under the rubric, "The Ground in General" for his Stockton Estate, he jots down: "Thin the trees. Cut out stumps and undergrowth. Remove old trees and other rubbish except

---

[57] William Howard Adams, *The Eye of Thomas Jefferson* (Washington, D.C.: National Gallery of Art, 1976), 322. Cf. Blair, who writes, "Why may not a whole estate be thrown into a kind of garden by frequent plantations, that may turn as much to the profit as the pleasure of the owner?" Hugh Blair, *Lectures on Rhetoric and Belle Lettres*, 248

[58] Thomas Jefferson, "A Tour of Some of the Gardens of England," in *Thomas Jefferson: Writings*, ed. Merrill D. Peterson (New York: Library of America, 1984), 624.

[59] Thomas Jefferson, *Thomas Jefferson's Garden Book*, ed. Edwin Morris Betts (Philadelphia: American Philosophical Society, 1944), 25.

where they may look well. Cover the whole with grass. Intersperse Jessamine, honeysuckle, sweetbrier, and even hardy flowers which may not require attention. Keep it in deer, rabbits, peacocks, guinea poultry, pigeons, &c." He also includes some ideas about beautifying the spring at the north end of the park and opening the land to the west and bedecking it with shrubs, trees, climbing plants, evergreens, and perennial flowers.[60] A certain Isaac Weld, Jr., who visited Monticello 25 years later—in May 1796—says, "The mountain whereon the house stands is thickly wooded on one side, and walks are carried round it, with different degrees of obliquity, running into each other."[61]

While president, Jefferson, having seen the English pleasure gardens during his stint in France, gave thought to beautify the entire landscape at Monticello. There is "a rich profusion" of prospect wherever one looks. "Mountains distant & near, smooth & shaggy, single & in ridges, a little river hiding itself among the hills so as to shew in lagoons only, cultivated grounds under the eye and two small villages." The principal difficulty, Jefferson notes, is satiety. "It may be successively offered, & in different portions through vistas, or which will be better, between thickets so disposed as to serve as vistas, with the advantage of shifting the scene as you advance on your way."[62]

His sketches show that Jefferson aimed at the sort of admixture of beauty and functionality at Monticello—to make the whole estate a garden—by creation of walkways, "roundabouts," around his farmed lots and by addition of a number of ornamental gardens around the roundabouts—thereby making a garden of his estate. There were four roundabouts. In his Garden Book (23 Oct. 1778), Jefferson says that the roundabout from Monticello's door to "the stone flood mark of 1778 by the river" is 1.5124 miles, "from the head of the Canal along my private road into public road by Shadwell thence down public road to where the mill road will come in" is 1.0426 miles, and "from the head of the Canal down the same to walnut where mill house will stand thence down the mill road along the riverside to Chapel branch thence up Chapel branch as the mill road is to be into the public road" is 1.5113 miles.[63] His measurements came from a survey "with a chain very exact," and we note his insistence on carrying out the measurement to the ten-thousandth degree. Decades later (1808), he writes in a note to overseer Francis Bacon, "In the open grounds on both the 3d. and 4th Roundabouts lay off lots for the minor articles of husbandry for experimental

---

60 Fiske Kimball, "The Beginnings of Landscape Gardening in America," *Landscape Architecture Magazine*, Vol. 7, No. 4: 182.

61 Merrill D. Peterson, ed., *Visitors to Monticello* (Charlottesville: University of Virginia Press, 1989), 19.

62 Thomas Jefferson, *The Garden and Farm Books of Thomas Jefferson*, 75.

63 Thomas Jefferson, *The Garden and Farm Books of Thomas Jefferson*, 75.

culture, disposing them into a ferme ornée [ornamental farm] and by interspersing occasionally the attributes of a garden."[64]

In a letter to William Hamilton[65] (31 July 1806), Jefferson writes of improving certain native-woods grounds, some 300 acres, "which are in a form very difficult to manage," to be done "in the style of the English gardens." These acres are "washed at the foot, for about a mile, by a river of the size of the Schuylkill [and] the hill is generally too steep for direct ascent, but we make level walks successively along on it's side, which in it's upper part encircle the hill, & we intersect these again by others of easy ascent in various parts."

Those lands, "chiefly still in their native woods," are majestic. There is too, "very generally, a close undergrowth, which I have not suffered to be touched, knowing how much easier it is to cut away, than to fill up." The upper third of the estate is mostly open, but there is, to the south, a dense thicket of Scotch broom that will make for "winter enjoyment" on sunny days. "you are sensible that this disposition of ground takes from me the first beauty in gardening," says Jefferson, "the variety of hill & dale, & leaves me as an awkward substitute a few hanging hollows & ridges. this subject is so original unique & at the same time refractory that to make a disposn analogous to it's character, would require much more of the genius of the landscape painter & gardener than I pretend to." The idea was to create a sort of ornamental forest, a grove, on the northern side of the monticule by cutting away, not filling up. Instead of clearing and grubbing a spot of land and then creating a garden through planting vegetation according to discretion, one begins with a densely wooded area and then removes, thins, trims, and prunes to create a wooded garden, pursuant to aesthetic taste, from what is already there. And so, Jefferson would remove understory, trim trees, and eliminate unsightly copse and do so "in the style of the English gardens."

We recall that during his stint as minister plenipotentiary from 1784 to 1789 in France, Jefferson thrice traveled to England. On one trip, as I note in chapter 1, he and John Adams toured the pleasure gardens of England and Jefferson recorded his impressions of gardens at Chiswick, Hampton Court, Twickenham Esher Place, Claremont, Paynshill, Woburn, Caversham, Wottom, Stowe, Leasowes, Hagley, Blenheim, Enfield Chase, Moor Park, and Kew. He took with him Thomas Whately's *Observations on Modern Gardening*[66]—an immensely popular book in Jefferson's day—because Whately had much to say about some of the gardens that Jefferson and Adams would see. Whately

---

[64] William Howard Adams, *The Eye of Thomas Jefferson*, 322.
[65] A disciple of landscape architect George Parkyns, who published *Six Designs for Improving and Embellishing Grounds. With sections and explanations*, in 1793.
[66] Jefferson owned the second (1770) edition.

begins his book with this prolix passage—prolixity was typical of the time—that aims to situate gardening among the fine arts. So much has gardening been brought to perfection in England that it is entitled for inclusion, and in no mean place, among the fine arts.

> It is as superior to landskip painting, as a reality to a representation: it is an exertion of fancy; a subject for taste; and being released now from the restraints of regularity, and enlarged beyond the purposes of domestic convenience, the most beautiful, the most simple, the most noble scenes of nature are all within its province: for it is no longer confined to the spots from which it borrows its name, but regulates also the disposition and embellishments of a park, a farm, or a riding; and the business of a gardener is to select and to apply whatever is great, elegant, or characteristic in any of them; to discover and to shew all the advantages of the place upon which he is employed; to supply its defects, to correct its faults, and to improve its beauties.[67]

Jefferson's tour of the gardens, as was the case with his study of buildings he saw in France and England, was for the sake of transporting what was useful and beautiful back to America, chiefly to his plantation at Monticello.

Yet English models, Jefferson continues to Hamilton, are problematic, because the climate is much different. "their sun-less climate has permitted them to adopt what is certainly a beauty of the very first order in landscape. their canvas is of open ground, variegated with clumps of trees distributed with taste. they need no more of wood than will serve to embrace a lawn or a glade." Virginia is dissimilar. "under the beaming, constant & almost vertical sun of Virga, shade is our Elysium. in the absence of this no beauty of the eye can be enjoyed. this organ then must yield it's gratificn to that of the other senses, without the hope of any equivalent to the beauty relinquished."

Jefferson, however, is undaunted by the enormousness of the task. Because of the heat of the unrelenting sun, most trees must remain, yet they can be trimmed "as high as the constitution & form of the tree will bear, but so as that their tops shall still unite and yield a dense shade." He adds that woods, opened from below, will appear to be an open ground. In that open area, there can be planted a clump of trees, a thicket of shrubs in the form of a hemisphere, "the crown of which shall distinctly show itself under the branches of the trees." Jefferson continues: "this may be effected by a due selection & arrangement of the shrubs, and will I think offer a groupe not much inferior to that of trees. the

---

[67] Thomas Whately, *Observations of Modern Gardening*, ed. Michael Symes (Woodbridge, UK: Boydell Press, 2016), 31.

thickets may be varied too by making some of them of evergreens, altogether. our red cedar made to grow in a bush, ever green Privet, Hyacanthus, Kalmia, Scotch broom." He has in mind, of course, Hutcheson's formula, "Uniformity amidst Variety."

The view, Jefferson imagines, will be spectacularly panoramic—a happy admixture of sublimity and beauty. A silver-tongued Jefferson writes:

> of prospect I have a rich profusion and offering itself at every point of the compass, mountains distant & near, smooth & shaggy, single & in ridges, a little river hiding itself among the hills so as to shew in lagoons only, cultivated grounds, under the eye and two small villages. to prevent a satiety of this is the principal difficulty. it may be successively offered, & in separate different portions through vistas, or which will be better, between thickets so disposed as to serve for vistas, with the advantage of shifting the scenes as you advance on your way.

I close this chapter with some thoughts on Jefferson's especial love of trees. As I note earlier in this section, Jefferson planted and groomed Monticello's trees to define its landscape. In 1769, he created the first orchard—comprising pomegranate, apple, nectarines cherry, pear, peach, apricot, almond and fig trees—on the southeast slope of the monticule.[68] He had some 160 types of tree, some native and some foreign, which he often aimed to put to both practical (food or shade) and ornamental use. Trees were native and exotic: e.g., ornamental trees were near the mansion and peach-tree fences bordered his fields. Margaret Bayard Smith recalls a sentiment of Jefferson in a dinner engagement with him in Washington, D. C., that betrays Jefferson large love of trees. "I wish I was a despot that I might save the noble, beautiful trees that are daily falling sacrifice to the cupidity of their owners, or the necessity of the poor. ... The unnecessary felling of a tree, perhaps the growth of centuries, seems to me a crime little short of murder."[69]

Upshot

"The greatest service which can be rendered any country is, to add an useful plant to its culture, a bread grain; next in value to bread is oil," says Jefferson in a memorandum around 1800.[70] It is clear that gardening, husbandry along

---

[68] Frederick Doveton Nichols and Ralph E. Griswold, *Thomas Jefferson, Landscape Architect* (Charlottesville: University of Virginia Press, 1978), 100.
[69] "Trees at Monticello," Thomas Jefferson Foundation. https://www.monticello.org/house-gardens/farms-gardens/landscape-features/trees-at-monticello/, accessed 9 June 2020.
[70] Thomas Jefferson, "Services to My Country," in *Thomas Jefferson: Writings*, ed. Merrill D. Peterson (New York: Library of America: 1984), 702–4.

with it, is a science of utmost utility, of significance perhaps even greater than architecture. Both allowed Jefferson to use his creativity and mathematical acumen. While stateliness and adherence to Classical standards predominate in architecture, the fine art of gardening allows for a more Protean, perhaps Hogarthian, expression of one's faculties. The two are complementary arts and should not be seen as expressions of different fine arts. The estates that he designed—and he designed or contributed to the designs of many residences other than his own—needed to be accompanied by gardens to give them aesthetic balance. Moreover, no estate could be discretionarily fitted into just any landscape.

The architectural landscaping around Monticello was never fully actuated, and we do not know how much effort Jefferson put into the project. After 1812, Jefferson's focus in his Garden Book is on vegetables, not ornament. Debt was likely the major reason, though physical infirmity was also certainly a factor.

Yet just prior to his death, Jefferson did propose to Dr. John Patten Emmet (27 Apr. 1826) of the University of Virginia for there to be established a botanical garden of roughly six acres, where Cabell Hall today sits. It was to be enclosed by a serpentine wall, leveled into terraces, and plants and trees from everywhere would be introduced over time. The aim was to teach students, hands-on, about native Virginian flora as well as about exotic plants and trees "as would suit our climate." Theirs was to be a lesson on ornament as well as on utility, medicine, and esculence.

In this chapter, we have seen that it would be forced to make a distinction for Jefferson between farming and gardening. Qua farmer, utility (yield) was always foremost, but beauty for Jefferson—and he saw beauty both in the ornament of his fields and in the efficiency of his workforce—was never neglected. Moreover, following Southcote, Jefferson certainly thought of his entire state, farmed fields included, as a sort of pleasure garden. Qua gardener, he followed the pattern of English pleasure gardens, and eschewing the bold geometry of most French gardens, he worked with nature to beautify his estate. Even here, beauty was partnered with utility. For instance, trees were planted for shade in the hot Virginian summers. They were also planted for fruits. In both farming and gardening, Jefferson sought to improve his estate, his state, and even his country by importing various sorts of plants or seeds to complement native Virginian plants. In beautifying Monticello, Jefferson was ever cautious to balance uniformity and diversity and ever chary of there not being too much art.

Chapter V

The Art of Architecture

"Here I am, Madame, gazing whole hours at the Maison quarrée [*sic*], like a lover at his mistress.." ~TJ to madame de Tessé, 20 Mar. 1787

Thomas Jefferson is reputed to have said, "Architecture is my delight, and putting up and pulling down, one of my favorite amusements."[1] If the wording here is true to his real utterance—that putting up comes before pulling down—it is indicative that Jefferson had an orientation that focused more on process than on outcome. Yet a process-orientation was not a matter of killing time, but of perfecting, that is, conviction to the notion that things, even the character of a person, could ever be perfected. Jefferson was always in the process of perfecting. As illustrations, not only was Monticello constantly being reconstructed and renovated during his life, but also were all other living spaces he occupied while in New York, Philadelphia, Paris, and Washington.

Thomas Jefferson's place as one of the leading American architects, perhaps the pioneer of American architecture, is firmly fixed. Architectural historian Fiske Kimball dubs him the "father of our national architecture,"[2] as Jefferson introduced Classicism into the American architectural landscape. In doing so, he focused on minutiae requiring mathematical exactness that would escape the attention of others. "Jefferson strove for correctness even in the shape of guttae, [and] his ideals were at once monumental and academic."[3] Jefferson left behind over 800 architectural drawings. Says architectural historian Frederick Nichols, "Jefferson learned to recognize and appreciate the beauty in architecture that derived from simplicity, regularity and proportion rather than from arbitrarily applied ornament, and he sought to instill this taste in his fellow citizens by providing architectural models."[4] As we shall see, he did that with astonishing success. His models set a standard for public and academic buildings that continues today and shows no signs of discontinuance.

---

[1] Margaret Bayard Smith, *A Winter in Washington*, Vol. 2 (New York: 1824), 261.

[2] Fiske Kimball, "Thomas Jefferson and the First Monument in the Classical Revival of America," *Journal of the American Institute of Architects*, Vol. II, No. 9 (1915): 371–81.

[3] Fiske Kimball, *Thomas Jefferson, Architect*, 35.

[4] Frederick Nichols, "Architecture," in *Thomas Jefferson: A Reference Biography*, ed. Merrill D. Peterson (New York: Charles Scribner's Sons, 1986), 215–32.

In this chapter, I aim to introduce readers to what was, to Jefferson personally, the most delightful of the fine arts: Architecture. I begin with a look at his education in Architecture, turn to his three most significant architectural projects—Monticello, the State Capitol of Virginia, and the University of Virginia—and end with a section on what I consider to be Jefferson's architectural oddment: his retreat at Poplar Forest.

"There never was a Palladio here ... till I brought one"

Jefferson's Architectural Education

It is strange that a man could live atop a monticule in what amounted to the middle of nowhere and still be one of the most enlightened men of his time and perhaps the country's foremost early architect. Yet Jefferson, qua "solitudinarian," accomplished prodigiously because he was an insatiable reader and a lifelong learner. He was a permanent student of agriculture, natural science, law, political science, morality, and the fine arts, especially architecture. He would collect throughout his life a large number of books on architecture and leave behind hundreds of architectural drawings from his hand.

If one is to write of Jefferson qua architect, one has to grasp what it meant to be an architect in Jefferson's day—especially in early America. First, it meant to be self-educated. There were no architectural schools in America at the time—MIT was established in 1865—so one had to learn on one's own and that usually was a matter of apprenticeship from the rank of builders. Second, given that most architects came from the rank of builders, it meant to be a builder. Jefferson knew well the ins and outs of building. Last, it meant not just to be a designer of buildings, but also to be an overseer of construction, though Jefferson's political duties often kept him from the latter. And so, Jefferson learned architecture from books, from observing construction and some degree of participation in it, from architectural friends like Benjamin Latrobe,[5] Dr. William Thornton, and Charles-Louis Clérisseau, from study of extant buildings in America and in Europe; and from overseeing construction, Monticello especially.

---

[5] His relationship with Latrobe was at times strained, especially from Latrobe's perspective. He dismissively called Jefferson "an excellent architect out of books" (Latrobe to Lenthall, May 3–4, 1805), which suggests a theoretical orientation that lacked the plasticity that praxis dictated. Benjamin Latrobe, *The Papers of Benjamin Henry Latrobe*, ed. T.E. Jeffrey (Clifton, NJ: Maryland Historical Society, 1976).

Those things noted, Jefferson would have had to know the raw materials of construction and the availability of certain materials for a particular project at a particular location, otherwise, his plans for construction would be cloud-built, not ground-built. For instance, Jefferson's frequent use of bricks for architectural projects was not necessarily a preference for bricks over stones, but based on the availability of bricks in Virginia due to the rich red clay in its soil and the relative scarcity of Virginian stone, like marble.

As the lion's share of his architectural education—and this comes as little surprise given his bibliomania—came from books, Jefferson had some 40 architectural volumes in his library. William Howard Adams states that his first books on architecture were likely James Gibbs' *Rules for Drawing the Several Parts in Architecture* and Giacomo Leoni's four-book compilation titled *The Architecture of A. Palladio.*

It is commonly known that the largest architectural influence was Andreas Palladio (1508–1580)—an Italian architect who followed Marcus Vitruvius Pollio's work *De architectura* and built in the Roman manner. As Palladio was heavily indebted to Vitruvius—"since I always held the opinion that the ancient Romans, as in many other things," says Palladio in the first sentence of his book, "had also greatly surpassed all those who came after them in building well, I elected as my master and guide Vitruvius"[6]—I have something first to say concerning the latter, whose influence on modern architecture, especially through Palladio, cannot be underestimated.

Vitruvius (c. 75–c. 15 B.C.) was a Roman architect of some note in his day, and has become an enormous architectural figure due to the discovery of his 10-book manuscript in the fifteenth century, *De architectura*—the only major architectural treatise from antiquity that has survived—and its subsequent influence.

Vitruvius begins Book I:

> Architecture is a science arising out of many other sciences, and adorned with much and varied learning; by the help of which a judgment is formed of those works which are the result of other arts. Practice and theory are its parents. Practice is the frequent and continued contemplation of the mode of executing any given work, or of the mere operation of the hands, for the conversion of the material in the best and readiest way. Theory is the result of that reasoning

---

[6] Andrea Palladio, *The Four Books on Architecture,* trans. Robert Tavernor and Richard Schofield (Cambridge, MS: MIT Press, 1997), 5.

> which demonstrates and explains the material wrought has been so converted as to answer the end proposed.[7]

A capable architect is both practitioner and theoretician. A practitioner without theory errs in being unable to explain the forms he gives to a work—*viz.*, he lacks knowledge. A theoretician without practice errs in taking epiphenomenon as phenomenon—*viz.*, he lacks experience with matter. And so, the right sort of architect, experienced in practice and knowing theory, considers both "the intention, and the matter used to express that intention." In grafting formal understanding with material experience, adds Vitruvius, a true architect must know writing, drafting, geometry, optics, arithmetic, history, natural philosophy, morality, music, law, medicine, and astronomy.[8] This is a theme that recurs in discussion of any of the fine arts in Jefferson's day. The best practitioners are the best because they are in effect polymathic.

Vitruvius asserts that public buildings—those for the sake of defense, religion, and safety—must be durable, functional, and pulchritudinous. Durability is secured through a strong foundation and proper selection of materials, and that takes Vitruvius to consideration of Greek *stoicheia* (elements): earth, water, air, and fire. Functionality happens when structure meets intended needs. Pulchritude is a matter of all the parts being duly proportions to each other, which results in a beautiful, unified appearance.[9] Much of Vitruvius' discussion is Aristotelian. The influences of Aristotle's epistemology, hylomorphism (matter/form dualism), and causation are clear.

In Book III, Chapter 1, of *De architectura*, Vitruvius describes what is now commonly called Vitruvian Man: "The design of Temples depends on symmetry, the rules of which Architects should be most careful to observe. Symmetry is dependent on proportion, which the Greeks call *analogia*. Proportion is due adjustment of the size of the different parts to each other and to the whole." It is with temples as it is with the human body. For instance, from the chin of the face to the top of the crown of the head is one-eighth of the height of the body, taken as a whole. From the upper part of the breast to the crown of the head is one-quarter of the whole body. the length of a foot is one-sixth of the whole body; the forearm, one-fourth; the breast's width; one-fourth. "The navel is naturally placed in the center of the human body, and, if in a man lying with his face upward, and his hands and feet extended, from his navel as the center, a

---

[7] Vitruvius, *The Architecture of Marcus Vitruvius Pollio: In Ten Books*, trans. Joseph Gwilt (London: Lockwood & Co., 1874), 3.

[8] Vitruvius, *The Architecture of Marcus Vitruvius Pollio*, 3.

[9] Vitruvius, *The Architecture of Marcus Vitruvius Pollio*, 13–16.

circle be described, it will touch his fingers and toes."[10] Vitruvius sums, "It is worthy of remark, that the measures necessarily used in all building and other works, are derived from the members of the human body, as the digit, the plan, the foot, the cubit, and that these form a perfect number, called by the Greek[s] *teleios* [perfect or complete]," and that number is 10.[11]

When published after its discovery, *De architectura* had a profound influence on the great Italians of that century: da Vinci, Alberti, and Michelangelo. Palladio in the sixteen century would bring to life Vitruvian architectural insights—Palladio was a compiler and not an original thinker—in his *Four Books on Architecture.*

So taken was he by Palladio's *Four Books* that Jefferson owned five distinct editions of Palladio's book. "It was a creative alliance of profound consequences," says William Howard Adams. "Through Palladio's plates, which conveyed architecture of timeless proportion and mathematical harmony, Jefferson envisioned a style and form based on antiquity but with a purity which left behind history's corrupting influences of rotten governments, benighted rulers and unenlightened institutions."[12] His favorite edition was Giacomo Leoni's *The Architecture of A. Palladio in Four Books,* which reworked Palladio's material in places and contained Leoni's own drawings.[13]

The Palladian architectural revolution in America was principally due to Jefferson. To James Oldham (24 Dec. 1804), who asked Jefferson for an edition of Palladio, Jefferson writes, "There never was a Palladio here even in private hands till I brought one." One of the significant lessons Palladio taught Jefferson when it came to residences was that a house must be "appropriate to the status of the person who will have to live in it." Significant men, especially public officials, should have houses with loggias and spacious, ornate halls so that someone waiting for the master of the house can pass pleasantly his time. That takes us to the entrance of Monticello. Another was the Virtruvian notion that the parts must "correspond to the whole and to each other."[14]

---

[10] Vitruvius, *The Architecture of Marcus Vitruvius Pollio,* 63–64.

[11] Vitruvius, *The Architecture of Marcus Vitruvius Pollio,* 64.

[12] William Howard Adams, *The Eye of Thomas Jefferson* (Washington, D.C.: National Gallery of Art, 1976), xxxv.

[13] Richard Guy Wilson, "Jefferson and England," in *Thomas Jefferson, Architect: Palladian models, democratic principles, and the conflict of ideals,* ed. Lloyd DeWitt and Corey Piper, (Norfolk: Chrysler Museum of Art, 2019), 44.

[14] Andrea Palladio, *The Four Books on Architecture,* Book II, chap. 1. There was a stiff bookishness to Jefferson's instructions to builders, says Carl Lounsbury. For instance, "He insisted on calling moldings by their classical rather than workbench names and specified the proportionate height of a surbase calculated precisely to the third decimal point."

Nonetheless, we must be cautious not to see Jefferson as a "passive user of Palladio's books," as "his employment of Palladio's schemes and details was a creative endeavor, involving comparison, choice, combination, and transformation. ... Palladio might have been his architectural bible, but the ultimate arbiter of truth and utility was Jefferson himself."[15] One such instance of deviation from the master was rejection of Palladian multifunctional rooms. Residents of mansions in Jefferson's day wanted rooms to fit specific needs—a dining room, a parlor, a library, a study, a dressing room, and so on—and that meant that residences needed to be large.[16] Jefferson followed that lead. Another instance of deviation was in employment of octagonal rooms and canted bays, and there Jefferson followed architect Robert Morris (1701–1754). The aim was to offer a larger view of the landscape and bring more light into the building.[17]

A second large influence on Jefferson's architectural thinking, especially as it relates to the construction of the University of Virginia, was Roland Fréart Chambray (1606–1676). Chambray published a complete translation of Palladio's *Four Books* (1650) as well as *Paraillèle de l'architecture antique avec la modern* (1650).

Chambray's *Paraillèle de l'architecture* was composed in the manner of Plutarch's *Parallel Lives,* as it compared 10 ancient writers with 10 modern writers on the use of Classical orders. Chambray argued contentiously for the superiority of the ancient writers. He maintained that the Classical Greek orders—Doric, Ionic, and Corinthian—were "perfect" and superior to the Roman orders—the Tuscan and the Composite.

In a letter to Nicolas Gouin Dufief (23 Mar. 1802), Jefferson requests a list of books from France. He says that he has Chambray's *Paraillèle de l'architecture* but adds that there has been promised a fifth volume "containing les elemens d'Architecture, painture & sculpture, and a 6th. under the title of le Manual des artistes." Jefferson requests "the whole work compleat."

Such bookish pedantry must have exasperated builders, used to "traditional," not arcane, terms. Carl Lounsbury, "Thomas Jefferson's Architectural Legacy," *Journal of Thomas Jefferson's Life and Times,* Vol. 1, Ed. 2, ed. M. Andrew Holowchak, Charlottesville: Thomas Jefferson Heritage Society, 2017: p. 28

[15] Howard Burns, "Thomas Jefferson, The Making of an Architect," in *Thomas Jefferson, Architect: Palladian models, democratic principles, and the conflict of ideals,* ed. Lloyd DeWitt and Corey Piper, (Norfolk: Chrysler Museum of Art, 2019), p. 12.

[16] It is not unlike some of today's fitness equipment, which is constructed to be multi-functional, though in being designed thus, a piece does poorly each thing of the several things it is supposed to do.

[17] Howard Burns, "Thomas Jefferson, The Making of an Architect," 21–22.

There are many other architects and builders who certainly influenced Jefferson on architecture, but space is prohibitive. It is enough to note that Jefferson chiefly looked to the past for architectural inspiration—to models of chasteness which passed the Vitruvian tests of durability, functionality, and pulchritude.

That noted, "there is a 'Jefferson look' or 'style,'" says Richard Guy Wilson, "which might be characterized as red brick, white trim, classical details, and frequently a full temple-fronted portico of large columns." Moreover, Wilson adds, there is also a Jeffersonian *modus operandi,* which includes agenda, precedent, training, vernacular, and site or landscape. Agenda includes the use of permanent materials such as brick or stone. Precedent involves the use of time-tested models such as the Maison Carrée and the Pantheon. Training for Jefferson involves apprenticeship or book training, and both include knowledge of constructive practices, as architects of the day oversaw construction. Vernacular involves the preservation of a Virginian flavor in seeking to find international styles. Use of brick is a fine illustration, as Virginians at the time lacked the technical skills to work with stone. Site involves working with a particular landscape.[18] Nothing of what Wilson says argues for the genius of architectural innovation. As was the case with everything he wrote, Jefferson was more of a compiler than an innovator, though as a compiler, he was ingenious and always added his touch.

To Wilson's expiscation of the Jeffersonian look, I add the mathematics in the minutiae of that look. Proportionality and rhythm follow from his love of mathematics and music. On the back of sheets with many of his architectural drawings, there are the calculations that Jefferson employed in drafting them.

There is no better illustration of the Jeffersonian look than in a passage from *Notes on Virginia,* in which Jefferson exemplifies that look by describing what good architecture is not. There is nothing, it seems, that is laudable in the buildings of Virginia—"the genius of architecture seems to have shed its maledictions over this land [Virginia]"—and so he begins with what is salvageable. His focus is Williamsburg. "The only public buildings worthy of mention are the Capitol, the Palace, the College, and the Hospital for Lunatics, all of them in Williamsburg, heretofore the seat of our government."[19]

Lukewarm praise quickly sours. All lack chasteness.

---

[18] Richard Guy Wilson, "Thomas Jefferson and the Creation of the American Architectural Image," in *The Cambridge Companion to Thomas Jefferson,* ed. Frank Shuffelton (Cambridge: Cambridge University Press, 2009), 115.

[19] Thomas Jefferson, *Notes on the State of Virginia,* ed. William Peden (Chapel Hill: University of North Carolina Press, 1954), 152.

The Capitol, he says, "is a light and airy structure, with a portico in front of two orders, the lower of which, being Doric, is tolerably just in its proportions and ornaments, save only that the intercolonnations are too large." The upper order, being Ionic, is "much too small for that on which it is mounted, its ornaments not proper to the order, nor proportioned within themselves." Its crowning pediment, however, is "too high for its span." Its dazzling defects notwithstanding, it is "the most pleasing piece of architecture we have."[20]

Next, there is the Palace, which is outwardly unassuming, though "is spacious and commodious within, is prettily situated, and with the grounds annexed to it, is capable of being made an elegant seat."[21]

Finally, "the College and Hospital are rude, misshapen piles, which, but that they have roofs, would be taken for brick-kilns."[22]

Besides those buildings, the public buildings and churches of Virginia—"no attempts are made at elegance"—are unassuming, ordinary. Yet even if there were a yen for elegance, it could not be actuated, since "a workman could scarcely be found here capable of drawing an order."[23]

Moreover, there is an "unhappy prejudice," says Jefferson, in favor of building with wood, because "houses of brick or stone are [deemed] less wholesome than those of wood." That prejudice has formed from the presence of dew on walls of stone or brick on rainy days.[24]

Jefferson explains, and it is worth following his explanation, if only to show his need to understand all things. Noting that dew forms on humid days without rain, on partitions as well as exterior walls, on pavements of brick or stone, and that the amount of dew is in proportion to the thickness of the walls, Jefferson goes on to give the correct explanation of the formation of dew. When cold water is poured into a pitcher of stone or glass, dew immediately forms on the outside of the pitcher. The same does not happen with a pitcher of wood. The immediacy of dew on the outside of a pitcher of stone or glass cannot be due to the exudation of water through the stone or glass. The water has formed from the circumambient air, "as the humid particles of vapour passing from the boiler of an alembic through its refrigerant, are precipitated from the air, in which they were suspended, on the internal surface of the refrigerant." Brick and stone, sufficiently cold, act as refrigerants; wood, insufficiently cold, cannot. The unwelcome dew, he

---

[20] Thomas Jefferson, *Notes on Virginia*, 152–53.
[21] Thomas Jefferson, *Notes on Virginia*, 152–53.
[22] Thomas Jefferson, *Notes on Virginia*, 153.
[23] Thomas Jefferson, *Notes on Virginia*, 153.
[24] Thomas Jefferson, *Notes on Virginia*, 153.

continues, can be eliminated easily by a small fire in the room in which it has formed.[25]

There is another "unhappy prejudice": the presumed cheapness of building with wood. Yet buildings of wood are often very expensive—many of the wooden buildings are festooned with "barbarous ornaments"—and they lack "symmetry and taste." Building with brick or stone "would not increase their cost," but "would only change the arrangement of the materials, the form and combination of the members." Furthermore, wood is not durable. And so, such wooden buildings are sometimes costlier than they would have been, if they were made at first of brick or stone.

The problems, then, are due to ignorance, which can be eradicated over time with schooling, and Jefferson has in mind a professorship of architecture at an institution of higher education, and a number of models of chasteness to stimulate notions of sturdiness and classical beauty. He writes: "Architecture being one of the fine arts, and as such within the department of a professor of the college, according to the new arrangement, perhaps a spark may fall on some young subjects of natural taste, kindle up their genius, and produce a reformation in this elegant and useful art."[26]

Jefferson appeals to European architecture for an illustration of the benefits of building with brick and stone. Europeans are at least as healthy as are Virginians, and they are warmer in the winter and cooler in the summer. In short, brick and stone are "cheaper in their first construction, where lime is convenient, and infinitely more durable." As the durability of wood is about 50 years, it follows that "every half century then our country becomes a tabula rasa, whereon we have to set out anew, as in the first moment of seating it."[27]

Jefferson's appeal to European architecture comes not just from reading about architecture, but also from seeing it, and here his visit to France as minister plenipotentiary much comes into play.

France would be a cultural shock for Jefferson that would lead to revivification of his appreciation of the fine arts—architecture especially. The French were doing innovative things in architecture that astonished Jefferson, so much so that it is safe to say that his tenure in France must be considered to be a second phase of his architectural education, though I do not use "phase" to imply mutually exclusive periods of time, for in his second phase, he applied direct experience of finished architectural projects to his repertoire as a designer of buildings. He studied much the "hotels"—that is, the apartments or houses—of

---

[25] Thomas Jefferson, *Notes on Virginia*, 153–54

[26] Thomas Jefferson, *Notes on Virginia*, 154.

[27] Thomas Jefferson, *Notes on Virginia*, 154.

Paris, where he learned of setting a house into a hillside, of alcove beds for maximizing space, of an indoor toilet inconspicuously located under the staircase, of windows that stretched from ceiling to floor, and of a large skylight for the house's central room (e.g., Poplar Forest).[28] It was one thing to appreciate the inexhaustible beauty of a particular design, but wholly another thing to build it where it does not belong or not to make physical accommodations for a different location. Arch de Triomphe would prove to be an architectural oddity, perhaps even an architectural nightmare, if it were constructed just anywhere in Paris.

In France and after a year of settling into Paris, Jefferson signed a lease at the palatial Hôtel Langeac, designed by Jean F. T. Chalgrin, designer of Arc de Triomphe, and on the corner of Avenue des Champs-Elysées and Rue Neuve de Berry, on September 8, 1785, and moved in on the seventeenth. It is described by Frederick Nichols as having a plain, elegant exterior with Neoclassical bas reliefs over its windows. The public rooms of the interior were oval and circular. The bedrooms, each of which had its own staircase, offered much privacy and were luxurious. There was a stately and large sitting room, and the hotel had flush toilets. The garden was sufficiently large for Jefferson to work it up to a small landscape enclosure. [29] Jefferson also availed himself of the opportunity to meet with some of France's foremost architects, such as Charles-Louis Clérisseau, and artists, such as Jean-Antoine Houdon, Jacques-Louis David, and Hubert Robert.

Frederick Nichols asserts that Jefferson "accepted [Parisians'] beliefs that good buildings made good people, that cruel ghettos made vicious people."[30] The wording strongly suggests that that was a lesson learned from his stint in Paris, whereas it was something he knew through the appropriation of an aesthetic sense and a moral sense (e.g., Kames and Hutcheson) which when both were rightly cultivated, worked in partnership: What was good was beautiful and inspired emulation; what was bad was unsightly and prompted aversion.

"Nothing handsomer or in chaster style"

Three Key Architectural Projects

In *Notes on Virginia*, as I note, Jefferson grouses about the sorry state of architecture in Virginia. Most of the buildings are of "scantling and boards,

---

[28] Travis C. McDonald, Jr., "Poplar Forest: Synthesis of a Lifetime," https://poplarforest.org/wp-content/uploads/Poplar_Forest_-_Synthesis_of_a_Lifetime.pdf, 5.
[29] Frederick Nichols, "Architecture," 218.
[30] Frederick Nichols, "Architecture," 219.

plaistered with lime." Houses of the poor are of logs, with interstices filled with mud. The only noteworthy architecture—and he cites as illustrations the Capitol, the Places, and the Hospital for the Insane—is in Williamsburg, and he is even critical of those three buildings.[31]

Yet lack of interest in architectural improvement is not the only problem. There are no architects to effect such improvements. "The first principles of the art are unknown, and there exists scarcely a model among us sufficiently chaste to give an idea of them," [32] hence the significance of Jefferson's trip to France and travels through Europe.

Jefferson's employment of "model" is significant. Sculptures need models—their subjects. Lawyers need models—their precedents. Moralists need models—moral cynosures. Architects too, for Jefferson, need models.

Why is that the case?

Jefferson writes to James Buchanan and William Hay (26 Jan. 1786) of the methods of designing public buildings. One can leave the design to the fancy of an architect. In such instances, "experience shews that about once in a thousand times a pleasing form is hit upon." On the other hand, an architect can take "some model already devised and approved by the general suffrage of the world." In that instance, success is not due to fortuity. That is wholly sensible. Design and construction of public buildings is costly, and leaving design to the caprice of a builder might prove devastating. Jefferson here has in mind a model for the new Capitol of Virginia in Richmond: the Maison Carrée of Nîmes, France—a building which "has pleased universally for nearly 2000 years." The test of time is crucial.

The Virginian capitol was one of Jefferson's three significant architectural projects—the other two were Monticello and University of Virginia. The aim of each design was unique, as each structure would have a different function, though it is safe to say that all structures were intended to be sublime in some Jeffersonian sense of the term. Richard Guy Wilson captures that sense of sublimity. Using Greek, Roman, Italian, French, and English models for inspiration, he developed "an architectural identity ... and an architectural language traditionally associated with monarchy, the church, and imperial power."[33] Wilson's wording implies aristocratic or royal power, yet I suspect, given Jefferson's disdain for imperialism and artificial aristocracy and his choice of words such as simplicity, lightness, and chasteness in describing his

---

[31] Thomas Jefferson, *Notes on Virginia*, 153.
[32] Thomas Jefferson, *Notes on Virginia*, 153.
[33] Richard Guy Wilson, "Thomas Jefferson and the Creation of the American Architectural Image," 124.

three main projects that the power of chasteness is most apt. They were also to be recognizable as a form of a new sort of architecture: American architecture. In this section, I cover Monticello, Virginia's State Capitol, and University of Virginia.

Jefferson's first significant project—his pet project, his most intimate project, and the one on which he cut his architectural eyeteeth—was Monticello. The site on which he was to build it, he first referred to as "Hermitage," because it was his personal retreat as a lad.[34] Margaret Bayard Smith captured this quote of Jefferson's daughter Martha who presumably said: "I have heard my father say that when quite a boy the top of this mountain was his favorite retreat. Here he would bring his books to study. Here would pass his holiday and leisure hours: that he never wearied of gazing on the sublime and beautiful scenery that spread around, bounded only by the horizon, or the far off mountains."[35]

Monticello, or "Monticule," was designed to awe. In his *billet doux* to Italian coquette Maria Cosway (12 Oct. 1786), Jefferson writes of the sublimity of Monticello:

> And our own dear Monticello, where has nature spread so rich a mantle under the eye? mountains, forests, rocks, rivers. With what majesty do we there ride above the storms! How sublime to look down into the workhouse of nature, to see her clouds, hail, snow, rain, thunder, all fabricated at our feet! and the glorious sun when rising as if out of a distant water, just gilding the tops of the mountains, & giving life to all nature!

The sense of sublimity—a concept which, for Jefferson, implies among other things largeness of size and stateliness, and inspires awe—is Olympian. Monticello has a perch "above the storms," and one which gives dwellers a godlike view of all natural phenomena, thereby making such persons, as it were, demigods. To enhance the effect of sublimity, the lawn to the rear sloped downward, though the downward sloping was also for the sake of not obscuring its "Olympian" view.

---

[34] Jefferson would have a lifelong need of quiet, personal space—especially when there was considerable work to be done. In 1776, Jefferson retired to the second floor of the Graff House at Seventh and Markets Streets when tasked with writing the Declaration of Independence. While in France years later, he retired to the Carthusian Monastery on Mont Calvaire to the west of Paris when there was the press of business. M. Andrew Holowchak, *Thomas Jefferson in Paris: The Ministry of an American "Looker-on"* (Wilmington, DE: Vernon Press, 2022), chap. 20.

[35] Margaret Bayard Smith, *The First Forty Years of Washington Society,* ed. Gaillar Hunt (New York: Scribners, 1906), 387.

There was a view of the mountains to the rear of Monticello from one of the round windows in the octagonal dome of the residence. One has only to consider what Richard Rush, son of Jefferson's dear friend Dr. Benjamin Rush, once said of Jefferson's residence. "Monticello is a curiosity! Artificial to a high degree; in many respects superb. If it had not been called Monticello, I would call it Olympus, and Jove its occupant. In genius, in elevation, in the habits and enjoyments of his life, [Jefferson] is wonderfully lifted above most mortals." "Richard Rush's Account of a Visit to Montpellier and Monticello, 9 October 1816," *Founders Online*, National Archives, https://founders.archives.gov/documents/Jefferson/03-10-02-0317, accessed 30 July 2022.

There were, for all intents and purposes, two main phases of construction: from 1768 to 1784 and from 1796 to 1809.

Prior to discussion of construction of Monticello, it is aidful to say something about the site of the estate. Here the influence of Palladio, whose *Four Books* he acquires in 1768, is evident. In Book II, Chapter XII, Palladio examines the conditions proper for the location of a country estate, where one can exercise his body on foot or on horseback and where the owner can revitalize his spirit through the tranquility of "study of literature and quiet contemplation."[36] What is plain is that Jefferson's Monticello fits Palladio's description of a villatic retreat.

In 1768, Jefferson began clearing the top of Monticello so that he could begin needed preparations for building his hilltop residence. He married in 1772 and hurried construction to accommodate his wife and the beginnings of his family. He continued building even after the death of his wife in 1782. It mostly came to a stop when he left for France in 1784 for what would become a post for Minister Plenipotentiary to France.

The first building of Monticello was constructed in 1770—the Southern Pavilion—which would function as a dwelling place, while the main house was under construction. It would be at the end of what would become the South Wing and it had beneath it a kitchen, which would be the kitchen at Monticello till 1808. It was in the Southern Pavilion that Jefferson took his new bride, Martha, on that blustering and snowy night in January 1772. It was there that first daughter, Martha, was born. It would later function as a study.

In 1796, Jefferson undertook a massive reconstruction of Monticello and that would double it in size by capping the house with a dome "in the stile of those of Armerico's [*sic*] house in Palladio"[37] and adding service buildings to

---

[36] Andreas Palladio, *The Four Books on Architecture*, 45.

[37] Jefferson means the Vicentine Paolo Almerico, whose house was square with a circular middle hall with a dome to receive light. Andrea Palladio, *The Four Books on Architecture*, 94–95.

the house to surround its lawn and to create, from the rear, the form of a Π (which would extend out and westerly from the South and North Terraces in Figure 5-1). The service buildings would comprise a kitchen, laundry, stables, and even a state-of-the-art ice house, with chunks taken from the Rivanna River in the cold of winter and stored. The wings were set partly into the ground so that the household and visitors would not be bothered by the various activities in and around those service buildings.

The additions were certainly driven by the architectural marvels he saw in his tenure in France—especially Hôtel de Salm and its striking dome—but also by plans to accommodate his grandchildren, who would stay with him at Monticello, when daughter Martha came to live with him, after the death of Jefferson's wife. In all, Monticello (Figure 5-1, bottom floor) would be transformed from eight rooms to 21 rooms. The Northern Pavilion, as a complement to the Southern Pavilion, would not be finished till 1809—thereby, for all intents and purposes, ending further major constructive projects. Jefferson was heavily in debt at the time, and what money or credit he could appropriate was spent on his residence, Poplar Forest, begun in 1806.

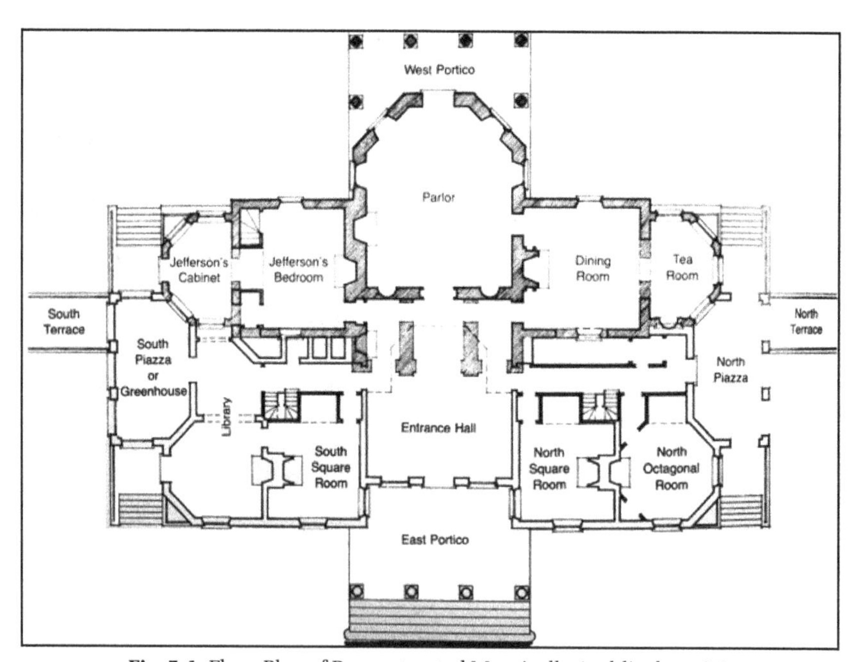

Fig. 5-1: Floor Plan of Reconstructed Monticello (public domain)

The reconstructive aim behind the hefty reconstructive project at Monticello was beauty with fullest functionality—*viz.*, beauty taking a back seat to functionality, though he always did what he could to admix the two. Jefferson's addiction to functionality is evident in his refusal to add a large, showpiece staircase in the Entrance Hall. Jefferson himself writes John Brown (5 Apr. 1797), "Great staircases are [to be] avoided which are expensive & occupy a space which would make a good room in every story."[38] In consequence, when Anna Maria Brodeau Thornton visited and she and her husband had to access their room on the second floor of the house, she grumbled, "We had to mount a little ladder of a staircase, about two feet wide, and very steep."[39] "Jefferson showed his admiration for the Romans by using a different order for the entablature of each room." The entablature in the parlor was modeled after Rome's Temple of Jupiter; his bedroom, after Rome's Temple of Fortuna Virilis.

Duc de la Rochefoucauld-Liancourt, who visited Jefferson at Monticello in 1796, sums Jefferson's European education on the design for Monticello:

> Monticello, according to his first plan, was infinitely superior to all other houses in America, in point of taste and convenience; but at that time Mr. Jefferson had studied taste and the fine arts in books only. His travels in Europe have supplied him with models; he has appropriated them to his design; and his new plan, the execution of which is already much advanced, will be accomplished before the end of next year, and then the house will certainly deserve to be ranked with the most pleasant mansions in France and England.[40]

Following biographer Nathan Schachner, we must marvel not just at the dream of such a villatic estate, but that its actualization. "The amazing thing with this particular young man is that he went through with it; and still more amazing is the practical particularity with which he drafted his plans, measured dimensions and calculated quantities with all the accuracy of an architect, a bricklayer and a working carpenter."[41]

---

[38] In the letter, Jefferson advises Brown to consider a single-story residence, instead of a multiple-story residence.

[39] Jack McLaughlin, *Jefferson and Monticello: Biography of a Builder* (New York: Henry Holt and Company, 1988), 5.

[40] Merrill D. Peterson, ed., *Visitors to Monticello* (Charlottesville: University of Virginia Press, 1989), 22.

[41] Nathan Schachner, *Thomas Jefferson: A Biography* (New York: Appleton-Century-Crofts, Inc., 1951), 66.

The Virginian Capitol (Figure 5-2) was his second significant project. It began after his appointment as chair of a committee to design public buildings for Richmond, the state's capital.

Jefferson writes to James Curie (18 Jan. 1786) concerning the model, an ancient Roman temple, for his state's Capitol. The designs of the capital are "simple & sublime," and "not the brat of a whimsical conception never before brought to light, but copied from the most precious, the most perfect model of antient architecture remaining on earth; one which has received the approbation of near 2000 years, and which is sufficiently remarkable to have been visited by all travellers."

The notion of sublimity is linked with simplicity, and one cannot help but believe that that sublimity to which Jefferson refers is merely lofty elegance, the result of meticulous and careful design that has had 2,000 years of approbation. Two thousand years of approbation show that what is beautiful about the building is not the effect of convention or vogue, but of something inherently stylish and grand—sublimity apropos of Classical beauty, which is both materially durable and stylishly resilient.

Fig. 5-2: Virginian Capitol (public domain)

The story of the history of Virginia's State Capitol is as follows. While governor of Virginia, a five-man board of Directors of Public Buildings added Governor Jefferson to the directors. He proposed separate buildings for each of the three branches of the Virginian government—something that was unprecedented at the time and due to his staunch belief in the relative independence of the three branches as political powers—but the proposal was rejected by the General Assembly after Jefferson went in Paris in 1784. In 1785, the General Assembly contacted Jefferson in Paris and asked for his advice for a proposed model for its new capitol. Jefferson discussed the issue with French architect Charles-Louis Clérisseau and subsequently chose as a model Maison Carrée—"one of the most beautiful, if not the most beautiful and precious morsel of architecture left us by antiquity," he told James Madison—though he enlarged the capitol and instituted plain, but stately, Ionian columns instead of the more elaborate Corinthian columns.[42] The difficulty, for Jefferson, was the interior partitioning. "Much time was requisite, after the external form was agreed on, to make the internal distribution convenient for the three branches of government."

The State Capitol was the first public building in the Classical manner in the United States and an overwhelming success insofar as it promoted neo-Classicism as the norm for public buildings in the United States. "A nobler marriage of landscape and architecture had not been consummated in colonial America," write Frederick Nichols and Ralph Griswold.[43] To Jefferson's original building, there have been added two flanking buildings as well as the steep steps.

Jefferson's University of Virginia—his Simeon's song[44]—was his final significant project. Though he employed other architects to assist him, for he sold his library and architectural books to create the Library of Congress—"we are sadly at a loss here for a Palladio," he wrote to James Madison (15 Nov. 1817), … [for] they are at Washington, and nobody in this part of the country has one unless you have"[45]—Jefferson designed every building, disregarded the advice of others to make changes to his original plan, and daily supervised construction inasmuch as his infirmities due to his dotage allowed.

Several passages in letters show that it possessed sublimity, Jefferson thought, which was the result not of size, but of comeliness and chasteness.

---

[42] He writes to James Sloan (15 June 1818): "to feast on [Maison Carrée], I went twice to Nismes, staid 10. days each time, & each day stood an hour, morning, noon & night, fixed as a statue to a single spot, and entransed in the beauties of it's form and symmetries."

[43] Frederick Doveton Nichols and Ralph E. Griswold, *Thomas Jefferson: Landscape Architect* (Charlottesville: University of Virginia Press, 1978), p. 16.

[44] See M. Andrew Holowchak, *Thomas Jefferson: Psychobiography of an American Lion* (Hauppauge, NY: Nova Science, 2019), chap. 9.

[45] Madison had an edition of Palladio, which he lent to Jefferson (TJ to James Madison, 30 Dec. 1817).

He writes to James Pleasants (26 Dec. 1821): "I can assure you there is no building in the US. so worthy of being seen, and which gives an idea so adequate of what is to be seen beyond the Atlantic. there, to be sure they have immensely larger and more costly masses, but nothing handsomer or in chaster style." To Judge Augustus B. Woodward (3 Apr. 1825), he says, "The form and distributions of its structure are original and unique, the architecture chaste and classical." It would have been easy for Jefferson to overwhelm architecturally through size, yet the sort of sublimity he aimed to achieve was not through bulk or heaviness, but instead through the innocence and purity that can only come from Classical inspiration. He writes to Charles Willson Peale (15 Feb. 1824): "greater works may be seen in the US. and in Europe. but you know the difference between magnitude and beauty. in the chastity of it's architecture, it's variety, symmetry, lightness and originality you will acknolege it's pre-eminence." Note here that Jefferson is drawing from Classical models to create a structure that is in the whole "original and unique."

Assisted by the architects Benjamin Latrobe and William Thornton—Jefferson followed their suggestions for the fronts of three pavilions[46]—the university was to be an "academical village." Jefferson says, "This village form is preferable to a single great building for many reasons, particularly on account of fire, health, economy, peace & quiet. the opportunity these small buildings will afford, of exhibiting models in Architecture of the purest forms of antiquity, furnishing to the Student examples of the precepts he will be taught in that art."[47]

Viewed from the Lawn, it was like Monticello Π-shaped in design. The Lawn (Figure 5-3), some 60 yards wide and sloping downward as one travels south from the Rotunda, was intended to have open space to allow for health in the manner of French hospitals he observed as minister plenipotentiary.[48] The east and west wings each had five pavilions to function as schoolrooms and living quarters for the 10 professors, and dormitory spaces between the pavilions to house students. Pavilions I (behind the tree at the left) through IV (far right and only partially shown) are visible to the left and right of the Rotunda (center). Each pavilion was to be architecturally unique with an admixture of present-day architectural innovations and Classical techniques,

---

[46] Fiske Kimball, *Jefferson the Architect,* https://archive.org/details/jeffersonarchite01kimb/page/n3/mode/2up, accessed 14 Apr. 2020.
[47] TJ to Wilson Cary Nicholas, 2 Apr. 1816.
[48] Burns maintains that the lawn at University of Virginia was inspired by the Governor's Palace at the end of the Palace Green, a long grassy space lined with trees and mansions, at Williamsburg. Howard Burns, "The Making of an Architect," 12.

based on Ionic, Doric, Corinthian, and Tuscan orders. The list of styles, taken from Palladio and Chambray (1606–1676), are as follows:

Pavilion I: Doric, following Diocletian's baths (Chambray)

Pavilion II: Ionic, with dentils from the temple of Fortuna Virilis (Palladio)

Pavilion III: Corinthian (Palladio)

Pavilion IV: Doric, of Albano (Chambray)

Pavilion V: Ionic, with modillions (Palladio)

Pavilion VI: Ionic, following the Theatre of Marcellus with dentils (Chambray)

Pavilion VII: Doric, with mutules (Palladio)

Pavilion VIII: Corinthian, following Diocletian's Baths (Chambray)

Pavilion IX: Ionic, with dentils following the Temple of Fortuna Virilis (Palladio)

Pavilion X: Doric, following the Theatre of Marcellus (Chambray)

Rotunda: Corinthian, following the Pantheon (Palladio)[49]

Fig. 5-3: UVa's Lawn, South View (author)

[49] Thomas Jefferson, "List of Styles of Pavilions at the University of Virginia, ca. 1820, December 1820," *Founders Online*, National Archives, https://founders.archives.gov/documents/Jefferson/98-01-02-1727, accessed 14 Apr. 2020.

Columns, following the lead of Palladio, would be composed of brick, covered by stucco. Jefferson writes to James Madison (12 May 1800), "In Ld. Burlington's edition of Palladio, he tells us that most of the columns of those fine building erected by Palladio are of brick covered with stucco, & stand perfectly. I know that three fourths of the houses in Paris are covered with plaister & never saw any decay in it."[50] Marble would have been much costlier and difficult to procure.

Centered at the top of the Π, where one might expect a chapel, there was the Rotunda, "a perfect sphere with a dome as the upper portion of the sphere," which functioned chiefly as a library. Says Jefferson to William Short (24 Nov. 1821), "the Library is to be on the principle of the Pantheon, a sphere within a cylinder of 70.f. diameter, to wit one half only of the dimensions of the Pantheon, and of a single order only." That the focal building, modeled after the Pantheon, should be a library, when it should have been a church, says much about Jefferson's profound, perhaps sacrosanct, love of books. Behind the buildings on the wings, there were serpentine walls for gardens and privacy (Figure 5-4). The walls were an illustration of Hogarthian elegancy and economy: A wavy wall would be one-brick thick and sturdy.

Fig. 5-4: UVa's Serpentine Wall (author)

[50] See also TJ to Benjamin Latrobe, 28 Feb. 1804.

To give an illustration of Jefferson's employment of mathematics in building and his large regard for minutiae, Jefferson writes to Arthur Brockenbrough in 1821: "Palladio's measures of the Fortuna virilis are not in Modules & minutes but in quarter inches of the Vicentina foot, the diameter of the column being 2 f–8½ I or 130 quarter inches which he calls minutes. then 130 ¼ I : 60′ :: 95 ¼ I his projection to 4317/20′ which is the projection of that cornice given by Palladio." He continues:

> Chambray's drawing of the same temple being expressed in modules and minutes, I had taken the projection of the cornice from his notation of 70′. measured from the center of the column. but measuring the projection from the face of the frize or of the diminished diameter as I generally do, one half of the diminished diameter, to wit, 26½′ must be deducted from Chambray's 70′, which leaves for the projection of the cornice beyond the face of the frize or of the diminished diameter as I generally do, one half of the diminished diameter, to wit, 26½′ must be deducted from Chambray's 70′, which leaves for the projection of the cornice beyond the face of the frize 43½′ = 21¾′ o that the frize if measured from the center of the column is 1 m–10′ = 2 f–11 I as noted if measured from the face of the frize is 43½′ = 1 f–9¾ I, but the difference between Palladio's and Chambray's projections is by 1/10 of a minute.

The chief difficulty of the project was that each pavilion was to be unique and showcase a different order of architecture so as to be a lesson of Classical architectural design, appropriable for students, professors, and visitors. Was it possible to do that without the whole being an architectural hodgepodge and an aesthetic nightmare?

Jefferson thought not. He writes to Robert Mills (3 Mar. 1826), "The plan has the two advantages of exhibiting a specimen of every fine model of every order of architecture, purely correct [the 10 pavilions], and yet presenting a whole entirely new and unique." The Rotunda, he tells John Trumbull (15 July 1823), was "the key-stone which is to give Unity to all that is already done." So, the Rotunda, he thought was the key to its unity—that which, to return to Hutcheson, gave the diverse buildings a sense of uniformity.

The overall effect of the layout and design of the University of Virginia was, and continues to be, stunning. In Jefferson's day, New Englander George Ticknor said, "They have ... a mass of buildings more beautiful than anything architectural in New England, and more appropriate to a university than can be found, perhaps, in the world." Architect and architectural historian Fiske

Kimball notes that many diverse elements are united by “a single impress of form” that has “an overwhelming aesthetic effect.”

> The grandiose symmetry of disposition, the rhythmic alternation of pavilion and colonnade, the jewel-like simplicity of the major units, square-faceted and round, with their contrast like diamond and pearl, the eternal recurrence of the white columns, as a rhythmic treble against the ground-bass of red walls are elements of this effect, which in its perfection surpasses analysis, and tells us we are in presence of the supreme work of a great personality and great artist.[51]

Monticello, the state capitol, and the University of Virginia were Jefferson’s three architectural gems, though he did much more to help to change the architectural landscape of his day, especially and directly in the burgeoning city of Washington, D. C., and indirectly through his influence on the construction of states’ capitols and other public buildings, and on college buildings as well as private residences.

“An object the most desirable for my comfort in this world”

Jefferson’s Getaway Villa

Then there is Poplar Forest, which is, in the words of Frederick Nichols, “the finest of his house designs” and “one of the most imaginative houses in America.” There, adds Nichols, Jefferson carries out “completely” octagonal design.[52] One might challenge Nichols’ assessment and say that octagonal design is carried out to the extreme—*viz.*, that Poplar Forest is an architectural oddment.[53]

Poplar Forest was so named because of the predominance of beautiful tulip poplars in the woodlands, prior to it being cleared for farming. Jefferson’s wife, Martha, inherited the 4,819 acres of land, owned by her father, John Wayles (1715–1773), on the death of Wayles on May 28, 1773, as well as other lands, 135 slaves, and Wayles’s substantial debt. That debt caused Jefferson to sell many of the inherited lands, much of the 2,042 acres along Judith Creek, but Poplar Forest was excepted, because of Jefferson’s favorable impression of the

---

[51] Fiske Kimball, *Jefferson the Architect,* https://archive.org/details/jeffersonarchite01kimb/page/n3/mode/2up, accessed 14 Apr. 2020.

[52] Frederick Nichols, “Architecture,” 224.

[53] For more on how Jefferson constructed the octagons for this residence, see Rachel Fletcher, “Thomas Jefferson’s Poplar Forest, *Nexus Network Journal,* Vol. 13 (2011): 487–98.

fecundity of the soil on a trip early in September 1773. Jefferson quickly made plans to improve agricultural yield with the hopes of making the land a source of considerable and stable revenue, through the chief crop over the years, tobacco, and other crops, such as wheat, as well as through domesticated animals like sheep, hogs, and cattle.[54]

Because of his decades of political involvement in Virginian and federal affairs, Jefferson was kept away from his land at Poplar Forest. Management of the farmed lands was indirect, from afar. He would only return to Poplar Forest, when British forces invaded Virginia in 1781 and essayed to capture Jefferson, then governor, other key officials, and significant papers.

Upon retirement in 1809, Jefferson tolerated uninvited visitors at Monticello and fed them, their horses, and put them up for the night and sometimes put them up for weeks. Overseer Edmund Bacon says: "After Mr. Jefferson returned from Washington, he was for years crowded with visitors, and they almost ate him out of house and home. ... They traveled in their own carriages and came in gangs—the whole family, with carriage and riding horses and servants; sometimes three or four such gangs at a time." The 36 stalls for horses, 10 of which were in use by Jefferson, were "very often ... full." All the beds in Monticello were often in use, and at times Bacon would have to lend his six spare beds for use at Monticello.[55] Jefferson's personal servant Wormley Hughes said to biographer Henry Randall that Monticello would be packed with visitors for at least eight months of the year.[56] Great-granddaughter Sarah N. Randolph relates that her grandmother Martha Jefferson Randolph once had to house 50 unexpected guests.[57] As to the objection commonly made that Jefferson's "generosity" was a rather poor excuse for extravagant spending—a rationalization—one could readily reply that he was brought up by his father in and accepted the tradition of, what great-granddaughter Sarah N. Randolph says was "primitive hospitality" or "Old Virginia hospitality."[58] Moreover, Jefferson, given to prévenance, was an unusually kind and generous person.

The problem of the intrusion of uninvited visitors was considerable. On one occasion, when there was to be a convention of Episcopalians in Charlottesville in 1822, and on hearing that there would be from 1,000 to 2,000 in attendance, Jefferson opted to retreat to his domicile in Bedford. He writes,

---

[54] For more on the early history of the region, see S. Allen Chambers, Jr., *Poplar Forest & Thomas Jefferson* (Forest, VA: Corporation for Jefferson's Poplar Forest, 1993), chap. 1.

[55] Hamilton Wilcox Pierson, *Jefferson at Monticello*, 113–14.

[56] Henry S. Randall, *The Life of Thomas Jefferson*, 332.

[57] Sarah N. Randolph, *The Domestic Life of Thomas Jefferson*, 346.

[58] Sarah N. Randolph, *The Domestic Life of Thomas Jefferson*, 8.

in an apologetic letter to Rev. Frederick W. Hatch (12 May 1822), that he wished to attend the convention, from which he would have "gladly profited," but "I have neither strength nor spirits to encounter such a stream of strangers from day to day [at Monticello], and must therefore avoid it by obeying the necessary call of my concerns in Bedford to which place I shall set out tomorrow morning."

In short, Jefferson's Monticello, after his presidency, had become somewhat of a place of pilgrimage that passersby would visit and exploit. When daughter Maria returned home after a visit to Washington, D.C., to see her father, she wrote (24 Jan. 1802), "With how much regret have I look'd back on the last two months that I was with you, more as I fear it will allways be the case now in your summer visits [to Monticello], to have a crowd." Maria, noting Jefferson's immense popularity on being president, anticipated that Monticello would no longer afford her famous father the peaceful retreat of a domestic residence. Hence, Poplar Forest would be that peaceful retreat, and so there was a need in Bedford for a residence.

Granddaughter Ellen Randolph Coolidge in a letter to biographer Henry Randall (c. 1856) told of the demands of mostly uninvited visitors on her grandfather whose leisure after many decades of service to his state and to his country was severely compromised. "That such a state of things entailed as a necessary consequence, the bustle and hurry of an almost perpetual round of company, wearied and harassed him in the end, whatever pleasure he may have taken, and it was sometimes great, in the society and conversation of his guests." His residence, thus, at Poplar Forest afforded him "a pleasant home, rest, leisure, power to carry on his favorite pursuits—to think, to study, to read—whilst the presence of part of his family took away all character of solitude from his retreat."[59]

A second reason, says S. Allen Chambers, for a residence at Bedford was financial. As president, his expenses far exceeded his salary and the income he had received from his lands. Jefferson built the house at Poplar Forest for the sake of directly overseeing production on the relatively profitable lands. "To ensure the greatest productivity, and consequently the greatest income, from his lands would necessitate firsthand supervision of the farm operations upon his retirement from public office. That, in turn, would mean numerous and lengthy visits to Bedford, and by extension, logical or otherwise, it would certainly be beneficial to have more comfortable lodging than those that had previously existed at Poplar Forest."[60] Chambers adds that there is "something

---

[59] Henry S. Randall, *The Life of Thomas Jefferson* (New York, 1858), 42.
[60] S. Allen Chambers, Jr., *Poplar Forest & Thomas Jefferson*, 30.

both appealing and appalling in Jefferson's completely irrational plan to achieve financial independence while building a house that would eventually cost as much, if not more, than the amount of the debt he sought to erase."[61]

There is, I suspect, a third reason for construction of the house in Bedford. In the 1806 letter to Trist in which he mentions preparation of his "occasional retreat" in Bedford, Jefferson also states that "this summer will entirely finish the house at Monticello." With construction at Monticello drawing to a close and his plans for a large-scale school of secondary education still more notional than actual, there would be nothing for him to put up and pull down. Poplar Forest would allow him some expression of his architectural talents, which ever cried out for expression. Architectural historian Travis C. McDonald writes: "The expense of a completely new villa retreat indicated a fundamental need, a necessity, for a private man long trapped in a public life. Had the need for a retreat been less of a psychological necessity, Jefferson could have deferred construction of Poplar Forest until better financial times."[62] In the words of Joan Horn, "Given his need for privacy, his desire for an idyllic place, his love of architecture and landscape design, and his awareness of the peace this place could offer him, it instead seems, upon reflections, inevitable."[63] That is how considerable and indispensable architecture had become for him.

Unlike Monticello, we know little about the interior of Poplar Forest. Ellen Randolph Coolidge gives in a letter perhaps the best extant description of folksiness of Poplar Forest to early biographer Randall in 1856:

> The house at Poplar Forest was very pretty and pleasant. It was of brick, one story in front, and, owing to the falling of the ground, two in the rear. It was an exact octagon, with a centre-hall twenty feet square, lighted from above. This was a beautiful room, and served as a dining-room. Round it were grouped a bright drawing-room looking south, my grandfather's own chamber, three other bedrooms, and a pantry. A terrace extended from one side of the house; there was a portico in front connected by a vestibule with the centre room, and in the rear a verandah, on which the drawing-room opened, with its windows to the floor.... It was furnished in the simplest manner, but had a very tasty

---

[61] S. Allen Chambers, Jr., *Poplar Forest & Thomas Jefferson*, 30.

[62] Travis C. McDonald, "Constructing Optimism: Thomas Jefferson's Poplar Forest," in *Perspectives in Vernacular Architecture*, Vol. 8 (2000): 190–1.

[63] Joan L. Horn, *Thomas Jefferson's Poplar Forest: A Private Place* (Forest, VA: Corporation for Jefferson's Poplar Forest, [2002] 2010), 16.

air; there was nothing common or second-rate about any part of the establishment, although there was no appearance of expense.[64]

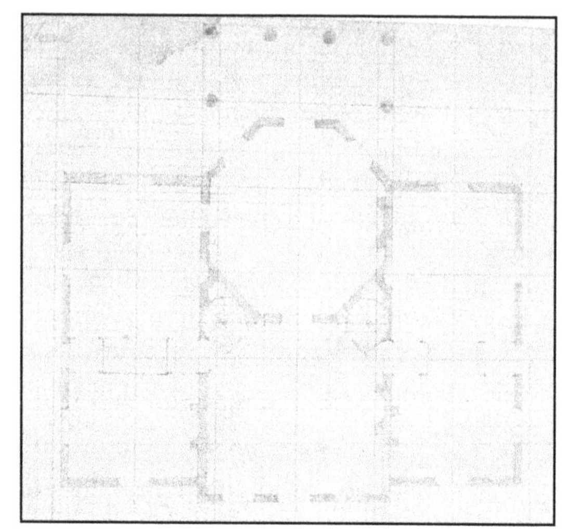

Fig. 5-5: Early Sketch of Retirement Home (public domain)

Unlike Jefferson's three key architectural projects, Poplar Forest, as his granddaughter's description shows, was an architectural oddity. It was not lavish, though it was not vernacular. It was not sublime, but being "pretty and pleasant," it was not without beauty. Its design was simple—he settled on an octagonal portion for his residence from a design he had earlier sketched (Figure 5-5)—and it was simply, though tastefully, furnished. In short, it was not, like other architectural projects, designed to awe, though it certainly awes architectural historians today.

Jefferson left behind many sketches for a possible design, and once he settled on a basic design—from the two-dimensional top-down view, an octagon which surrounded four octagons, which surrounded a square (Figure 5-6)—he moved forward with that design. It would not undergo critical changes to its basic structure or continual changes for improved efficiency. With the exception of the east wing (Jefferson's "service offices"), which was added in 1814, there were no large additions. For all intents and purposes, the construction of Poplar Forest ended in 1816 and he began with his granddaughters his summer sojourns.

---

[64] Henry S. Randall, *The Life of Thomas Jefferson* (New York, 1858), 342.

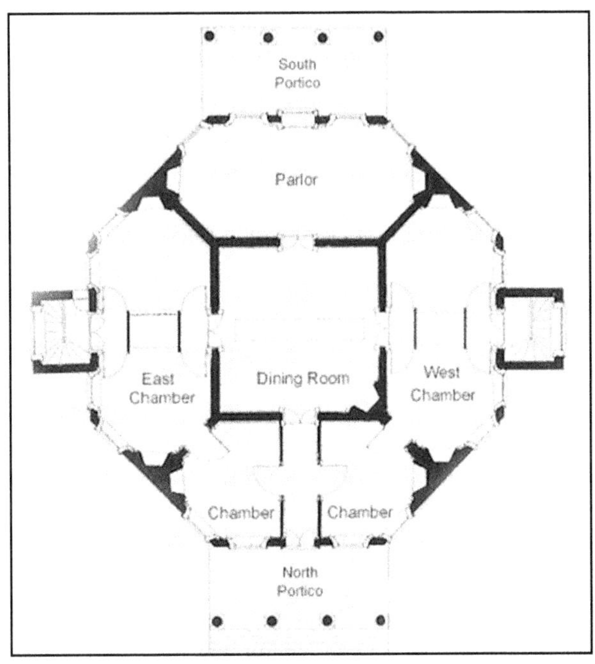

Fig. 5-6: Poplar Forest, Floor Plan (public domain)

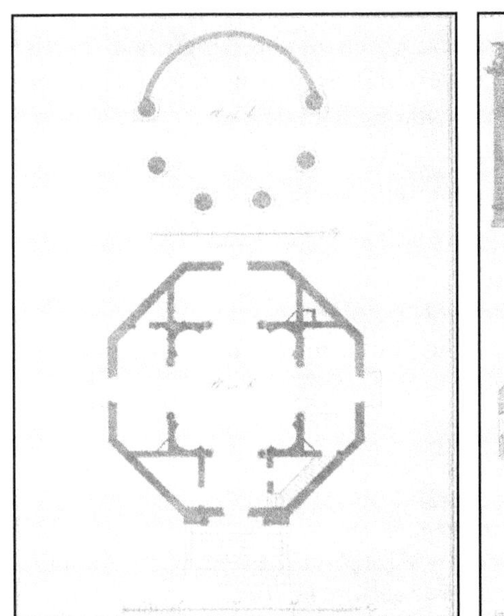

Fig. 5-7: Becker's Garden Temple (public domain) (left)
Fig. 5-8: Plate 30, Moriss' *Select Architecture* (public domain) (right)

Given Jefferson's penchant for drawing from models, it is apposite to ask this question: From what model did Jefferson draw in designing Poplar Forest?

C. Allan Brown has shown strong similarity between the basic structure of Poplar Forest and a plan for a garden temple in Wilhelm Gottlieb Becker's *Neue Garten-und-Landschafts-Gebäude* (1798–1799, Figure 5-7).[65] Chambers notes that Jefferson bought the book in June 1805—just before the construction was begun on the landscape of Poplar Forest. It might be that his notion of an inner and perfectly square room was inspired by Becker.

There is another drawing that might have inspired Jefferson. That is Plate 30 (Figure 5-8) of Robert Morris' *Select Architecture,* which Jefferson owned. Morris writes of the building: "The general Construction of this Plan is formed from a Square of 45 Feet *from out to out,* and the inscribing Part of 4 Octagons, 22 Feet Diameter in the Clear; 3 Sides of each of these Octagons break beyond the square Part 7 Feet, the other Sides forming 5 Spaces, each 8 Feet 6 Inches square, as is more particularly described by the Plan. The Ground or Parlour is 13 Feet, and the Chambers 10 Feet high in the Clear, the middle Square or Vestible is illuminated in each Story from the Staircase."

Travel from room to room is fast and easy. Yet such a residence "would be habitable only a Part of the Year, [for] Summer's extream Heat, and Winter's bleak and piercing Cold and Winds, would render it an uncomfortable or disagreeable Residence." Moreover, it could house only a very small family, though offices for staff could be built into the ground.[66] By removing the upper and lower squares to the right and left of the design and thereby preserving the general octagonal pattern and by making the inner square much larger, the inscribed octagons would be flattened, as it were, and one has the basic design of Poplar Forest.

Why was Jefferson continually tinkering with Monticello and not with Poplar Forest?

The reasons are many—e.g., its relatively late construction, lack of money, and it being a villa and not a permanent residence—and they have been discussed by others. One reason, touched on in the literature, has not been

---

[65] C. Allan Brown, "Thomas Jefferson's Poplar Forest: The Mathematics of an Ideal Villa. *Journal of Garden History,* Vol. 10 (1990): 120–21.

[66] Robert Morris, *Select Architecture: Being Regular Designs of Plans and Elevations Well Suited to both Town and Country; In Which the Magnificence and Beauty, The Purity and Simplicity of Designing for Every Species of that Noble Art, Is Accurately Treated, And with Great Variety Exemplified, From the Plain Town-House to the Stately Hotel, And in the Country from the Genteel and Convenient Farm-House to the Parochial Church, With Suitable Embellishments* (London, 1755), 5.

given full consideration: Jefferson's residence at Poplar Forest, upon his retirement, was more his own than was his residence at Monticello. Even though Jefferson often aimed for it to be the future residence of one of his grandchildren, it was a villa, *Jefferson's* villa, in the manner of a retreat from a Roman aristocrat's primary urban estate.

According to James Ackerman, the function of a villatic residence, though it might have a farm, is simple relaxation and enjoyment. "The villa is typically the product of an architect's imagination and asserts its modernity."[67]

In sum, Jefferson's house in Bedford needed only to be built to accommodate his needs as well as those of companions—e.g., his beloved granddaughters and his grandson Francis Wayles Eppes, who would inherit the residence. The relative simplicity of structural design and the plainness with which it was furnished tell us much of those needs—of the character of Thomas Jefferson. Whereas the buildings at Monticello, the Virginian Capitol, and the University of Virginia were intended, other than their obvious purposes, to be models of durability, stateliness, and chasteness from which others could learn, and they did, Poplar Forest was designed with the chief function of pleasing Thomas Jefferson and accommodating his basic needs in retirement. It was a place principally for reading, writing, reflection, and enjoyment of family.

Jefferson's library at Poplar Forest reflected that. It included many volumes on history and philosophy, and was weighted toward ancient authors. There were volumes of his beloved Ossian; the Greeks Homer, Plato, Demosthenes, Epictetus, Aurelius, Sophocles, Euripides, Aristophanes, Pindar, Xenophon, Aesop, Plutarch, and Hippocrates; the Romans Cicero, Seneca, Juvenal, Livy, Tacitus, Lucretius, Horace, Seutonius, Ovid, and Quintus Curtius; the French authors Descartes, Voltaire, Fontaine, Pascal, Corneille, Moliere, Volney, Buffon, and Diderot; and the English authors Bacon, Shaftesbury, Burke, Shakespeare, Hume, and Milton; collections of English and Italian poets; and an Edinburgh version of the Bible—many of those in small books to be fitting into his Petit Format Library, so as to be readily transported and once transported, to take up little space.[68] The collection strongly intimates that the books were culled to rest the mind, not test the mind.

Poplar Forest was, more than Monticello, Jefferson's architectural play-toy. While changes to Monticello were often with an eye to greater functionality, given the needs of the ever-growing family of his daughter Martha and later

---

[67] James S. Ackerman, *The Villa: Form and Ideology of Country Houses* (Princeton: Princeton University Press, 1990), 9.

[68] http://tjlibraries.monticello.org/transcripts/poplarforest/poplarforest.html, accessed 18 Apr. 2020.

the uninvited visitors who would disturb his retirement, Poplar Forest was Jefferson's own residence—his private getaway or hermitage—and so he lost himself in the project.

Proof comes with certain liberties Jefferson took in the process of construction. The entablature of the middle, square room at Poplar Forest was based on Doric order and modeled after the Diocletian Baths. Yet Jefferson had plaster-cast ox sculls, made by sculptor William Coffee, in the entablature, in strict violation of the Doric order. Coffee protested (25 June 1822), "In the example by Nicholson from the Baths of Dioclesian no ox scull is shown or can I find it so in any other work that I have looked at in fact this mistake of mine. If it is one would Extend to Every frize [*sic*] of that order and Example, and therefore I see the Necessity of your opinion, the way I looked at the subject was that you Intended to ornament two rooms at Bedford One as in the North." Jefferson replied (10 July 1822): "You are right in what you have thought and done as to the metopes of our Doric pavilion. Those of the baths of Diocletian are all human faces, and so are to be those of our Doric pavilion [Pavilion I of University of Virginia]. But in my middle room at Poplar Forest I mean to mix the faces and ox-sculls, a fancy which I can indulge in my own case, although in public work I seem bound to follow authority strictly."

Another oddity was Jefferson's choice of order at Poplar Forest. He went with the Tuscan order, which is the simplest and plainest of orders. He articulated detestation for the Tuscan order—it was suitable for barns, but not for a dwelling house—and yet he used it at Poplar Forest.[69] It is perhaps in its simplicity and plainness that Jefferson considered it the quietest order. It certainly was cheapest.

The project was not merely personal, but also intimate. Writes Travis McDonald: "While all his architectural projects can be called personal, this one was intimate. Its creation was one of private pleasure, both in the autobiographical nature of its architecture and in the anticipated peace and quiet the retreat would afford him in retirement. Poplar Forest provided the privacy Jefferson had always craved."[70]

Fiske Kimball called it a building "excessively rational," to such extent that its rationality impeded its functionality. With the octagonal design, "nearly every room was a passageway."[71] That excess of rationality reminds one of Palladio's La Rotonda (Figure 5-9)—a square structure, capped with a dome, and having

---

[69] S. Allen Chambers, *Poplar Forest & Thomas Jefferson*, 48.
[70] Travis C. McDonald, Jr., "Constructing Optimism", 176.
[71] Fiske Kimball, *Thomas Jefferson, Architect*, 71.

four identical porches.[72] The building, which has the "magnificence and abstraction of a celestial dwelling," says Guido Beltramini, yet has bad internal organization and is poorly lit.[73]

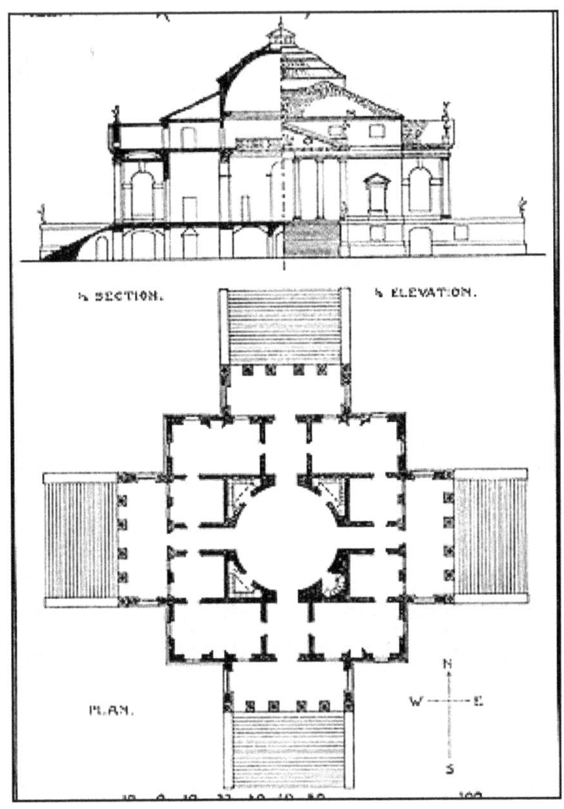

Fig. 5-9: Palladio's La Rotonda (public domain)

It is hard to believe that Jefferson did not anticipate those nodi.

The centermost space, the dining area, was a cube with each line of the cube being 20 feet in length. The exterior walls, dictated by the constraints of the inner cube, were each 20 feet in length and formed a perfect equilateral

[72] Jefferson merely reverses Palladio's design and puts the square inside and the circle, in the form of an octagon, on the outside.
[73] Guido Beltramini, "The Palladians," in *Thomas Jefferson, Architect: Palladian models, democratic principles, and the conflict of ideals,* ed. Lloyd DeWitt and Corey Piper, (Norfolk: Chrysler Museum of Art, 2019), 33.

octagon. Thus, the floor space of the dining area was 400 square feet while the floor space of the house was 1,931 square feet. Conjoining the cube to the outside walls were four elongated octagons, fitted to accommodate the inner squared walls and having a square footage of roughly 382.75. Moreover, as Figure 5-7 shows, the dining room would have been more than just a dining area. It was the only room by which one could access any other room: *viz.*, the parlor or the three chambers, if we treat the north chamber as one, not two, rooms. It is difficult, however, to believe that Jefferson did not anticipate that problem. If so, it was likely not a problem, but a desideratum. He may have had in mind something like critic Marc-Antoine Laugier's criticisms of the old royal squares of Paris. "For a square to be beautiful it should be a communal center from which people can make their way into different quarters and were, coming from different quarters, they can get together."[74]

Furthermore, given that the sloping southern lawn would have been the recreational area for his granddaughters, relaxing in the southern parlor would not always have been a secluded retreat for Jefferson. What we can say is that any disturbances to his time for study would have been less than those at Monticello, always overrun with visitors in the summer months.[75] Poplar Forest was designed for intimacy of living, and the giggling of an interloping granddaughter would have been happily tolerated.

In 1814, Jefferson added his "offices"—that is, a 100-foot left wing to the house with several functional rooms. "I have engaged a workman to build offices," he writes to son-in-law John Wayles Eppes (18 Apr. 1813). There would be a kitchen, smokehouse, laundry room, and a room for storage (Figure 5-10).

"I have laid off a handsome curtilage connecting the house with the Tomahawk, have inclosed and divided it into suitable appendages to a Dwelling house, and have begun its improvement by planting trees of use and ornament," Jefferson continues to Eppes. The curtilage of which Jefferson speaks is a 61-acre enclosure in the middle of which was a circular 540-yard road, lined with mulberry trees. The curtilage was defined by a split-rail fence. Outside the fence, there were his farmed lands. Inside the fence, there were the house and his gardens.

---

[74] William Howard Adams, *The Paris Years of Thomas Jefferson* (New Haven, CT: Yale University Press, 1997), 39.

[75] Laying out the outermost octagon proved no simple task, as Jefferson's master-builder, Jefferson noted in a June 16 (1806) letter to daughter Martha, was "not equal to himself" in setting up the foundation. The problem would be materially decupled by requiring squint bricks—a brick with one end cut to a 45-degree angle.

The overall design, says Joan Horn, is "the Palladian idea that house and grounds should be joined into a seamless whole."[76] That was achieved at Jefferson's magnificent university, as we saw, by inclusion of its "keystone"—the Rotunda. That was also the aim of the grand residences of the pleasure gardens that Jefferson toured in England with John Adams, though Jefferson's application of geometric regularity at Poplar Forest was *de trop*. Thus, it is impossible to believe that Jefferson did not have plans for a 100-foot right wing, scuttled due to lack of monetary resources.

To the east and west of the house, whose front faced due north, there were planted on each side a row of paper mulberry trees. Each row ended with an artificial earthen mound, with willow and aspen trees and shrubs. Beyond each mound, there was an octagonal privy.

To the north, Jefferson left the grove of tulip poplars, though he trimmed them so that their growth would occur atop and allow for maximal shade. He writes in the 1806 letter to William Hamilton: "Let your ground be covered with trees of the loftiest stature. Trim up their bodies ... so that their tops shall still unite and yield dense shade." There were oval beds, thickly planted with shrubs and roses, and "Athenian & Balsam poplars ... locusts, common & Kentucky, redbuds, dogwoods, calycanthus, and liriodendron." We see again some effort to make the estate as a whole a pleasure garden and the intimate interplay of landscape gardening and architecture.

Fig. 5-10: Mounds and Paper Mulberries of Poplar Forest (author)

To the south, things opened and Jefferson again used geometry for control of the landscape. The south lawn, 90 feet wide and over 200 feet long,

---

[76] Joan L. Horn, *Thomas Jefferson's Poplar Forest* (Forest: VA, The Corporation for Jefferson's Poplar Forest, 2002), 50.

Jefferson had sloped in the manner of The Lawn at the University of Virginia. Sloping the lawn, dubbed "forced perspective," gives the impression, from the southernmost end of the lawn, that the house is farther than it is, and from the house, and that the lawn extends farther than it does. In 1812, he directed his overseer to plant "lilacs, Althaeas, Gelder roses, roses, calycanthus." The choice of plants was intelligent, as each grows well in the Virginian red-clay soil, each grows at a similar rate, and each blooms at a different time, so that there would be efflorescence through much of the year. Jefferson, as we have seen in the chapter prior, was no dilettante when it came to botany.

Finally, the garden at Poplar Forest, only some 240 square feet, was certainly diminutive in comparison to that of Monticello, which was 1,000 feet in length. He grew lettuce, spinach, tomatoes, squash, beans, artichokes, asparagus, and of course peas—Jefferson's favorite vegetable.

Upshot

In this chapter, we have seen Jefferson's love of architecture through inspection of four of his key projects—Monticello, the Virginian Capitol, University of Virginia, and his architectural oddment, Poplar Forest, to which I have given especial attention—though he certainly designed wholly or in part other buildings, especially residences, and had a profound influence on the architectural landscape of his day that continues to ours. He was inspired by Palladio to bring Classicism to America and he did so remarkably well in each of those projects, though to each, he added personal touches. Each project balanced the Vitruvian needs of durability, functionality, and pulchritude. To the objection that Poplar Forest was excessively rational, perhaps obsessively rational, one might counter that it filled Jefferson's modest need to build in his retirement years. Moreover, building Poplar Forest gave Jefferson industrious use of his time after work on Monticello, for the most part, ended and prior to engagement with designing and constructing the University of Virginia.[77]

Jefferson, overall, was a capable critic of all the fine arts, but had not what Hugh Blair called "universal genius" for all of them—one who is equally and indifferently turned towards several different … arts" and active in them. Such a genius, says Blair, is likely not able to excel in any art.[78] Jefferson possessed no discernible capacity for poetry, painting, and sculpture; was an able critic, landscape architect, and orator (though better by much at writing, not

---

[77] For other buildings Jefferson designed or might have designed, see Ihna Thayer Frary, *Thomas Jefferson, Architect and Builder* (Richmond: Garrett and Massie, 1950), 53–58.
[78] Hugh Blair, *Lectures on Rhetoric and Belles Lettres* (Philadelphia: Troutman & Hayes, 1853), 27–30.

delivering, orations); and a very talented musician, till the injury to his wrist, but kept from pursuit of music as a profession by his status as a Southern gentleman (chapter 7). It was only in architecture that he excelled enormously in genius, for Blair, a sort of capacity for actualizing through imagination. While architecture might not have been the most important of the fine arts, it was clearly Jefferson's favorite art in praxis—one which allowed ample expression for his aesthetic imagination and his passion for math. It also allowed the expression of Jefferson's insistence on combining beauty and utility.

Chapter VI

The Arts of Painting and Sculpture

"In all human activity the violent and transitory develops first; repose and profundity appear last. The recognition of these latter qualities requires time; only great masters have them, while their pupils have access only to violent passions."[1] ~Jacques-Louis David

Writes American painter John Trumbull: "It is universally allowed that we [Americans] very much excel in the force of natural genius: And although but few among us are able to devote their whole lives [*sic*] to study, perhaps there is no nation, in which a larger portion of learning is diffused through all ranks of people. For as we generally possess the middle station of life, neither sunk to vassalage, nor raised to independence, we avoid the sordid ignorance of peasants, and the unthinking dissipation of the great." It is the love and cultivation of liberty which fuels love of education—the fine arts included. "The encouragement, which is given the Arts and Sciences, affords the prospect of our future glory."

No American painter captured the American spirit of revolutionary times as well as Trumbull, called "Painter of the Revolution." His *Declaration of Independence, Surrender of Lord Cornwallis, General George Washington Resigning His Commission,* and *Surrender of General Burgoyne* hang today in the Rotunda of the U.S. Capitol.[2] It is Thomas Jefferson who inspired him to be the painter who captured the revolutionary spirit.

Unlike gardening and architecture, Jefferson considered painting and sculpture to be among the least important of the fine arts, valued in his day because they promoted beauty without utility. America was for him to be an expansive nation of self-sufficient husbandmen whose days would be suitably occupied by farming, which would leave little time for aesthetic cultivation. Nonetheless, Jefferson had a lifelong interest in painting and sculpture, he befriended and even supported Trumbull in France, and he acquired and displayed a significant collection of artwork at Monticello.

---

[1] "Jacques Louis David," *Art & Popular Culture,* http://www.artandpopularculture.com/Jacques-Louis_David, accessed 13 May 2022.

[2] John Trumbull, *An Essay on the Use and Advantages of the Fine Arts: Delivered at the Public Commencement, in New-Haven, September 12, 1770* (New Haven: T. and S. Green, 1770), pp. 12–13.

Was Jefferson behaving inconsistently?

This chapter aims to answer that question. I begin with a discussion of Jefferson's proposed early gallery of artworks for Monticello, turn to elaboration of his education in painting and sculpture as minister plenipotentiary while in France (1784–1789), and end with an account of his collection of artwork at Monticello by the time of his retirement from the presidency early in 1809.

"The Whole Ecology of Greatness..."

Jefferson's Early Gallery of Art

Jefferson's first plan for Monticello was a design in many respects radically different from what we see today. Construction began around 1768, yet by 1772, the only functional space was a room at the end of the small southwest pavilion, which Jefferson inhabited after Shadwell had burned on February 1, 1770. It is there that Jefferson brought his lovely wife Martha and that snowy night after they were wed on January 1, 1772, to begin their life together.

With plans for Monticello materializing, Jefferson planned to festoon its interior with significant works of art. Around 1771, he composed a list of copies of works he aimed to acquire.[3]

- ✓ Venus of Medicis. Florence
- ✓ Apollo of Belvedere. Rome
- ✓ Hercules Farnese. Rome
- ✓ Antinous. Florence
- ✓ Dancing Faunus
- ✓ Messenger Pulling out a Thorn
- ✓ Roman slave whetting his knife
- ✓ The Gladiator at Montalto
- ✓ Myrmillo expiring. Rome
- ✓ The Gladiator reposing himself after the/engagement.
- ✓ Hercules & Antaeus

---

[3] Thomas Jefferson, *Building Notebook for Monticello*, Thomas Jefferson Papers: An Electronic Archive (Boston: Massachusetts Historical Society, 2003), p. 12.

- ✓ the two wrestlers
- ✓ the Rape of the Sabines

The other pieces were paintings or prints.

- ✓ St Paul preaching at Athens
- ✓ St Ignatius at Prayer
- ✓ Jephtha meeting his dautr.
- ✓ Sacrifice of Iphigenia
- ✓ History of Seleucus giving his beloved wife Stratonice to his only son Seleucus who languished/for her. Florence
- ✓ Diana Venatrix

Though copies of many of the items Jefferson had listed were available to dilettantes and mavens of art in his day, Jefferson, for reasons unknown, never acquired any of the works on his list.

What do the listed works of art tell us about the aesthetic taste of the young Thomas Jefferson?

First, we note that 13 of the 19 items listed were works of sculpture. That suggests a decided preference for sculpture in early life. His growing appreciation for painting later in life was perhaps due to the influence of Hogarth (see preface), who preached that aesthetic understanding has been stifled in his day due to a lack of appreciation of painting.[4]

Next, as with his architectural ideals, Jefferson preferred pieces that had universally received the approbation of scholars of art in his time and whose subject matter was rooted in Greek and Roman antiquity. Shut up in villatic Virginia, books were again his primary source of information. The *Venus of Medici*—a first-century B.C. marble copy of a bronze statue in the tradition of Praxitelean sculptors—was one of the most commonly copied pieces in Jefferson's day. The *Farnese Hercules* (Figure 6-1)—by a certain Glycon from the third century A.D. and a copy of a bronze by the Greek Lysippos or an understudy from the fourth century B.C.—is one of the most famous pieces from antiquity and so named because it was situated for many decades at the Palazzo Farnese in Rome. Other definitely identifiable pieces in Jefferson's list are also well-known pieces from antiquity that have passed the approbation

---

[4] Jefferson lists Hogarth's *The Analysis of Beauty* in a letter to Robert Skipwith (3 Aug. 1771), so his acquaintancy with Hogarth goes back at least to 1771.

of critics over millennia and that showcase Jefferson's respect for his education in Greek and Roman antiquity. That began with Revs. William Douglas and James Maury and continued in his tenure at William and Mary College under the tutelage of Dr. William Small, lawyer George Wythe, and Gov. Francis Fauquier during his tenure at the school from 1760 to 1762. The proposed collection also displays his relative naïveté with respect to contemporary art and artists of his day.

Art historian Seymour Howard says Jefferson was likely also influenced in his list by Dr. John Morgan (1735–1789). Jefferson was probably introduced to the Classical scholar during a trip north in 1766 with a letter of recommendation by George Gilmer, since Jefferson's list includes some of the items collected by Morgan.[5]

What do the works of art tell us about the psychological "trappings" of the young Thomas Jefferson?

Howard, who offers a description and commentary on the 19 works,[6] includes an appendix on the "subjective bases for Jefferson's interests in the arts." Jefferson's large creativity, he states brusquely, "stems ultimately from its appeals to his eros, anima, and narcissism." He fails to expatiate, though he appeals to renowned psychoanalyst Erik Erikson in support of that statement.[7]

Fig. 6-1: *Farness Hercules* (public domain)

[5] Seymour Howard, "Thomas Jefferson's Art Gallery for Monticello," *The Art Bulletin*, Vol. 59, No. 4, 1977, p. 584.
[6] Seymour Howard, "Thomas Jefferson's Art Gallery for Monticello," Appendices A & B.
[7] Seymour Howard, "Thomas Jefferson's Art Gallery for Monticello," p. 596.

In a series of lectures on Jefferson and following Freud's study of Leonardo, Erikson states that the "artistic gift as such escapes analysis." He adds, "The whole ecology of greatness ... transcends many of the assumptions which clinical work has suggested regarding the inner economy of a person." The analysis extends only insofar as a great person exhibits psychologically damaging symptoms outside of conscious control. "Otherwise, the facile or biased use of psychiatric terms can only blind the observer to the historical issues at stake."

Like any other person, Jefferson had narcissistic tendencies, says Erikson, yet "whatever dangers of narcissism he may have harbored, as he sees himself mirrored in the imagery of a present and vital people, [he] answers their call for leadership artfully and competently."[8] Thus and *pace* Howard, Erikson says nothing definitive concerning the eros, anima, and narcissism of Jefferson.

Howard continues, "He [Jefferson] is recognized as a man of sentiment as well as reason." To illustrate Jefferson's that, Howard quotes from Jefferson's letter to Maria Cosway (24 Apr. 1788), "I am but a son of nature, loving what I see and feel, without being able to give a reason, not caring much whether there be one," and another letter to the Countess de Tessé (20 Mar. 1787).[9]

While the letter to Tessé does exhibit an excess of emotional display, as Jefferson describes himself as being in love "with a house," but one must be cautious, as we saw in chapter 1, about Jefferson's refusal to proffer a reason for aesthetic indulgence in the letter to Cosway. Aesthetic assessments for Jefferson were not a matter of reason, but of the aesthetic sense—*viz.*, they were sensed or felt, not ratiocinated—and the pronouncement of beautiful or sublime, or of repugnancy, though shaped by a person's experiences, was immediate. So, Jefferson, not caring whether there was a reason for his love, was not a measure of devil-may-care, syrupy sentimentality, but an expression of aesthetic sensibility, which being immediate, needed no justification. And so, the critical comments of Howard are in the main disobliging.

What about Jefferson's 1771 list of works?

As Jefferson's picks have had universal approbation, his list is conservative, riskless. It would have been difficult for anyone in his day to criticize it. Yet one can ask this: Why did Jefferson include piece x and not piece y?

---

[8] Erik Erikson, *Dimensions of a New Identity: Jefferson Lectures, 1973* (New York: W.W. Norton & Co., 74), pp. 55–56.
[9] Seymour Howard, "Thomas Jefferson's Art Gallery for Monticello," p. 597.

Fig. 6-2: *Boy with Thorn* (public domain)

Second, the list reflects his budding democratic ideals. In addition to such notable mythical figures such as Venus, Apollo, Hercules, and Ares, there are common figures such as a thorn puller, a knife sharpener, a gladiator, two wrestlers, and a dying Gaul.

Third, the selections seem to evoke an array of emotional responses other than the immediate impressions of beauty and sublimity. Jefferson's "Messenger with thorn," more commonly known as *Boy with Thorn* (Figure 6-2), incites the instantaneous impression of sympathy until one sees the look of relative nonchalance on the face of the boy. The statue of the two wrestlers (Figure 6-3) directly incites edgy tension, as the copy of the lost Greek original in the Uffizi Museum highlights the extraordinary muscular strain of the two engaged-to-the-limit athletes. *Hercules of Farnese* (Figure 6-1) depicts brilliantly the toil of battle on an indomitable demigod. Hercules, with the skin of the Nemean lion draped over his massive club, is no celebrating victor, but a war-weary combatant, perhaps even more weary in anticipation of his next labor. *Rape of the Sabine Woman* by Giambologna (Figure 6-4), which was in the Loggia dei Lanzi in Florence, is an extraordinary depiction of the link between eroticism and violence.

Fig. 6-3: *The Wrestlers* (public domain)

Fig. 6-4: *Rape of the Sabine Woman* (public domain)

Among the paintings included in Jefferson's list, there was Raphael's *St. Paul at Athens* (Figure 6-5), which shows an animated Paul and an engaged and reflective, but sparse audience—for Jefferson, most likely, an illustration of toleration of free discussion in Athens, a significant aspect of Jeffersonian republicanism.[10]

Fig. 6-5: *St. Paul at Athens* (public domain)

"The smaller they are, the more agreeable"

Jefferson's Parisian Years

Jefferson's stint in France after the death of his wife, Martha, was for many reasons a turning point in his life. As minister plenipotentiary, he was removed from Monticello, where so many things would remind him of his departed wife, and was thrust into the bustling milieu of one of the world's most "enlightened" and cosmopolitan cities, Paris. It was in some sense a recrudescence of his years at William and Mary College, but this time the setting was international and cosmopolitan, not parochial and vernacular. There he met cognoscenti from all persuasions: e.g., belle lettres, agriculture, natural science, philosophy, and art. There he would meet, among numerous other notables, John Trumbull, A.L.C. Destutt de Tracy, Voltaire, Comte de Volney, and Pierre-Georges Cabanis—aka, Condorcet. It was in Paris that Jefferson *qua* intellectual thrived. It was in Paris that Jefferson the aesthete

[10] Jefferson would later write to William Short (13 Apr. 1820), "Paul was the great Coryphaeus, and first corruptor of the doctrines of Jesus."

could mature. With exceptions such as Tuscan immigrant Filippo Mazzei and Carlo Bellini, the aesthetic climate of Virginia in his day was, for all intents and purposes, nonexistent.

The intellectual climate of Paris forthwith piqued Jefferson's slumbering aesthetic sense. On October 19, 1784, he purchased "2 small laughing busts" and later a statue in plaster of Hercules. His first painting he bought on October 29 and soon thereafter he acquired five paintings with religious themes at an auction in 1785. He would continue to collect works of art, along with books and furniture, during his tenure. Without the material resources for artistic originals, he satisfied himself with first-rate copies of masterpieces. William Howard Adams explains, "Jefferson's initiation into the realm of aesthetic judgments came too late for him to develop any real originality into his artistic taste."[11]

Adams' sentiment, beguiling, is nonetheless deceptive. A man capable of deep deliberation and of wide understanding, Jefferson's gift was not creativity. He profoundly appreciated imagination, yet his own imagination was not innovative, inasmuch as he could not begin from scratch, so to speak. In everything that he created—e.g., University of Virginia, the pleasure gardens of Monticello, and his moldboard for plowing—he worked from models. His celebrated Declaration of Independence, he admitted, was persuasive only because he captured the pulse of the American colonists of his day. "Neither aiming at originality of principle or sentiment, nor yet copied from any particular and previous writing," he writes to Henry Lee (8 May 1825), "it was intended to be an expression of the American mind, and to give to that expression the proper tone and spirit called for by the occasion. All its authority rests then on the harmonizing sentiments of the day, whether expressed in conversation, in letters, printed essays, or in the elementary books of public right, as Aristotle, Cicero, Locke, Sidney, &c." His much-ballyhooed *Notes on Virginia* was birthed and patterned by 22 questions of François Barbé de Marbois. One wonders what Jefferson would have done with his copious notes over the decades of things noteworthy had he not come upon Marbois' queries. Also, it is aidful to recall Jefferson's concern in crafting his own pleasure gardens, in the letter to William Hamilton (31 July 1806) from chapter 2. He writes that English models are of limited assistance on account of Britain's "sun-less climate." He sums, "This subject is so original unique & at the same time refractory that to make a disposn analogous to it's character, would require much more of the genius of the landscape painter & gardener than I pretend to." Again, his architectural gems—the Virginian

---

[11] William Howard Adams, *The Paris Years of Thomas Jefferson* (New Haven: Yale University Press, 1997), p. 84.

capitol, Monticello, Poplar Forest, and the University of Virginia—were based on models.

In France, Jefferson came under the spell of world-renown sculptor Jean-Antoine Houdon.

In 1784, Jefferson received a letter from the Virginian governor and future president, Benjamin Harrison (July 20), concerning the Virginian Assembly to commission a statue of George Washington. Harrison writes that the assembly has unanimously decreed that completing the task should devolve on Jefferson with the aid Dr. Franklin, for both know well the history of the war and Gen. Washington's role in it. Harrison has asked Peale to send to whoever is commissioned to craft the statue a full-length picture of Washington from which to work. "The intention of the assembly is that the Statue should be the work of the most masterly hand. I shall therefore leave it to you to find out the best in any of the European States."

The significance of the letter is twofold. Harrison writes to Jefferson because he wholly trusts the latter's aesthetic sensibility. Yet it also is suggestive that there is no American sculptor equal to the task, so Harrison writes to Jefferson, in France, to find a French sculptor of greatest preeminence.

Jefferson replies on January 12, 1785, and the letter is an unqualified endorsement of Houdon: "There could be no question raised as to the Sculptor who should be employed, the reputation of Monsr. Houdon of this city being unrivalled in Europe. He is resorted to for the statues of most of the sovereigns in Europe."

Jefferson then turns to discussion of crafting the statue from a painting. He, Franklin, and Houdon agree that any statue from a painting would be worthless. "No statue could be executed so as to obtain the approbation of those to whom the figure of the original is known, but on an actual view by the artist." Statues manufactured from paintings, when figures are living, are "always condemned by those who know him for a want of resemblance," and that is large evidence that statues of the dead from paintings are equally misrepresentative.

Houdon, Jefferson continues, was so excited by the prospect of crafting a statue of Washington (Figure 6-6) that "he offered to abandon his business here [France], to leave the statues of kings unfinished, and to go to America to take the true figure by actual inspection and mensuration." The expense of transporting and accommodating Houdon, he adds, will not be exorbitant. Houdon's excitement at the prospect of doing a statue of Washington shows the enormous celebrity of the general in Europe at the time.

Jefferson, Franklin, and Houdon again agree that "the size shall be precisely that of the life," though statues are customarily made somewhat larger than of life, because they are generally elevated. Yet he adds, "We think it important that some one monument should be preserved of the true size as well as figure, from which all other countries (and our own at any future day when they shall desire it) may take copies, varying them in their dimensions as may suit the particular situation in which they wish to place them."[12]

Fig. 6-6: Houdon's statue of Washington (public domain)

On the same day of his reply to Harrison, Jefferson offers some critical insights into statuary, properly done, in keeping with the sentiments to Harrison. If a person is alive, a statue ought not to be done, as it is often done, from a painting, he writes to the Virginian Assembly and to Gov. Patrick Henry, who had just once again assumed governorship of Virginia on December 1, 1785, in replace of Harrison. Moreover, "the smaller they [statues] are, the more agreeable." He cites a "small" statue of Louis XV—"the best in the world,

---

[12] One of the large difficulties was Washington's garb. As Adams notes, "The American Republic's identification with its ancient Roman counterpart was reflected not only in architecture, painting, and sculpture but in the popular decorative arts and fashions." It was not uncommon for portraits to be done in Roman costume. Washington preferred common dress, and West, Copley, Brown, and Trumbull agreed. It was so commissioned. William Howard Adams, *The Paris Years of Thomas Jefferson*, pp. 90–1.

and it is the smallest here." Still, the statue is a "monster" from every point of view, unless one is far removed, because it deviates too much from life. When far removed, one then loses the "features and finer lineaments of the face and body." He continues: "A statue is not made, like a mountain, to be seen at a great distance. To perceive those minuter circumstances which constitute its beauty you must be near it, and, in that case, it should be so little above the size of the life, as to appear actually of that size from your point of view." Keeping the statue small—and Jefferson means close to lifelike size—has the additional gain of largely reducing the cost of the piece. The sentiments are equally applicable to busts.

Fig. 6-7: Houdon's bust of Jefferson (public domain)

In his collection of works of art at Monticello, Jefferson would eventually have busts, completed by Houdon, of Anne Robert Jacques Turgot, Voltaire, John Paul Jones, Benjamin Franklin, George Washington, Marquis de Lafayette, and himself along with a small nude Diana, with which Jefferson became much infatuated on a visit to the sculptor's studio.[13] Houdon's bust of Jefferson (Figure 6-7), an unqualified masterpiece, though certainly idealized, depicts the

[13] Due to its stark nudity, this was never on display at Monticello and eventually given to a friend. Alf J. Mapp, *Thomas Jefferson: America's Paradoxical Patriot* (Lanham, MD: Rowman & Littlefield, 1987), p. 216.

minister as somber, stately, confident, and dignified, and with a slight manly Alexander of Macedon cock of the head. The eyes are friendly and expressive of wisdom, while the mouth sits uneasily between a frown and smile.

Fig. 6-8: Brown's painting of Jefferson (public domain)

In summer 1786, John Trumbull, whom Jefferson had met in England in spring 1785, came to France at the invitation of Jefferson, and he stayed with the minister at Jefferson' residence—Hôtel de Langeac. During Jefferson's trip to England, Trumbull took Jefferson to visit his mentor Benjamin West as well as John Singleton Copley, who painted both Samuel Adams (1772) and John Adams (1783), and Mather Brown, another student of West. Jefferson would pose for Brown in the now well-known painting, finished in 1786 and in the possession of John Adams and his family till 1999 (Figure 6-8).[14] In stark contrast to the bust by Houdon, Brown's portrait depicts a solemn-to-the-point-of-sadness, vulnerable, and effete, perhaps even effeminately so, Jefferson with powdered wig. The eyes, focused but inattentive, are tired, and the mouth intimates disappointment. Of that painting, William Short said it is "an étude [as] it has no feature like him."[15]

---

[14] It is now in Monticello, next to Brown's painting of Adams.
[15] William Short to John Trumbull, 10 Sept. 1788.

Trumbull's stay in France would be a large furtherance of Jefferson's education in the Fine Arts. "Your friend Mr. Trumbul [*sic*] is here at present," writes Jefferson to David Humphreys (14 Aug. 1786). "He brought his Bunker's hill and Death of Montgomery to have them engraved here. He was yesterday to see the king's collection of paintings at Versailles, and confesses it surpassed every thing of which he even had an idea. I persuaded him to stay and study here, and then proceed to Rome." Of his stay with Jefferson, Trumbull writes in his journal:

> In the summer of 1785, political duties had called Mr. Jefferson, then minister of the United States in Paris, to London, and there I became acquainted with him. He had a taste for the fine arts, and highly approved my intention of preparing myself for the accomplishment of a national work. He encouraged me to persevere in this pursuit, and kindly invited me to come to Paris, to see and study the fine works there, and to make his house my home, during my stay.
>
> I now availed myself of this invitation, and went to his house, at the Grille de Chaillot, where I was most kindly received by him. My two paintings, the first fruits of my national enterprise, met his warm approbation, and during my visit, I began the composition of the Declaration of Independence, with the assistance of his information and advice.[16]

As Trumbull's entry in his journal indicates, he would be the chief beneficiary of his stay with Jefferson. The artist was given his own studio at Hôtel de Langeac, and there he could work on paintings on the history of the fledgling country, thereby capturing on canvas the spirit of the times from the American perspective for posterity. It was, as William Howard Adams notes, "a casual yet significant gesture that was without precedent,"[17] just another instance of Jefferson's prévenance, for as perusal of Trumbull's *Autobiography* shows, the young and talented artist struggled through much of his life to win the sort of notoriety and fame that would enable him to be financially stable and relatively self-sufficient. Jefferson's "sponsorship" of Trumbull was likely not remunerative, but he did have food to eat and a place to stay while Trumbull studied his art in France.

---

[16] John Trumbull, *Autobiography: Reminiscences and Letters of John Trumbull, from 1756 to 1841* (New Haven: Wiley and Putnam, 1841), pp. 96–97.
[17] William Howard Adams, *The Paris Years of Thomas Jefferson*, 91.

Trumbull's most famous painting is probably the twelve-by-eighteen-foot *Declaration of Independence* (1818), which depicts the five-man committee—including Adams, Franklin, and Jefferson—presenting the document to the Congress for its assessment on June 28, 1776.[18]

The painting began decades earlier as a "small picture."[19] Trumbull left for London in November 1786—"my brain half turned by the attention which had been paid to my paintings in Paris, and by the multitude of fine things which I had seen"—and "arranged carefully the composition for the Declaration of Independence, and prepared it for receiving the portraits, as I might meet with the distinguished men, who were present at that illustrious scene. In summer 1787, "I took that opportunity to paint his [Adams'] portrait in the small Declaration of Independence." He would return to Paris in the fall to paint Thomas Jefferson in the picture. He would also include Franklin's likeness from "the Life," as well as several other notables over time.[20]

Fig. 6-9: Trumbull's *Declaration of Independence* (public domain)

---

[18] On October 23, 1818, Trumbull writes Jefferson to tell him that his painting is completed.
[19] For Trumbull's account of how the picture came to be, see "Enclosure: John Trumbull to 'Detector,' October 1818, enclosure no. 2 in John Trumbull to Thomas Jefferson, 23 October 1818," in *The Papers of Thomas Jefferson, Retirement Series, Vol. 13, 22 April 1818 to 31 January 1819*, ed. J. Jefferson Looney (Princeton: Princeton University Press, 2016), pp. 331–34.
[20] John Trumbull, *Autobiography*, p. 148.

The small picture would morph many years later into a life-size painting (Figure 6-9). In 1816, Trumbull showed the small original to certain members of "the Government, in the expectation that it might attract their attention."[21] It did, and Trumbull was commissioned to paint a large twelve-by-eighteen-foot version of the small picture. In the new painting, Trumbull wished to include in it all of the signers of the Declaration, but he could include only 47 of the 56 men, as he worked from likenesses, not imagination—hence the extraordinary value of the painting today.

Trumbull writes of the painting—one of four commissioned in 1817 at the behest of the U. S. House of Representatives,[22] as "the Government" liked what they saw—to Thomas Jefferson (28 Dec. 1817):

> the Committee who drew up the Declaration form the principal Group, by which means I place yourself & some other of the most eminent Characters conspicuously—the figures large as Life:—The Picture will contain Portraits of at least Forty seven members,—for the faithful resemblance of Thirty Six I am responsible [*sic*], as they were done by myself from the Life, being all who Survived in the year 1791—of the remainder Nine are from pictures done by others:—One Gen[l] Whipple of New-Hampshire, is from memory;—and One Mr B. Harrison of Virginia, from Description aided by Memory.
>
> I at first dreaded the Size of my Work—but I have proceeded far enough to have conquered my timidity, and to be Satisfied that this Picture as a mere work of Art will be superior to those which have been heretofore engraved.

Trumbull would also paint a miniature of Jefferson (Figure. 6-10) in 1788. It is an oil on wood (4″ x 3¼″), which Trumbull left behind for Jefferson, when Trumbull travelled to England late in 1788. Trumbull writes Jefferson (Dec. 19) of a box, which Jefferson will receive on the day next, that contains, among other things, a "little case with two pictures"—one of Thomas Paine for Jefferson and the other of Jefferson for his daughter Martha. The portrait of Jefferson was suggested to Trumbull by William Short (10 Sept. 1788). As with Houdon's bust and Brown's portrait, Jefferson's dress is casual and his shoulders squarely face the viewer, while his head is turned left. The face is serious, and the cheeks, nose, and chin, ruddy by the sun. In sharp contrast to Brown's picture, the eyes are focused and highly attentive, the lips are pursed,

---

[21] Enclosure: "John Trumbull to 'Detector,'" 1818.

[22] See TJ to John Trumbull, 3 Mar. 1817.

and brows, stern. The portrait suggests readiness for momentous action. The miniature was created from Trumbull's depiction of Jefferson in his *Declaration.* He made two other miniatures of Jefferson, each distinct.

Fig. 6-10: Trumbull's miniature of Jefferson (public domain)

"The collection of pictures is precious"

Art Jefferson Did Eventually Acquire for Monticello

Following aestheticians such as Lord Kames, Edmund Burke, and Thomas Whately, Jefferson always recognized that cultivation of the aesthetic, especially in sculpture and painting, could be overdone, and if overdone, would be a corruptive monetary indulgence. Writes Horace M. Kallen, "Too expensive for the state of wealth in the home country, these nonproductive arts did not call for the same connoisseurship as architecture and gardening."[23]

Painting and sculpture were luxuries for a jejune country like the United States, for, unlike architecture and gardening, they in general had little practical value. Yet the right sort of painting or sculpture cataloged significant events like Gen. John Burgoyne's surrender at Saratoga on October 17, 1777, in John Trumbull's *Surrender of General Burgoyne* (1821) or left to posterity an image of

[23] H.M. Kallen, "The Arts and Thomas Jefferson," *Ethics*, Vol. 53, No. 4, 1943, p. 275.

a personage like François-Marie Arouet in Jean-Antoine Houdon's *Seated Voltaire.* It also provided, said Jefferson to Thomas Sully (8 Jan. 1812), "a pleasing and innocent direction" for those few persons with "accumulations of wealth which could otherwise be employed in the nourishing of course and vicious habits"—a sentiment commonly uttered by critics of art in Jefferson's time.[24]

Jefferson's letter was in reply to a prior communication by Sully (22 Dec. 1811), as head of a committee of artists in the Society of Artists of the United States, that announced Jefferson's unanimous election as honorary member of the society. Sully would send another letter (6 Jan. 1812) indicating that Jefferson was appointed president of the society for the year 1812. Sully in the letter was candid about the political nature of the letter. "I have no hesitation candidly to acknowledge that the Society expect to recieve much benefit from your acceptance of the office of President, although at a distance, and your time doubtless employed in important persuits [*sic*]; we nevertheless hope to derive much solid advantage from such communications as your leisure may permit you to make on the subject of the Arts."

Sully would also paint a portrait of Jefferson (Figure 6-11). His painting of Jefferson, completed in 1821, depicts a somber Thomas Jefferson in his senior years. There is a heaviness to the picture, as the lower body is too large for the rest of the body, the head is too small, and the colors are earthy, deep, and grave, not cheery.[25] The full-length picture hangs at U.S. Military Academy at West Point, New York. A truncated version is hung at Benjamin Franklin Hall at the American Philosophical Society in Philadelphia.

By the time of Jefferson's retirement from the presidency, Monticello was almost tawdrily decked out with busts, portraits, paintings, and other tokens of art. In a memoranda book, Jefferson listed his "Catalogue of Paintings &c. at Monticello," which is as complete a list of the pieces he owned as we have.

I have chosen in this section not to go the dry route of merely replicating Jefferson's list. I have opted instead to give readers a sampling of the artwork of Monticello through the eyes of contemporaries of Jefferson who visited Monticello and left to posterity their impressions of the artwork in his parlor.[26] To that end, lengthy quotes here are needed to capture the museum-like atmosphere of Monticello and the amazement, even awe, of visitors.

---

[24] E.g., Hugh Blair, *Lectures on Rhetoric and Belles Lettres* (Philadelphia: Troutman & Hayes, 1853), p. 14.
[25] TJ to Thomas Sully, 8 Jan. 1812.
[26] For Jefferson's list of artwork, see "Catalog of Paintings," *Thomas Jefferson Encyclopedia,* https://www.monticello.org/site/research-and-collections/catalogue-paintings.

Fig. 6-11: Sully's painting of Jefferson (public domain)

Academician George Ticknor (1791–1871) offers this account of the wonders of Monticello in a visit with fellow Bostonian Francis Calley Gray (1790–1856) as they enjoyed Jefferson's company early in 1815. Ticknor was given a letter of recommendation by John Adams, dated December 20, 1814, as well as a letter from Caspar Wistar, which Jefferson received in early February 1815. Ticknor writes of the Entrance Hall (Figure 6-12):

> You enter, by a glass folding-door, into a hall which reminds you of Fielding's 'Man of the Mountain,' by the strange furniture of its walls. On one side [there] hang the head and horns of an elk, a deer, and a buffalo; another is covered with curiosities which Lewis and Clarke found in their wild and perilous expedition. On the third, among many other striking matters, was the head of a mammoth, or, as Cuvier calls it, a mastodon, containing only the *os frontis,* Mr. Jefferson tells me, that has yet been found. On the fourth side, in odd union with a fine painting of the Repentance of Saint Peter, is an Indian map on leather,

of the southern waters of the Missouri, and an Indian representation of a boldly battle, handed down in their traditions.[27]

As the passage shows, the house was as much a museum of Natural History as it was a gallery of paintings, sculpture, and other memorabilia.

Fig. 6-12: Entrance Hall of Monticello (courtesy, Thomas Jefferson Foundation)

"Through this hall—or rather museum," continues Ticknor, "we passed to the dining room," where Jefferson soon appeared with Madison.

He took us to the drawing-room,—a large and rather elegant room, twenty or thirty feet high,—which, with the hall I have described, composed the whole centre of the house, from top to bottom. The floor of this room is tessellated. It is formed of alternate diamonds of cherry and beech, and kept polished as highly as if it were of fine mahogany.

Here [there] are the best pictures of the collection. Over the fireplace is the Laughing and Weeping Philosophers [Democritus and Heraclitus], dividing the world between them; on its right, the earliest navigators to America,—Columbus, Americus Vespuccious, Magellan, etc.,—copied, Mr. Jefferson said, from originals in the Florence Gallery. Farther

[27] George Ticknor, *Life, Letters, and Journals of George Ticknor,* Vol. 1 (Boston: Houghton Mifflin Company, 1909), p. 34.

> round, Mr. Madison in the plain, Quaker-like dress of his youth, Lafayette in his Revolutionary uniform, and Franklin in the dress in which we always see him. There were other pictures, and a copy of Raphael's Transfiguration.[28]

When Baron de Montlezun visited Monticello in 1816, he had this to say of Jefferson's "museum." I include much from his descriptions.

> I went back inside with Mr. Randolph Jr., who showed the museum in the entrance hall of the house to me. It contains both extremely rare items and others that you could find nowhere else, among them the upper jaw of a mammoth. It was discovered in Kentucky, and Mr. Peale used a copy of it to complete his mammoth at the Philadelphia Museum. The head is complete, but the lower jaw is not from the same individual. Two other infinitely curious pieces are: 1. An Indian painting representing a battle; it is on buffalo hide, about five feet square, and shows four lines of combatants. Each facing line has horses painted red and green and warriors armed and dressed in the manner of the savages.[29] 2. A geographical map without the slightest flaw, also on buffalo hide and six feet square. It depicts a section of the Missouri River, and, although roughly drawn, is easy to understand. The explanations have been written in French by interpreters.
>
> One also sees there a tusk from a mammoth and one from an elephant, with a tooth from the latter animal to show how different it is from those of the former, which are conical and designed for a carnivorous animal, whereas the others have flat and scratched crowns, as is characteristic of a fructivore.
>
> A head of a gigantic ram; one supposes that it is from the primitive breed that used to live in North America.
>
> Mr. Randolph next showed me the pictures and portraits that decorated the different rooms. The portraits of Washington, Lafayette, Adams, Franklin, Walter Raleigh, Amerigo Vespucci, Columbus, Bacon, Locke, Newton, etc., etc.

---

[28] George Ticknor, *Life, Letters, and Journals of George Ticknor,* pp. 34–35.

[29] For more, see Joyce Henri Robinson, "An American Cabinet of Curiosities: Thomas Jefferson's 'Indian Hall at Monticello,'" *Winterthus Portfolio,* Vol. 30, No. 1, 1995: pp. 41–55.

> Pictures: a dead man emerging from the tomb to tell his story; The surrender of Cornwallis in October 1781 at Yorktown, Virginia; Diogenes looking for a man; Alexander and Diogenes; Democritus and Heracleitus, etc., etc., etc.
>
> I also saw: A bear's claw from Missouri. This species is larger and much more ferocious than the others; A mammoth's tusk; Several teeth from the same animal; The thighbone of the same. The mammoth's head is constituted, as I said before, of a perfect upper jaw and two lower half-jaws from different animals; one of the latter is much larger than the other. A European coat of mail used by those who fought the Indians early on. With it, they were in no danger of being wounded by their arrows.
>
> Antlers of the American elk and other animals of that sort. ... Two stone busts sculpted by the savages, one representing a man and the other a woman. The faces are hideous and quite coarsely made. They were no doubt used for worship and have a lot in common with the Egyptian and oriental divinities, whose images are engraved in most of the books that deal with those peoples. A small Indian hatchet made from a kind of polished porphyry, with the top in the shape of a pipe; A figure of an animal in the same type of stone; Various petrifactions. Bows, arrows, spears, and lots of objects made by the savages; A life-size marble statue similar to that of Cleopatra. She is lying down, and a snake encircles her left arm. This is a copy from the ancients. Mr. Jefferson believes that she represents Ariadne.[30]

Montlezun adds that he saw busts of Voltaire and Turgot in plaster and a model of the Great Pyramid of Egypt.

In the drawing room, there were busts of Czar Alexander I, Bonaparte, and a sleeping Venus (actually, Ariadne).

In the dining room, there were busts of Washington, Franklin, Lafayette, and Paul Jones. "The collection of pictures is precious," adds Montlezun. There are Possin's Ascension, Raphael's Holy Family, Rubens' Flagellations of Christ, Reni's Crucifixion, "along with several other subjects drawn from the Bible

---

[30] Baron Montlezun, "Montlezun's Account of a Visit to Monticello, 20 September 1816," in *The Papers of Thomas Jefferson, Retirement Series, Vol. 10, May 1816 to 18 January 1817*, ed. J. Jefferson Looney (Princeton: Princeton University Press, 2013), pp. 397–404.

and history, executed by the outstanding masters, and a large number of pints, medals, medallions, etc., of distinguished people and famous events."[31]

I turn now to Jefferson's parlor, which was also bedecked with various pieces of artwork.

Jefferson's parlor was built for social activities from dances and wedding to more modest activities such as playing games, music, casual conversation, and reading. It was a room of 645 square feet in Corinthian Order and with a ceiling just over 18 feet, and it contained some of his most significant pieces of art—according to Jefferson, "Portraits—24; Paintings—17; Medals—10; Busts—2; Miscellaneous—4." Paintings/prints include Daphne being transformed into laurel, Septimia Zenobia, Hector and Andromache, and the Cyclops crafting thunderbolts; American politicians, Benjamin Franklin, John Adams, James Madison, and the Brown and Trumbull Jeffersons; explorers Amerigo Vespucci, Christopher Columbus, Ferdinand Magellan, Fernando Cortez, and Sir Walter Raleigh; foreigners of importance like Castruccio Castracani and Andrea Doria of Italy, Count Rumford of Germany, Marquis de Lafayette and Napoleon Bonaparte of France; biblical events such as Herodiade with the head of John the Baptist, Jephtha and his daughter, a crucifixion, Christ from the cross, the Prodigal Son, Susanna and the elders, Jesus' baptism, Jesus bearing a cross, and Mary Magdalene, penitent; philosophers/scientists Democritus and Heraclitus, Francis Bacon, John Locke, Isaac Newton, and Thomas Paine; grandson Thomas Jefferson Randolph; Trumbull's *Surrender of York*, and two pictures of birds of Virginia. Sculptures include *Hope with Cupid* (on the fireplace mantle, Figure 6-13), Napoleon Bonaparte, and Tsar Alexander I. There are also engravings of Liberty, Louis XVI, Thaddeus Kosciuszko, David Rittenhouse, and James Monroe, as well as other artworks, such as Count Volney in pencil, and artsy memorabilia like medallions.

I end this section with Jefferson's thoughts on framing pictures.

There is a sentiment today by mavens of paintings—and a sound sentiment it is—that no frame should detract from the beauty of a painting, if the painting is of any significance, by showing up that painting—that is, if a painting is worth being framed and hanged, then the frame should not fight with what it frames. Jefferson in an 1818 letter to Trumbull (Jan. 8), offers his thoughts on excessively ornamental frames, but limits his discussion to prints.

Americans are discouraged, says Jefferson, from purchasing prints of by "the tawdry taste prevailing for gew-gaw gilt frames. these flaring things injure greatly the effect of the print. a narrow fillet of gilt on the inner & outer edge,

---

[31] Merrill D. Peterson, ed., *Visitors to Monticello* (Charlottesville: University of Virginia Press, 1989), p. 70.

merely to relieve the black of the main breadth, permits the eye to rest in composure on the field of the print, undisturbed by the glare of a massive, refulgent border." In sort, excessively ornate frames place the focus on the frame, not the print. Moreover, excessively ornate frames are of an expense equal to or more than the print.

What Jefferson says concerning frames one must assume applies also to pedestals for statues or busts.

Fig. 6-13: *Hope with Cupid* (public domain)

Upshot

Says William Howard Adams, "Because he grew up in a province with almost no paintings and sculpture, it is remarkable that Jefferson was able to develop an eye for the visual arts at all."[32] Villatic Virginia in Jefferson's day was a fine-arts desert.

Yet Jefferson did, over time, develop a relatively sharp eye for the visual arts and an attentive ear for harmony, first through books, which shaped his early

[32] William Howard Adams, *The Eye of Thomas Jefferson* (Washington, D.C.: National Gallery of Art, 1976), p. xxxiv.

vision of a fine-arts gallery, never actualized, for Monticello, and then through his peripatetic travels in Europe, which refined his appetite.

In the European tradition of the time, the fine arts were "fine" because of their purity, as it were—that is, they were not contaminated by considerations of practicality. And so, they were the province of the gentry—the wellborn and wealthy—and were measures by which the *bon ton* distinguished themselves from the many.

Though he often cautioned that the fine arts, especially painting and sculpture, were of limited value in a country like America,[33] envisioned to be chiefly agricultural, that did not stop Jefferson from adorning the floors, sills, and walls of Monticello with numerous paintings, prints, statues, busts, medallions, pieces of Natural History, and other artwork. In that, it seems impossible not to fault him for some measure of two-facedness.

Is it possible to rescue Jefferson from the charge of hypocrisy?

Early in life, Jefferson, I suspect, was moved by a passion to showcase certain budding aristocratic ideals: hence, for instance, his choice of the location of Monticello atop a monticule—though as we saw in chapter 3 that the mountaintop was special to him since his childhood—and his early catalog of time-tested art for it as a source of pleasure for visitors and as evidence of his taste.

However, things changed when Jefferson, after involvement in numerous cases of litigation concerning land as a lawyer, became a politician and began to delve into, adopt, and refine his republican ideals around the principle of *vox populi*. He did not cease to love and enjoy art, but in the main, the sorts of pieces he collected were a reflection of his republican standards, based on his moral ideals: freedom of speech, partnership of science and politics, and fighting for liberty. Yet it would be difficult to make a case for the 19 pieces he wished to collect in his circa 1771 catalog to be anything more than aesthetic self-promotion—*viz.*, immodest evidence of Jefferson's aesthetic refinement as a young man.

The gallery of pieces that Jefferson eventually would showcase at Monticello after he returned from France in 1789 was part of a story he wished to tell of a struggling young nation and the personages who helped birth it, and that story was to be told in an aesthetically pleasant, self-indulgent manner. Writes William Howard Adams, "Sculpture, like architecture, had a symbolic, elevating role to play in a republic to remind a free people of its achievements and

---

[33] E.g., Thomas Jefferson, "Travelling Notes for Mr. Rutledge and Mr. Shippen," in *Thomas Jefferson: Writings*, ed. Merrill D. Peterson (New York: Library of America, 1984), pp. 659–60.

sacrifices, and it would be important for future generations to have the very best examples of creative genius."[34] Jefferson sought out the best European and American artists to tell that story.[35]

Here perhaps we find an answer to a question that has perplexed and continues to perplex historians: why Jefferson ended his autobiography with the French Revolution. The answer is certainly etiologically complex, and I proffer here another piece, what I take to be a significant one, of the etiological explanation.

When he returned from France in 1789, Jefferson had 86 crates of household goods to be shipped back to Monticello at the discretion of William Short, and there were many pieces of fine art among those goods. Unlike his proposed gallery circa 1771, those items were not to be some of the most remarkable pieces of artwork by some of the most acclaimed artists over millennia. The sculptures, portraits, and artifacts that he brought to Virginia were mostly contemporaneous, and the pieces were part of the story, ever in the making, of Jefferson's own struggle on behalf of his country for liberty. Thus, the pieces he acquired were personal, and as he resettled in America, he would incessantly add to his "museum."

With the enlargement and maturity of his museum, there was no longer any need to continue his autobiography, which I suspect he increasingly found to be an onerous task, given that it was undertaken late in life. That story could be in some sense fullest explained by the pieces bedecking Monticello—pieces like the painting of beloved grandson Thomas Jefferson Randolph by friend Charles Willson Peale and Marquis de Lafayette by *pientre du roi* Joseph Boze—and by Monticello itself: *viz.*, its walls, its ceilings, its floors, its brickwork, its gardens, its fields, its grove, and its walkways. Monticello was alive so long as Jefferson lived, and the putting up and pulling down he was so fond of doing was ever for the sake of its revitalization. There could be no once-and-for-all version of Monticello, any more than there could be an once-and-for-all version of Thomas Jefferson, for him and today for us.

Still Jefferson would never have thought to have Monticello void of art. If we follow the partitioning of Francis Bacon adopted by Thomas Jefferson, Fine Arts, concerning imagination, was deemed one of the three axial categories of learning in his day—History, concerning memory, and Philosophy, concerning

---

[34] William Howard Adams, *The Eye of Thomas Jefferson*, p. xxxvii.

[35] It is illustrative to note that from the evidence that we have at our disposal, Poplar Forest was quite unlike Monticello. Jefferson did not concern himself with adorning it with works of art. It was a place for relaxed living.

reason, being the others—and no one in his day could be considered learned and rounded without some degree of immersion in Fine Arts.

Given his belief that that man-crafted beauty which was of utmost utility was most beautiful, Jefferson opted, if only subconsciously, for some sort of reconciliation between beauty and usefulness apropos of the fine arts, with a lean toward usefulness. The portraits and sculptures that he collected and showcased, unlike his first plan for a collection for Monticello, were mostly contemporary and they told the story of the birth of liberty in the United States and its contagion in the world. Bacon, Locke, and Newton were chosen because they were his philosophical/scientific heroes—each paving the way for liberty through augmented understanding of nature and society—and Rittenhouse he considered the American Newton. Vespucci, Magellan, Cortez, Columbus, and Raleigh were the early explorers of the American continents. Washington, Franklin, Paine, Adams, Madison, Monroe, and even Hamilton were early patriots in the American cause.[36] Even biblical themes were likely chosen for philosophical/political reasons—e.g., John the Baptist's beheading is an indication of the horrors associated with lack of free speech.

If this reading is correct, then Jefferson collected works of art like he collected books, and later in life, like he collected poems: Concern for their utility trumped any aesthetic consideration and their utility at Monticello concerned telling the story of the efflorescence of liberty in the youthful United States and the advance of knowledge in Enlightenment times. Still, as with the case of the pavilions at the University of Virginia, there was nothing prohibitive about both telling a momentous story and cultivating aesthetic refinement at the same time. That said, we see a similarity between Jefferson's cultivation of painting and sculpture and poetry. As his interest in "fine" poems gave way to an interest in useful poems, so it was too with paintings, sculptures, and sketches and other artifacts.

---

[36] As one enters Monticello, one is greeted by a bust of Jefferson facing a bust of Alexander Hamilton—"opposed in death as in life"—both by Italian sculptor Giuseppe Ceracchi. The statue of Hamilton is life-size, while the statue of Jefferson is much larger, and that suggests not merely Jefferson's opposition, but political victory over Hamilton. Neither was listed by Jefferson in his "Catalog of Paintings, &c."

Chapter VII

The Art of Music

"If music be the food of love, play on, / Give me excess of it; that surfeiting, / The appetite may sicken, and so die."[1] ~ William Shakespeare

On February 1, 1770, Thomas Jefferson's house at Shadwell was razed by fire. His books and papers of account were lost in the fire, and that makes biography concerning his early life a labyrinthine task. We know that Jefferson was devastated about the loss of his books—quite unsurprising, from such a philobiblist—estimated at some 200 pounds sterling. "Would to God it had been the money [then] had it never cost me a sigh!" wrote Jefferson in a letter (21 Feb. 1770) to boyhood friend John Page. Yet according to early biographer Henry S. Randall, Jefferson was fond of relating an anecdote of a different sort apropos of the incident. When an out-of-breath slave rushed to him to inform him of the devastation, Jefferson said, "Were none of my books saved?" "No, master, but *we saved the fiddle*!"[2]

Jefferson's fondness of relating the story about his fiddle speaks abundantly about the man's love of music. Although his books were foremost in his mind, his violin was not far behind the books.

Jefferson had a Stoic demeanor—as I note earlier, many who visited the man for the first time relate that he came off at first "cold and reserved" or "at first serious, nay even cold"[3]—but to the right sort of visitor, he would speedily warm and then the time spent together through polite conversation would be quite agreeable. When not engaged in conversation, he tended to sing or hum. Says overseer Edmund Bacon: "I have rode over the plantation, I reckon, a thousand times with Mr. Jefferson, and when he was not talking he was nearly always humming some tune, or singing in a low tone to himself. And it was just so with [daughter] Mrs. Randolph. As she attended to her duties about the house, she seemed to be always in a happy mood. She had always her father's

---

[1] William Shakespeare, *Twelfth Night*, ed. Barbara A. Mowat and Paul Werstine (New York: Simon & Shuster, 2019), p. 7.
[2] Henry S. Randall, *The Life of Thomas Jefferson*, Vol. 1 (New York: Derby & Jackson, 1858), p. 59.
[3] Marquis de Chastellux and Lieutenant Francis Hall, in Merrill D. Peterson, ed., *Visitors to Monticello* (Charlottesville: University Press of Virginia, 1989), pp. 28 and 74.

pleasant smile and was nearly always humming some tune."[4] Thus, Jefferson's temperament was, as it were, "songful," and a songful temperament could only have been equable, contented, and perhaps even unflappable.

That again comes out of Bacon's memoirs. "His countenance was always mild and pleasant. You never saw it ruffled. No odds what happened, it always maintained the same expression." Bacon, for instance, relates an incident where a large freshet swept away a dam Jefferson had built and in which he had invested thousands of dollars. "'Well, sir,' said he, just as calm and quiet as though nothing had happened, 'we can't make a new dam this summer, but we will get Lewis' ferryboat, and with our own, and get the hands from all the quarters, and boat in rock enough in place of the dam to answer for the present and next summer, I will send to Baltimore and get ship bolts, and we will make a dam that the freshet can't wash away.'"[5]

This chapter is about the fine art, music. I begin, perhaps somewhat unusually, with Jefferson's love of the music of nature—*viz.*, his love of birds—turn to his early education in music, and end with some thoughts on the status of music as a fine art. Music, in some sense, posed a singular problem as a fine art for Jefferson. If the best of the fine arts were those which combined beauty with functionality—a handsome tree could also offer shade from oppressive summer's heat, a painting could tell a story, and a poem could inspire moral activity—it is unclear just what functionality music could have had for Jefferson, a dyed-in-the-wool musical man throughout his life. At the chapter's end, I offer some Kamesian thoughts on the significance of music in Jefferson's, or any person's, life.

"Filled with nightingales in full song"

Jefferson's Love of Birds

Plutarch, in "The Life of Lycurgus," writes of the Spartan practice of laconics. In one instance, someone recommended to a Spartan that he go and see a performer who brilliantly mimicked a nightingale. Hutcheson, as we saw in chapter 1, would remark that the performer's art was genuine only insofar as his mimicry was close to the real thing. Yet the Spartan merely replied, "Sir, I have heard the nightingale itself."[6] The implication, *pace* Hutcheson, is that a

---

[4] Edmund Bacon, "The Private Life of Jefferson," in *Jefferson at Monticello*, ed. James A. Bear (Charlottesville: University Press of Virginia, 1967), pp. 83–84.
[5] Edmund Bacon, "The Private Life of Jefferson," pp. 71–72.
[6] Plutarch, *The Lives of the Noble Grecian and Romans*, trans. Thomas North (New York: Heritage Press, [1930] 1941), p. 155.

copy, howsoever good, is inferior to the real thing, so there is no need to attend to the copy, when the real thing is nearby.

Jefferson would have agreed. On May 21, 1787, and while sailing on the Canal Royal en Languedoc (today, Canal du Midi)—a 150-mile long canal in the south of France and considered to be one of the largest architectural achievements of the time—Jefferson took some time to pen a letter to his daughter Martha, who was with him in France, but with her sister Maria at l'Abbaye Royale de Panthemont, a prestigious convent where she was schooled with some 60 other girls in music, drawing, dancing, and Italian. The waters are limpid, begins Jefferson, and the skies are cloudless, "and on each hand a row of nightingales in full chorus." Their singing then brings to mind another delightful episode, where nightingales regaled Jefferson with song at the Fountain of Vaucluse at Avignon (Figure 7-1; painting by Hubert Robert, 1783, at Musée Calvet in Avignon). Jefferson, fatigued, arrived at Avignon and sat for repose by the fountain. "It gushes, of the size of a river, from a secluded valley of the mountains, the ruins of Petrarch's chateau being perched on a rock two hundred feet perpendicular above. To add to the enchantment of the scene, every tree and bush was filled with nightingales in full song."[7]

Fig. 7-1: *Fountain at Vaucluse* (public domain)

---

[7] See also TJ to William Short on the same day. There he adds: "What a bird the nightingale would be in the climates of America! We must colonize him thither."

Jefferson then enjoins his daughter to attend to the nightingales that might be perched and singing in the trees of the convent, for it is the time of year for their songs. By attending to the nightingales, Martha then will be able to recognize their music and compare it to that of the mockingbirds of Virginia. "The latter has the advantage of singing through a great part of the year, whereas the nightingale sings about five or six weeks in the spring, and a still shorter term, and with a more feeble voice, in the fall."

The letter is significant for several reasons. First, repose for Jefferson was not merely a matter of recovery through rest. Jefferson preferred to find an enchanting spot for repose: a gushing fountain in a secluded valley, nestled in the mountains, with the ruins of the chateau of Petrarch "two hundred feet perpendicular above." The "nightingales in full song," something that others might not have noticed or that might have been a botheration to them, is for Jefferson extra delight. Second, Jefferson bids Martha to attend to the music of the nightingale and to compare it to the Virginian mockingbird. He expresses here no preference for the music of one over the other, but notes that mockingbirds sing for most of the year, while nightingales sing only for five or six weeks in the spring and a few more weeks in the fall, though then with an enfeebled voice. One might say that his tendency to arithmetize in the letter shows that he cannot just leave alone a beautiful moment and appreciate it without critical commentary of some sort. That might be the case, but it also might be the case that he expects his daughter to develop a discerning ear for the music of nature that surrounds her wherever she might be.

Jefferson, elsewhere, does express preference for mockingbirds. In an earlier letter (TJ to Abigail Adams, 1785 June 21), he says, "I heard there [in France] the Nightingale in all it's perfection: and I do not hesitate to pronounce that in America it would be deemed a bird of the third rank only, our mockingbird [Linnaeus, *Turdus polyglottus*[8]], and fox-coloured thrush [Linnaeus, *Turdus rufus*[9]] being unquestionably superior to it."

Years later, Jefferson writes to his daughter Maria (9 Mar. 1791) from Philadelphia and castigates her for not writing more to him. He then adds: "On the 27th of February I saw blackbirds and robin-redbreasts, and on the 7th of his month I heard frogs for the first time this year. Have you noted the first appearance of these things at Monticello?" The music of birds was not only enjoyable in itself, but also the first songs of certain birds marked out different times of a season for Jefferson. Moreover, the music of birds very likely served as Jefferson's alarm clock. Though Jefferson is noted to have arisen when the

[8] "Many-tongued thrush."

[9] "Reddish-brown thrush," another bird with a large musical "vocabulary."

rays of the sun reached the clock near his bed,[10] he doubtless woke to the varied songs of the Virginian birds just prior to the sun hitting his clock.

Jefferson loved birds—especially the mockingbird, which he considered a "superior being"[11] and of which he had at least four as pets. His favorite mockingbird was Dick, which stayed with him in his solitary hours of study. Margaret Bayard Smith describes his cabinet of the President's House. There were carpenter's tools, garden tools, maps, globes, charts, and numerous books. There too was Dick.

> In the window recesses [there] were stands for the flowers and plants which it was his delight to attend and among his roses and geraniums was suspended the cage of his favorite mocking-bird, which he cherished with particular fondness, not only for its melodious powers, but for its uncommon intelligence and affectionate disposition, of which qualities he gave surprising instances. It was the constant companion of his solitary and studious hours. Whenever he was alone he opened the cage and let the bird fly about the room. After flitting for a while from one object to another, it would alight on his table and regale him with its sweetest notes, or perch on his shoulder and take its food from his lips. Often when he retired to his chamber it would hop up the stairs after him and while he took his siesta, would sit on his couch and pour forth its melodious strains. How he loved this bird![12]

Jefferson doubtless loved mockingbirds because Jefferson loved music and they were hearty and versatile musicians with an endless repertoire of songs. They mimicked animals around them, usually birds—e.g., cardinals, blue jays, shrikes, blackbirds, wrens, orioles, killdeer, and hawks—but sometimes even other animals such as frogs and today other sounds such as car alarms. While in France on January 24, 1785, Jefferson records that he paid 18 francs for a bird organ (aka, serinette, Figure 7-2)—a miniature barrel organ that would sit in a box of about six inches square, with wind pipes and a hand crank, that would play a variety of tunes that birds could mimic—doubtless for his mockingbirds.[13] The songs of mockingbirds are customarily short whistles, but they also trill, rasp, and scold, and can extend a song for as long as 20

---

[10] TJ to Vine Utley, 21 Mar. 1819.

[11] TJ to Martha Jefferson, 10 June 1793.

[12] Margaret Bayard Smith, *The First Forty Years of Washington Society* (New York: Charles Scribner's Sons, 1906), p. 57.

[13] Thomas Jefferson, "Memorandum Books, 1785," *Founders Online*, National Archives, https://founders.archives.gov/documents/Jefferson/02-01-02-0019, accessed 29 May 2020.

seconds. Songs are generally repeated a few or more times, before the birds move on to another.[14]

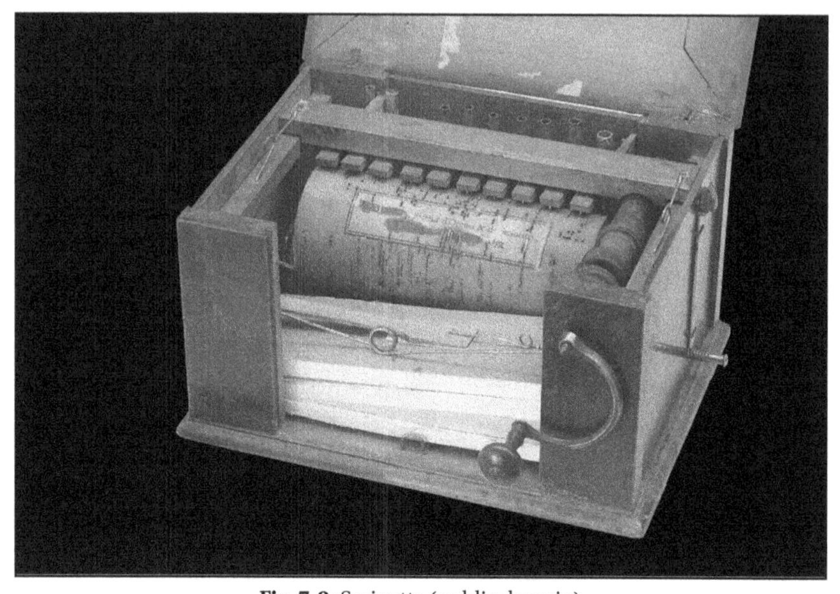

Fig. 7-2: Serinette (public domain)

As the letter to Abigail Adams intimates, Jefferson's ornithophilia was not on account of bird's physical beauty—blue jays exceed in pulchritude mockingbirds and nightingales—but on account of the pleasantness and versatility of the music they made. In that too, he prized practical beauty, that is, utility, over absolute beauty. In that too, he followed William Hogarth, who noted that nature tended to pair beauty with utility. "In nature's machines how wonderfully do we see beauty and use go hand in hand."[15] That is not to say that he misprized the striking coloration of many birds—e.g., the Northern Cardinal, the Red-bellied Woodpecker, the American Goldfinch, and the Eastern Bluebird—but he valued birds' musical abilities more than their looks, hence his ranking of thrushes ahead of European nightingales.

---

[14] Mark Mancini, "Why Mockingbird's Mock," How Stuff Works, https://animals.howstuffworks.com/birds/why-mockingbirds-mock.htm, accessed 22 May 2020; Mark Mancini, "Northern Mockingbird," All about Birds, https://www.allaboutbirds.org/guide/Northern_Mockingbird/sounds, accessed 22 May 2020.

[15] William Hogarth, *The Analysis of Beauty* (Cambridge: Oxford University Press, [1753] 1955), p. 86.

Jefferson's love of birds is also evident in Query VI of *Notes on Virginia*, where he proffers a list of 93 Virginian birds, drawn from Mark Catesby, and adds, at the end of the list, 34 more birds, missed by Catesby.[16]

Were he alive today, he would unquestionably appreciate and be fascinated by our cell phones and the many uses to which they can be put. Yet I am certain that he would be much disturbed and dismayed by our inability to stroll quietly, though vigilantly, through a natural park without earphones and music, downloaded to our cell phones. He likely considered the music of nature to be superior to the music of man.

"They took their hats and retired, to return no more"

Jefferson's Early introduction to Music

"Although he referred to music as a 'delightful recreation,' it was far from a casual or peripheral concern," writes Douglas Wilson.[17] That sentiment is spot on. Music was an art to which Jefferson was exposed early in life and it was a passion throughout his life. He was dyed-in-the-wool musical.

Jefferson's exposure to music began very early in life. His father, Peter Jefferson, a self-made man, was insistent that his son should be a well-rounded gentleman, so the fine arts could not be neglected. By the time he was a teenager, Jefferson was fairly proficient with the violin and could play both Classical music, and like Patrick Henry,[18] fiddle tunes. He would become sufficiently accomplished by his matriculation at William and Mary College to be invited by Lieutenant Governor Francis Fauquier to be among the amateur musicians to perform weekly at the Governor's Palace.

What was music in Colonial America like?

With the diversity of the colonial population, there came a diversity of musical tastes. Colonists, of course, brought with them the popular music and folk songs of their culture, but also the music of Classical composers such as Bach, Haydn, and Mozart.

Some Colonists made music a profession by proffering musical entertainments like recitals, operas, choirs, and orchestral performances to Colonial audiences, starved for musical enjoyment. Other musicians were

---

[16] Thomas Jefferson, *Notes on Virginia*, ed. William Peden (Chapel Hill: University of North Carolina Press, 1954), pp. 65–70.
[17] Douglas L. Wilson, introduction to *Thomas Jefferson: Musician & Violinist*, by Sandor Salgo (Charlottesville: Thomas Jefferson Foundation, 2000), p. xii.
[18] Henry also played the flute.

itinerant and tutored the well-to-do. Businesses opened to cater to the musical appetence of Americans by publishing and printing music. Others got into the business, part-time or fulltime, of constructing instruments or of fixing or maintaining them.[19]

Other Colonial musicians, like Jefferson, maintained an amateur status. Some were amateurs because they possessed insufficient skill to make music a profession, and so they played when they could for whatever income they might earn. Among them, there were those who had no formal training, but could "play by ear" (e.g., Patrick Henry)—that is, blend in and harmonize with formally trained musicians. Others were amateurs because they were gentlemen and a gentleman could not accept money for music. Jefferson fit into the latter class. Says Cynthia Collins: "He had upper-class social status and did not use music as a source of income. Though his ability to read music and his violin training were excellent, because of his position in society, he never performed for payment. He generally played and sang for enjoyment at gatherings with family and friends. When he played in public, he played as a patron or in benefit concerts."[20]

Early in life, Jefferson cultivated his love of music with his older sister Jane (b. 1740), to whom he was much attached and who died at the youthful age of 25.[21] Says Dumas Malone, "She, more than any other member of the family, stimulated his boyish ambitions and encouraged him in his reading and his cultivation of music."[22] Henry S. Randall says that Jane, "a singer of uncommon skill and sweetness," excelled in the singing of Psalms of the Church of England. "Many a winter evening, round the family fireside, and many a soft summer twilight, on the wooded banks of the Rivanna, heard their voices, accompanied by the notes of his violin, thus ascending together."[23]

While at William and Mary College from 1760 to 1762, Jefferson befriended philosopher Dr. William Small (1734–1775), lawyer and lifelong friend George Wythe (1726–1806), and Governor Francis Fauquier (1703–1768), who, after noticing his young friend's talent for the violin, soon invited Jefferson to

---

[19] Helen Cripe, *Thomas Jefferson and Music* (Charlottesville: University Press of Virginia, 1974), 14.

[20] Cynthia Collins, "Thomas Jefferson: Ambassador for Musical Education in Early America," *The Journal of Thomas Jefferson's Life and Times*, Vol. 2, No. 2, 2019.

[21] When Jane, unwed, prematurely died on October 1, 1765, Jefferson was crushed. He crafted an epitaph: "O Jane, best of youthful women, / Ah, taken prematurely in the prime of youthful vigor, / Let the earth be light on you; / farewell forever and forever."

[22] Dumas Malone, *Jefferson the Virginian* (Boston: Little, Brown and Company, 1948), 39.

[23] Henry S. Randall, *The Life of Thomas Jefferson*, Vol. 1 (New York: Derby & Jackson, 1858), 41.

participate in the weekly amateur ensemble at the Governor's Palace. Of Fauquier, Jefferson says, "The Governor was musical also & a good performer, and associated me with 2. or 3. other amateurs in his weekly concerts."[24]

Jefferson's 12-years-younger brother, Randolph (1755–1815), was also to some extent musical. An entry in Jefferson's account book (3 May 1773) shows that Randolph took lessons in the violin from Jefferson's tutor Francis Alberti (d. 1785),[25] a violinist and harpsichordist who had immigrated to America from Italy.[26] Jefferson first met Alberti while at William and Mary College in Williamsburg. According to Henry Randall, Jefferson convinced Alberti to remove to Charlottesville, where the latter instructed Jefferson and members of his family for many years.[27] Slave Isaac Jefferson, in his memoirs, says, "Old Masser's brother, Mass Randall, was a mighty simple man: used to come out among black people, play the fiddle and dance half the night; hadn't much more sense than Isaac."[28]

Mutual love of music was one critical reason that Jefferson was able to woo and win the favor of the young widow Martha Wayles Skelton (1748–1782)—"she favored Jefferson over several other suitors in part because he shared her love of music"[29]—whom he married on January 1, 1772, and who could play several keyboard instruments as well as the guitar. According to oral tradition, two rivals for Martha's hand met at her doorstep at The Forest. Writes Henry S. Randall: "They were shown into a room from which they heard her harpsichord and voice, accompanied by Mr. Jefferson's violin and voice, in the passages of a touching song. They listened for a stanza or two. ... They took their hats and retired, to return no more on the same errand!"[30]

On February 20, 1771, Jefferson asks Richmond businessman Thomas Adams to order a clavichord for his wife-to-be when Adams arrived in London. "The things I have desired you to purchase for me I would beg you to hasten, particularly the Clavichord which I have directed to be purchased in Hamburgh [*sic*] because they are better made there, and much cheaper." Yet

---

[24] TJ to Louis H. Girardin, 15 Jan. 1815.

[25] Thomas Jefferson, *Thomas Jefferson and His Unknown Brother Randolph* (Charlottesville: University of Virginia Press, 1942), 8.

[26] Thomas Jefferson's Monticello, "Francis Alberti," https://www.monticello.org/site/research-and-collections/francis-alberti, accessed 25 May 2020.

[27] Henry S. Randall, *The Life of Thomas Jefferson,* Vol. 1, 131–32.

[28] This is a passage that suggests that Randolph, not Thomas, fathered children with Sally Hemings. Isaac Jefferson, "Memoirs," *Jefferson at Monticello,* ed. James A. Bear, Jr. (Charlottesville: University Press of Virginia, 1967), 22.

[29] Merrill D. Peterson, *Thomas Jefferson and the New Nation: A Biography* (Oxford: Oxford University Press, 1970), 27.

[30] Henry S. Randall, *The Life of Thomas Jefferson,* Vol. 1, 64.

the Colonists at the time were in the midst of a series of Non-importation Agreements, which severely restricted trade with the mother country. Those agreements were in response to taxes, deemed unjustly excessive, imposed unwillingly on them. When Adams arrives in London, Jefferson sends to him another missive (1 June 1771), in which he notes that "the restrictions will be taken off everything but the dutied articles." He then mentions the clavichord. "I have since seen a Forte-piano and am charmed with it. Send me this instrument then instead of the Clavichord. Let the case be of fine mahogany, solid, not veneered… and the workmanship of the whole very handsome, and worthy the acceptance of a lady for whom I intend it." The forte-piano that caught Jefferson's attention was an early version of today's piano. It was invented by Bartolomeo Cristofori at the start of the eighteenth century.

In his early years with Martha, Jefferson spent hours each day in practice of music, and he wished, as was the case with architecture and pleasure gardening, to cultivate that fine art in America. In a letter to Italian agronomist Giovanni Fabbroni (8 June 1778), Jefferson says: "If there is a gratification which I envy any people in this world it is to your country its music. This is the favorite passion of my soul, and fortune has cast my lot in a country where it is in a state of deplorable barbarism." He adds that "a passion for music might be reconciled with that economy which we are obliged to observe."

Jefferson then bids Fabbroni to consider exporting musicians of "sobriety and good nature" to America. "In a country where like yours music is cultivated and practised by every class of men I suppose there might be found persons of those trades who could perform on the French horn, clarinet or hautboy & bassoon, so that one might have a band of two French horns, two clarinets, & hautboys & a bassoon, without enlarging their domestic expenses." He concludes, "If you think such a plan practicable, and will be so kind as to inform me what will be necessary to be done on my part I will take care that it shall be done."

During his tenure as governor (1779–1781), Jefferson had to accommodate some 4,000 transplanted German and British prisoners of war in Charlottesville. When the prisoners, being removed from Boston, were eventually situated—the scenario in Charlottesville in January 1779 was at first despicable, as the barracks were not readied and meat was scarce—and the officers settled into residences rented or newly built, Jefferson, who became governor on June 1, treated the captured officers with singular civility. He entertained them, loaned out books to them, and even formed ensembles with the musicians among them. German officer Jacob Rubsamen wrote of his experience as prisoner of war:

> I have free Access to a Copious and well chosen Library of Colo. Jefferson's[,] Governor of Virginia. As all Virginians are fond of Music, he is particularly so. You will find in his House an Elegant harpsichord Piano forte and some Violins. The latter he performs well upon himself, the former his Lady touches very skillfully and who, is in all Respects a very agreable [*sic*] Sensible and Accomplished Lady.[31]

Under the direction of Governor Jefferson, the prisoners, officers especially, were only nominally prisoners. They were well treated. "Public questions were never discussed. Music was the happy *divertissement* when the Europeans were guests at Monticello."[32]

As minister plenipotentiary in France, Jefferson wrote to Charles Bellini (30 Sept. 1785), about the fine arts in Europe: "Were I to proceed to tell you how much I enjoy their architecture, sculpture, painting, music, I should want words. It is in these arts they shine. The last of them particularly is an enjoiment, the deprivation of which with us cannot be calculated. I am almost ready to say it is the only thing which from my heart I envy them, and which in spight of all the authority of the decalogue I do covet."

In Paris, Jefferson certainly availed himself of "everything musical that Paris had to offer." He saw Pierre Beaumarchais' *Le mariage de Figaro* on August 4, 1786, which was the must-see musical at the time.[33] His daughters were given harpsichord lessons from the celebrated harpsichordist and organists Claude Balbaster, as well as guitar and dancing lessons. He bought music and attended concerts given by some of the foremost violinists of the day: Rodolphe Keutzer, Giovanni Battista Biotti, and Madame Gautherot.[34]

It was also in Paris that Jefferson met Maria Cosway (1760–1838, Figure 7-3, self-portrait), who was not only a recognized painter but also an accomplished musician. Married to artist Richard Cosway, who was 20 years her senior and recognized by many as a rake—it was mostly a marriage of convenience, as Maria's mother, upon the death of her husband, recognized the social utility of such a marriage—she sang and composed music and played artfully the harp and harpsichord. Writes John Kaminski, "The Cosways regularly entertained the *haut monde* in their fabulously decorated mansion

---

[31] Merrill D. Peterson, ed., *Visitors to Monticello* (Charlottesville: University Press of Virginia, 1989), 8–9.

[32] Merrill D. Peterson, *Thomas Jefferson and the New Nation*, 164.

[33] John B. Boles, *Jefferson: Architect of American Liberty* (New York: Basic Books, 2017), p. 134.

[34] Helen Cripe, *Thomas Jefferson and Music*, 22–23 and 35. See also her Appendix III, "Jefferson's Note on Tickets Purchased for Musical Performances while Minister to France," pp. 131–35.

on Pall Mall. Maria would sing and play the harp and harpsichord, often to music she composed."[35] As many of the well-to-do became smitten with Maria, practiced in the art of coquetry, they would agree to have their portrait painted by Richard so that they could see more of her. Maria focused her time more on music than painting, as her husband forbade her a professional career in the latter.

Fig. 7-3: Maria Cosway, self-portrait (public domain)

After they were introduced in 1786 by John Trumbull, Jefferson too became smitten with Cosway and he would spend whatever time he could free, from mid-August to mid-September, to be with her. In his infamous and lengthy *billet doux* to Cosway (12 Oct. 1786), Jefferson's "Heart" notes that Cosway is of utmost moral integrity and that she is in full possession of "music, modesty, beauty, and that softness of disposition which is the ornament of her sex and charm of ours." It is clear that her musical abilities, like those of his departed wife's, were a major reason for attraction.

[35] John P. Kaminski, introduction to *Thomas Jefferson and Maria Cosway, Jefferson in Love,* ed. John P. Kaminski (Lanham, MD: Rowman & Littlefield, 2001), 11.

Jefferson's preference for women with musical abilities too is evident in an early letter to boyhood friend Will Fleming (c. Oct. 1763). Jefferson writes: "Last Saturday I left Ned Carter's where I had been happy in other good company, but particularly that of Miss Jenny Taliaferro: and though I can view the beauties of this world with the most philosophical indifference, I could not but be sensible of the justice of the character you had given me of her. She has, in my opinion, a great resemblance of Nancy Wilton, but prettier. I was vastly pleased with her playing on the spinnette and singing, and could not help calling to mind those sublime verses of the Cumberland genius: 'Oh! how I was charmed to see / Orpheus' music all in thee.'"

Jefferson's "career" as amateur violinist for the most part ended in his Paris years. The ruinous moment was the day that he fractured his wrist in 1786. Though we know nothing definitive apropos of his talent with the violin, emeritus professor and violinist Sandor Salgo maintains that Jefferson must have been quite good. "Mastery of the violin was surely consistent with his basic drive towards excellence in all things. ... When Thomas Jefferson took up his violin he must have set the highest standards for himself as a performer on that instrument."[36] He later adds, "Until he broke his wrist, Thomas Jefferson was an excellent violinist—and could well have been a professional musician, had not such a vocation been inappropriate for an eighteenth-century Virginia gentleman."[37] It was not gentlemanly for a brewstered Virginian to accept money for performing musically.

While Jefferson was president of the United States, the country had a Marine Band, founded during John Adams' administration. The band would perform at varied celebrations, but with uneven results. One story recounts President Jefferson riding his horse with Lt. Col. William Ward Burrows, who established the band, and suggesting ways to improve the band. Jefferson fell back on his 1778 plan to Fabronni that Burrows recruit and bring in Italian musicians. Burrows did that. He enjoined Capt. John Hall, who was in the Mediterranean Sea at the time, to enlist musical Italians into the Marines and then to bring them back to America. In September 1805, around 15 musicians arrived in Washington, and of them, some were eventually integrated into the Marine Band.[38]

Passion for music Jefferson passed on to his daughters and to his granddaughters. While in France, he writes to John Paradise in London (25 May 1786) about purchase of a harpsichord for Martha: "I have yet another favour to ask, which is to get Kirkman [*sic*] to make for me one of his best

---

[36] Sandor Salgo, *Thomas Jefferson: Musician & Violinist,* 14–15.
[37] Sandor Salgo, *Thomas Jefferson: Musician & Violinist,* 50.
[38] Helen Cripe, *Thomas Jefferson and Music,* 28–30.

harpsichords with a double set of keys, and the machine on the top resembling a Venetian blind for giving a swell. The case to be of mahogany, solid not vineered, without any inlaid work but deriving all it's beauty from the elegance of the wood." Both Martha and Maria would eventually own Kirckman harpsichords—the latter, receiving hers in 1789. "Do not neglect your music," he says to his daughter Martha (4 Apr. 1790). "It will be a companion which will sweeten many hours of life to you." For granddaughter Virginia Randolph Trist, he purchased a guitar, which he had desired for a long time. "One morning, on going down to breakfast," writes she, "I saw the guitar. It had been sent up by Mrs. ***** for us to look at, and grandpapa told me that if I would promise to learn to play on it I should have it. I shall never forget my ecstasies. I was but fourteen years old, and the first wish of my heart was unexpectedly gratified."[39]

As music was an important part of Jefferson's life, he made sure that his daughters and grandchildren, females especially, had access to music, musical instruments, and musical training.

"Music is invaluable where a person has an ear"

The Status of Music as a Fine Art

Thomas Jefferson, it seems, never made music the object of critical analysis, as he did, for instance, language,[40] statuary,[41] pleasure gardening,[42] and poetry.[43] In keeping with his passion for architectural creation and his enjoyment of the process more than the product, Jefferson also had a process-orientation vis-à-vis music. "So far as the present available evidence goes, musician Thomas Jefferson was much more articulate about the processes of musical production than about the enjoyment of the musical product; his delight was more in the how than in the what of music."[44] As was the case with architecture, Jefferson enjoyed making music more than he enjoyed listening to it. It is not that he never appreciated a finished product, but instead, he thought that a finished product, like a person's character, could always be improved.

---

[39] Virginia J. Randoph Trist to Nicholas P. Trist, 26 May 1839, in Henry S. Randall, *Life of Thomas Jefferson, Vol. 3* (Boston, 1858), 349–51.
[40] TJ to John Waldo, 16 Aug. 1813.
[41] TJ to William Hamilton, 31 July 1806.
[42] Thomas Jefferson, "A Tour of Some of the Gardens of England," *Thomas Jefferson: Writings*, ed. Merrill D. Peterson (New York: Library of America, 1984), pp. 624–28.
[43] "Thoughts on English Prosody," in *Thomas Jefferson: Writings*, 593–622.
[44] H.M. Kallen, "The Arts and Thomas Jefferson," 273.

Jefferson, as we have seen, was by nature musical. He was a skilled violinist, who also could play the cello. He participated in weekly concerts at the governor's residence, while at William and Mary College. While married, he and Martha would sing together. She would play her piano; he, his violin. He was wont to sing or hum throughout the day. Granddaughter Ellen Wayles Coolidge reports. "My chamber at Monticello was over his, and I used not unfrequently [*sic*] to hear him humming old tunes, generally Scotch songs, but sometimes Italian airs or hymns."[45] Slave Isaac Jefferson says: "He kept three fiddles; played in the arternoons and sometimes arter supper. ... Mr. Jefferson always singing when ridin' or walkin'; hardly see him anywhar outdoors but what he was a-singin'. Had a fine clear voice; sung minits and sich; fiddled in the parlor."[46]

Music as a fine art, for Jefferson, had a special status, which comes out superbly in a letter to granddaughter Ellen Wayles Randolph (19 Oct. 1807): "I have nothing better to send you than an old song. But indeed, I could send you nothing better. It was much in vogue when I was of your age, and has lost nothing of it's pathos by time. It shews the wonderful sources of comfort which open themselves to every condition of man."

For Jefferson, music was not as significant as gardening and architecture—in addition to beauty, art in gardening could also provide food or shade and art in architecture could have the function of durability—yet, losing none of its pathos over time, it had a more elevated status than painting and sculpture, both of which seemed to require considerable cultivation to be enjoyed. Music in some form could be enjoyed by all, and it had an uncanny capacity to rest and rejuvenate, or in the words of Lord Kames, "not only to revive the spirits when sunk by sensual gratification, but also to relax them when overstrained in any violent pursuit."[47] And so, while it perhaps theoretically occupied a fine-arts status in the manner of sculpture and painting, it was for Jefferson as significant as gardening and architecture, and thus, warranted large cultivation in America.

Music was especially important for genteel women in Enlightenment times. They were to be particularly educated in the fine arts, precisely because they were by definition undertaken for appreciation of beauty. In a word, men were to be chiefly useful, and women, chiefly beautiful. We have only to revisit Jefferson's description of the virtues of Maria Cosway: her music, modesty, beauty, and softness of disposition.

---

[45] Cyntian H. Burton, *Jefferson Vindicated* (Cynthia H. Burton, 2005), 100.

[46] Isaac Jefferson, "Memoirs of a Monticello Slave," *Jefferson at Monticello*, ed. James A. Bear, Jr. (Charlottesville: University Press of Virginia, 1967), 3.

[47] Henry Home, *Elements of Criticism* (New York: A.S. Barnes & Burr, 1865 [1762]), 22–23.

Jefferson might have been a futurist when it came to governmental reforms, but he was no futurist when it came to the role of women in American society, even if he envisioned that society to be chiefly agrarian. A refined woman's education was to be essentially in the fine arts, whose aim was appreciation of beauty.

In a 1783 letter to his daughter Martha (Nov. 28, Figure 7-4), Jefferson proffers certain instructions to his daughter, who is staying with a certain Mrs. Hopkinson. Among those instructions, there is a recommended "distribution of your time."

> From 8 to 10, practice music.
> From 10 to 1, dance one day and draw another.
> From 1 to 2, draw on the day you dance, and write a letter next day.
> From 3 to 4, read French.
> From 4 to 5, exercise yourself in music.
> From 5 till bed-time, read English, write, &c.

Fig. 7-4: Martha Jefferson Randolph (public domain)

The "distribution" is hastily composed. Among other things, there is nothing said about the slot from 2 to 3—was that an oversight due to haste in composition of the letter?—it is not clear what the "&c" entails, and "write a letter the next day" seems as if it was added as an afterthought to encourage a letter by her to him every other day. Yet her "education"—and here she is 11 and there is no allowance for spontaneous play—is nearly wholly in the fine arts.[48] There are two hours of drawing each day, one and one-half hours of dancing, one hour of reading French, an unspecified amount of reading English and writing, and three hours of practicing music each day. Martha is to begin the day, with refreshed mind, with music, and for all intents and purposes, end the day with music.[49] The aim is to shape her into the sort of woman who will attract a man of large ambition, much education, and great spirituel. The letter shows little imagination and betrays Jefferson's conservative bent of mind concerning women. A progressive liberal in so many ways, he was nowise visionary when it came to the role of women in American society.

In a letter to Nathaniel Burwell (14 Mar. 1818), Jefferson offers some thoughts on female education. Burwell has written Jefferson on February 17, 1818, to request the latter's thoughts on "a system of female education, best adapted to the present state of our society." The request is again in keeping with the American sentiment of the day that female education must be different from male education, as a genteel woman's role is domestic, not social.

Jefferson's reply, though not short, does not exhibit the sort of thoughtfulness and regard for minutia which, for instance, he often gave to the subject of the education of a would-be lawyer.[50] His views on women's social role were always conservative and he was much distrustful of empleomania in women—hence, his amicable, but arm's-length relationship with Abigail Adams. Says Jon Kukla, "Jefferson did nothing whatsoever to improve the legal or social condition of women in American society, and he was always wary of female influence in government."[51]

Jefferson's reply to Burwell begins with a caveat. "A plan of female education has never been a subject of systematic contemplation with me. It has occupied my attention so far only as the education of my own daughters occasionally required." In a villatic setting, females required an education to be mothers, teachers of their daughters, and even directors of their sons, when a father passed too early.

Noting that novels poison the mind and that reading should be confined to works that reinforce "sound morality," Jefferson says that female education for a countryside girl should focus on dancing, drawing, household economy, and music. The first is important in that it offers a girl sufficient "healthy exercise,

---

[48] For more on the letter, see M. Andrew Holowchak, "The ornaments … and amusements of life": Jefferson, Female Felicity, and the Proper Education of a Genteel Woman," *The Journal of Thomas Jefferson's Life and Times*, Vol. 2, No. 1 (2017): 87–96.
[49] The slot from 5 until bedtime seems discretionary.
[50] E.g., TJ to John Minor, 30 Aug. 1814.
[51] Jon Kukla, *Mr. Jefferson's Woman* (New York: Vintage Books, 2008), p. 4.

[which is] elegant and very attractive for young people. Drawing "is an innocent and engaging amusement," though it is less appreciated in America than in Europe. Household economy, following a line of thought that dates back to Aristotle in his *Politics,* is obviously important. "The order and economy of a house are as honorable to the mistress as those of the farm to the master, and if either be neglected, ruin follows, and children destitute of the means of living." Last, there is music. "Music is invaluable where a person has an ear. Where they have not, it should not be attempted. It furnishes a delightful recreation for the hours of respite from the cares of the day, and lasts us through life. The taste of this country, too, calls for this accomplishment more strongly than for either of the others."

The benefits of music are several. First, it is a welcome rejuvinative tonic for the drain caused by the rigors of the day. Again, unlike dancing, one can enjoy music at all periods of life. Furthermore, it is a refined pastime that is significant for improving the taste of Americans much more than are dancing and drawing.

Yet then, there is the puzzlesome qualification "where a person has an ear." What precisely is the intended scope of that remark?

It is unlikely that Jefferson thinks that many people—there is no reason to believe that the comment is restricted to females—have no appreciation of music. It is instead very probable that Jefferson believes that a person who shows neither desire nor aptitude for music should not be forced to study music or to learn a musical instrument—e.g., to learn the fiddle or piano forte.[52] If that is what Jefferson meant, then the qualification is innocuous, even superfluous.

Yet Jefferson was not given to superfluity, and so there must be more to the explanation. As a skilled musician and patron of that art, Jefferson attended numerous performances of all sorts throughout his life and he was certainly often disappointed by what he heard, and by what he observed. Thus, the comment very probably also is a measure of Jefferson's own disappointment, after listening to would-be musicians over the years. The comment of course is also equally applicable to the practice of the other fine arts, but is applied here to music because of it being globally treasured.

The enclosure to Burwell limns over 60 works/authors, and there is a large dose of history and some study of geography and math. There are also some works on morality, English and French dictionaries, works on grammar, and novels by, among others, Miss Edgworth and Madame Genlis. Concerning the fine arts, Jefferson lists Whately's book on pleasure gardening as well as over a

---

[52] The forte piano differed from the harpsichord in that its strings were struck, not plucked.

dozen of the great poets and tragedians from Homer and Virgil to Milton and Molière. A genteel young lady is also to read *Don Quixote* in French.

None of the books listed, perhaps surprisingly, are about music. Musical education was to come through private tutelage: though ear more than through eye. The study of the theory of music is left for critics of the fine arts—for men.

Jefferson did have many books on music in his library and they are aidful in apprehending Jefferson's thoughts on music. Among the books under "Theory of Music" in his 1783 catalog, there were John Holden's *An Essay Towards a Rational System of Music* (1770), comprising "The Rudiments of Practical Music" and "The Theory of Music," William Jackson's *A Preliminary Discourse to a Scheme, Demonstrating the Perfection and Harmony of Sounds* (1726), Robert Bremner's *Rudiments of Music: or, A Short and Easy Treatise on that Subject* (1762), Charles Burney's *The Present State of Music in France and Italy* (1771) and *The Present State of Music in Germany, The Netherlands, and United Provinces* (1775), Francesco Geminiani's *The Art of Playing the Violin* (1771) and *Rules for Playing in a True Taste* (1748), Charles and Samuel Thompson's *The Compleat Tutor for the Harpsichord or Spinnet* (1770), Nicolo Pasquali's *Thorough-Bass Made Easy* (1757) and *The Art of Fingering the Harpsichord* (1760), Johann Caspar Heck's *The Art of Playing the Harpsichord* (1779), and Pierre Hoegi's *A Tabular System whereby the Art of Composing Minuets Is Made so Easy that Any Person, without the Least Knowledge of Musick, May Compose Ten Thousand, All Different, and in the Most Pleasing and Correct Manner* (1770), and Carlo Zuccari's *The True Method of Playing Adagios* (1762).

Those works, however, tell us little about the appreciation of music at Monticello or the value of music in its omniformity in American culture. The best way to grasp the music that Jefferson and his family enjoyed and the importance of music for cultural enrichment is through inspection of Monticello's vocal and instrumental music, much of which survives in the Monticello Music Collection. As Helen Cripe notes, "The collection reflects the tastes of a man who, by means of copious purchases and constant exchange with friends, accumulated a potpourri of every kind of music available and in every possible arrangement that he, his family, and friends could play or sing."[53]

Upshot

Music was problematic among the fine arts. Jefferson, I maintain, considered it to be inferior to architecture and gardening, as it was more dispensable than both, but superior to painting and sculpture, which might be considered needless trappings, especially when not moderated.

---

[53] Helen Cripe, *Thomas Jefferson and Music,* 10–11.

Yet that ranking is difficult to grasp. Jefferson clearly appropriated Hogarth, who noticed how nature partnered beauty with utility, and Jefferson seemed always to have a preference for utility over beauty, and distaste for or aversion to fruitless beauty—*viz.*, beauty without utility or an art that was truly fine. Yet painting and sculpture could be historically availing—we have only to consider Jefferson's collection of artworks at Monticello, covered in the chapter prior—and it is not clear that music was in that regard as useful as painting and sculpture. If anything, music is perhaps the most useless of the fine arts, and it might seem to be categorized best at the bottom of the fine arts.

What was it about music for Jefferson that elevated it above painting and sculpture?

It was the pathos of music—its capacity to evoke like no other fine art the depths and extremes of emotion. Lord Kames notes in *Elements of Criticism* that "the objects of the eye must so far yield preference to those of the ear," because of the power of speech to move people emotionally. He continues: "Music, having at command a great variety of emotions, may, like the many objects of sight, be made to promote luxury and effeminacy ... especially in vocal music. But, with respect to its pure and refined pleasures, music goes hand in hand with gardening and architecture and her sister arts, in humanizing and polishing the mind; of which none can doubt who have felt the charms of music."[54] Thomas Jefferson clearly concurred. He doubtless thought that music of the right sort could not only provide repose from the strenuous intellectual activities of the day, but also encourage morally sensible actions.

Few of us today, I suspect, would disagree with Jefferson, placing music ahead of painting and sculpture as a fine art. Music in some form or other appeals to and moves emotionally every person. Many persons have developed "an ear" for it in its omniformity, and are better positioned to value its beauty in the manner of an anthophile, valuing the multifarious beauty and natural function of flowers.

---

[54] Henry Home, *Elements of Criticism,* ed. Rev. James R. Boyd (New York: A.S. Barnes & Burr, 1965), 46.

Postscript

Given that Jefferson, following Francis Bacon, thought that all knowledge was subsumable under the rubrics of History, Philosophy, and the Fine Arts—related to the human faculties of memory, reason, and imagination—it is incredible that scholarly discussion of Jefferson and Fine Arts, other than numerous essays and several books on Jefferson and architecture, has been over the decades almost nonexistent. Perusal of 15 of the indices of some of the best books in my library on Jefferson, including books on Jefferson and one of the particular fine arts—such as works by Malone, Peterson, Lehmann, Cripe, Nichols, Kimball, Gutzman, Mapp, Ellis, Koch, Shackelford, Onuf, and Boles—showed "fine arts" not listed in any one. (I stopped after 15.) One might remonstrate that many of the books I have limned have some discussion of certain of the particular fine arts. Here I counter-remonstrate that discussion of painting, say, without a generic grasp of what Jefferson thought about Fine Arts and the aesthetic sense is as availing as Plato discussing a particular virtue, "courage," without an understanding of "virtue" and human rationality.

That in gist is the incentive for *Thomas Jefferson, Taste, and the Fine Arts*. My aim is to introduce readers to the eight particular fine arts, and in doing so, to explicate what makes each of those arts "fine," according to Jefferson, who, as I show, had a unique take on "fine arts." Along the way, I try to tease out some understanding on how the faculty of taste, independent of rationality and the moral sense, functions.

This undertaking has enabled me to make some singular disclosures.

The most singular disclosure, which I have aimed to thread throughout the book, is that Jefferson wished to import to America the fine arts only inasmuch as they would enhance, not impeded, human flourishing in what he envisaged—or at least hoped—to be predominantly agrarian living. Hence, he was insistent that any fine art couples fineness with utility. Works of fiction without moral content were not only desultory, but also potentially corruptive. Oratory, exemplified by the fiery speeches of Patrick Henry, could be pressed into service of republican ideals. Architecture, like the pavilions at the University of Virginia, could house professors and educate students apropos of the beauty and functional durability of Classical designs. Even seemingly inutile arts like music and pleasure gardening could, following Lord Kames, have a restorative function, when done with the aim of moderation. Art, he frequently noted, could be "too much"—especially for a young nation, aiming to escape the ills of social stratification and coercive governing. In the words of Carl Richard, "Republican art and architecture must also represent republican simplicity, not monarchical opulence. The republican way was Aristotle's 'middle way.' Jefferson's ambivalence concerning paintings and statues reflected this anxiety concerning the proper republican balance."[1]

Yet this Redefinitional Thesis, as I have come to call it, has more than mere parochial implications. Jefferson was advocating a conception of Fine Arts that not only better suited the American understanding of beauty, but also suggesting a redefinition that better suited the nature of humans. Jefferson's redefinition of Fine Arts was, thus, a universal human ideal. Functional or heterotelic beauty was for Jefferson always and everywhere preferred to fine or autotelic beauty. Jeffersonian redefinitionalism, therefore, ineluctably placed him in position of a rational critic of the fine arts in spite of the fact that beauty (and sublimity) were immediately recognized by the aesthetic sense without any assistance from rationality. That is in keeping with my thesis in *Thomas Jefferson in Paris: The Ministry of a Virginian "Looker on"*—that Jefferson, ever vigilant and ever critical, approached his time in France as well as everyday life with the dispassionate circumspection of an investigative scientist, looking to improve ever the human condition.

A second disclosure of significance is what I have called Jefferson's epistemology of the sublime as it relates to taste. Objects that naturally immediately incite feelings of sublimity (awe, dread, horror, and fear), for Jefferson, are fundamentally beautiful—*viz.*, feelings of sublimity soon give way to feelings of beauty for a patient observer. The dread one feels on observing Natural Bridge morphs soon into a perception of beauty, and acquaintancy over time softens the initial dread. That invites some discussion of whether, following the lead of Hugh Blair, feelings of sublimity are vestiges of early human interaction with the world, where numerous unfamiliar objects incited fear and whether they might at some future time evanesce.

I call this study in the preface preliminary, because it is inaugural—the first of its kind. As such, some of the points I make might not pass the test of future critical analysis. That, however, does not diminish its significance, so long as this book incites other scholars to take up the study of Jefferson on Fine Arts, the aesthetic sense, and the particular fine arts as species of Fine Arts—those especially that have been much overpassed: poetry, rhetoric and oratory, and criticism.

---

[1] Carl J. Richard, The Founders and the Classics: Greece, Rome, and the American Enlightenment (Omaha, NE: Classics of Liberty Library, 2014), 51–52.

Index

D

E

F

G

H

J

K

L

M

N